Structuring Islamic Finance Transactions

Structuring Islamic Finance Transactions

Edited by
Abdulkader Thomas, Stella Cox and Bryan Kraty

Published by Euromoney Books

Published by
Euromoney Books
Nestor House, Playhouse Yard
London EC4V 5EX
United Kingdom

Tel: +44 (0) 20 7779 8999 or USA +1 800 437 9997
Fax: +44 (0) 20 7779 8300
www.euromoneybooks.com
E-mail:hotline@euromoneyplc.com

ISBN 1 84374 213 6

Printed by Hobbs the Printers

Contents

Foreword xi

David E. Upton

Recent history of Islamic finance xii

Faith, ethics, law and finance xiii

Compatibility xv

Shari'a boards and *fatawa* xvi

Intellectual curiosity and personal growth xvii

Internationalisation of finance xviii

Conclusion xix

Introduction: the origins and nature of the Islamic financial market 1

Abdulkader Thomas, based upon the work of Bryan Kraty, Stella Cox and Lawrence Oliver with Mustafa Hussain

Introduction 1

The growth of the Islamic finance industry 3

Islamic finance principles 6

Core mechanisms 6

Islamic finance instruments 7

What is money? 9

What does this mean for banking and finance? 9

Systemic challenges 9

Notes about the book 11

1 **Examining the role of Islamic law** 13

Abdulkader Thomas

Introduction 13

Maqasid al Shari'a 14

Sources of law 15

Islamic schools of law 19

The concerns of *Shari'a* 20

Contracts 23

The rule of possession (*qabd*) 26
Forbidden contracts and accountability 27
Conclusion 27

2 Understanding the *Shari'a* process 32
Abdulkader Thomas
Introduction 32
Shari'a boards 32
Preparing for the process 35
Two case studies: exceptions to the rule 36

3 Equity finance vehicles: *mudaraba* and *musharaka* 45
Abdulkader Thomas with M. Ikram Thofeek
Introduction 45
Limited liability and corporate personality 46
Mudaraba 47
Syndication by *mudaraba* 49
Retail fund aggregation 51
Non-bank financial institutions 52
Musharaka 53
Musharaka deposits 54
Deposit profit distribution methods 55
Other forms of bank account 56
Declining-balance partnership 56
Shares and certificates 57
Pre-emption 57
Conclusion 58

4 The *murabaha* and simple sales transactions 60
Abdulkader Thomas and Bryan Kraty, with Sudin Haron, Mustafa Hussain, and Stella Cox
Introduction 60
Murabaha 60
Murabaha and cash management 63
Murabaha in a banking context 65
Murabaha in trade financing 66
Murabaha versus *bai' bithaman al muajjal* 68

The case of Malaysia 69
Less widely applied sales concepts 71
Problematic sales types 72
Letters of credit 73
Conclusion 74
Checklist: *murabaha* transaction steps 74

5 Lease finance and *ijarah* 77
Abdulkader Thomas and Bryan Kraty, with Mustafa Hussain, and Stella Cox
Introduction 77
Lease finance and *ijarah* 77
Islamic lease structure 79
Ijarah-wa-iqtina'a 80
Project finance applications 82
Main differences between Islamic and conventional leases 88
Conclusion 90

6 *Salam* 93
Abdulkader Thomas and Bryan Kraty, with Mustafa Hussain, and Stella Cox
Introduction 93
Salam 93
Checklist: *Salam/istisna'a* financing transaction steps 94
Parallel *salam* and liquidity management 97
Commodity financing 97
Working capital applications 98
Conclusion 100

7 Complex transactions: *istisna'a*, pre-export or manufacturing finance working capital and project finance 102
Abdulkader Thomas with Bryan Kraty
Introduction 102
Istisna'a 102
Ju'ala as a sub-set of *istisna'a* 105
Securitised and syndicated project finance transactions 105
Syndicated and securitised pre-export and export finance transactions 110
Syndicated and securitised corporate finance transactions 113

8 **Real estate** 125

Abdulkader Thomas with appreciation to Mohammed Asaria

Introduction 125

Mudaraba and *musharaka* 125

Istisna'a and *intifa'a* 127

Murabaha 127

Musharaka and declining-balance partnership 128

Ijarah and leveraged *ijarah* 129

Securitisation of real estate 130

Conclusion 136

9 **Islamic asset management** 137

Stella Cox and Lawrence Oliver with Abdulkader Thomas

Introduction 137

Islamic principles 137

Creating an Islamic asset base 137

Islamic fund management 138

Structure, marketing and distribution 148

Jurisdiction of registration and regulation 150

Disclosure 151

Islamic global asset management 151

Addressing the issues 152

Conclusion 152

10 **Opportunities with *sukuk* and securitisations** 154

Abdulkader Thomas, with appreciation to Mohammad Asaria and Tamara Box

Sukuk – legal structure 154

Sukuk securitisation 156

Receivables securitisation 159

Rating *Shari'a* securitisations 161

Historical data and rating risk 162

Legal and regulatory issues with *Shari'a*-compliant securitisations 164

Tax and accounting issues 165

Jurisdiction and trustee issues 165

Shari'a securitisation opportunities 166

Conclusions and challenges for *sukuk* and Islamic securitisations 168

11 Liquidity management: developing the Islamic capital market and creating liquidity 171

Stella Cox with Abdulkader Thomas

Introduction 171

Liquidity management and mainstream financial services 171

Challenges of Islamic liquidity operations 171

Murabaha as a liquidity management tool 172

Murabaha – asset or liability? 173

Salam 174

Tawarruq 174

Islamic 'debt' securities 175

Defining liquidity strategies 176

Ijarah lease finance 177

Short-term investment programme 178

Islamic investment asset base 179

Disclosure, regulation and rating 179

The International Islamic Financial Market 181

Islamic capital market – multinational institutions 181

Conclusion 182

12 Risk management and derivatives 184

Abdulkader Thomas

Introduction 184

Takaful and insurance 185

Derivatives 186

Principal 192

Synthesising derivatives or the effects 195

Derivative market risks 198

Hedge funds 199

Legal 200

Conclusion 200

13 The regulatory constellation and challenges 204

Abdulkader Thomas, with special thanks to Helmi Talib, Rifaat Abdel Karim, Umer Chapra and Tariqullah Khan

Introduction 204

General supervisory standards 205

Emerging Islamic network 206

Risk monitoring and measurement 210
The analytical challenge of profit-sharing deposits 214
The regulatory capital equation 217
Securitisation 218
Approaches governing Muslim minorities 219
Conclusion 220

14 Changes and challenges 222
Abdulkader Thomas
Introduction 222
Key developments 222
New opportunities 223
Standardisation 223
New markets 224
Conclusion 224

Glossary 226

Foreword

David E. Upton, Virginia Commonwealth University, Richmond, Virginia

Is there a need for this book on Islamic finance? If so, why should a non-Muslim be interested in reading such a book? These would seem to be reasonable questions to many, even to finance professionals. The typical reaction to a mention of Islamic finance is that it is an arcane topic involving dogmatic religious pronouncements, incompatible with finance as generally practised and possibly an obstacle to economic growth. After all, hasn't Islamic finance resulted in a stultified Mid-East economy, a business backwater except for the oil sector? Isn't Islamic finance just a side-show, hemmed in by religious strictures? Isn't it often based on conflicting *fatawa* (legal opinions) issued by rival clerics that result in archaic rules and procedures? To the casual observer it seems to be a topic of interest to religious Muslims or sociologists, perhaps, but of little interest elsewhere. Surprisingly, these views can sometimes be found even among secular Muslims, especially among finance professionals who have been trained in western finance. Such attitudes are, of course, largely misinformed and exaggerated. The actual situation is very different. In fact, Islamic finance has emerged from a period of inertia, and is undergoing a period of renewal and vigorous growth. It has become a dynamic field that will change the face of finance everywhere. As with any change, there are opportunities to grasp and adjustments to make. But grasping opportunity, and making the right adjustments, requires an understanding of the reasons for and nature of the change.

One of the motivations for this book arises from the need to overcome outmoded and uninformed impressions. But there is also a need to provide a more realistic picture of Islamic finance as it exists today and how it will evolve in the future. *Structuring Islamic Finance Transactions* provides the background and understanding necessary for the reader to find the opportunities and to make informed proactive adjustments.

Even for those who manage to get past their early misconceptions and begin a study of Islamic finance, however, the going can be difficult. The reasoning may seem cryptic, especially to those used to the thought processes of western finance. Unfamiliar concepts are described by unfamiliar words, such as *riba* and *gharar*, making the topic seem impenetrable. Much of the problem lies in the fact that comprehensive, straightforward explanations of Islamic finance have been scarce and sometimes incomplete. The revival of interest in Islamic finance has been comparatively recent, and many of the instruments and procedures are new or have a relatively short history. Islamic scholars who first attempted to bridge the cultural gap were struggling with western financial concepts that, to them, were as difficult to grasp as Islamic concepts are for those approaching the problem from the West. This is no longer the case, and boundary-spanning expertise now exists in both groups. The recent growth and development of the field has been rapid, however, and the literature has not been able to keep pace with the changes. As a result, much of the material that is available tends to be overly simplified. The more sophisticated treatments that provide an advanced knowledge level usually assume some previous background, and are often too specific and esoteric in nature. Lacking a comprehensive source, readers were forced to link together scattered treatments, mentally switching gears among different authors. This has also contributed to misunderstandings. One example is the oversimplified description of *riba* as 'no interest.' The subsequent explanation that this only applies to a return on money, and not to a return on assets, may go unheard or even not be offered. To many, the meaning of 'interest' is much broader than intended, and the description is mistakenly taken as 'no rate of return.' This misinterpretation usually evokes an incredulous 'Then how can they make any money?' and the suspicion that the requirement is a sham that is ignored in practice. Another example is the explanation of *gharar* (roughly, avoidable uncertainty), which often includes *hadith* (quotes) that are in the formal and indirect form of expression found in religious writings. This leaves the mistaken impression that 'It's a Muslim thing,' and not meant for outsiders.

How can a novice get past these obstacles? Both the rapid development of new techniques, and the misconceptions which have arisen over time, have created a pressing need for a clear and concise treatment of the conceptual underpinnings and state of the art in Islamic finance and an indication of possible future developments. *Structuring Islamic Finance Transactions* fills that need, drawing on many diverse sources to provide a treatment that is thorough and understandable, without resorting to oversimplification or becoming bogged down in detail.

Recent history of Islamic finance

Islamic finance is not new, and actually rests on over 1,500 years of philosophical and legal reasoning. During its classical period, Islam made great contributions to science and industry, including the concept of zero and the concept of an algorithm. Trade in the Mediterranean region was strong and flourishing under the Islamic commercial law of the time. Unfortunately, this system became stagnant, and withered after the rise of colonialism and the emergence of large, sophisticated international companies. Together these powers created an environment that led to western financial concepts and techniques being superimposed over the existing financial structures. Under this pressure, while the traditional Islamic financial structures continued to exist, they were relegated to a minor role. For many, this resulted in an impression that the only real business in the Mid-East was supported by and conducted through western finance. The disconnect and clash between western practices and the underlying Islamic practices of traditional business sectors made access to capital difficult, discouraged innovation and entrepreneurship, and obscured the existence of the more traditional sectors. It is not surprising that smaller domestic business failed to flourish and that growth of Islamic financial solutions was inhibited.

Perhaps nature abhors a vacuum, but certainly finance abhors unemployed resources and frustrated entrepreneurship. Demand for financing techniques acceptable to the Islamic faith began to increase. Some attempts were made to mobilise capital in an Islamic fashion that was more acceptable to domestic business owners, but it was not until the 1960s that these attempts became widespread and began to bear fruit. Since that time, there has been a continued and accelerating development of Islamic finance, resulting in a growing number of increasingly sophisticated instruments and procedures compatible with Islamic precepts. New ways to reconcile Islamic and western thought in solving shared business problems have been discovered. These new techniques are providing acceptable alternatives to western finance and permit greater flexibility in problem solving, making it possible to free up previously untapped sources of capital. The financial effect of many of these instruments is virtually identical to the financial effect of western instruments, but they remain within the bounds of *Shari'a* (Islamic law). The close similarity of financial effects is not at all surprising; it is simply a function of the similarity of the problems being solved. While there remain areas in which Islamic alternatives are not yet available or are still somewhat difficult to use, Islamic finance has proven itself flexible and applicable to the modern business world. This growth process is continuing, with solutions to many remaining problem areas already under development.

The benefit of these developments is not restricted to Muslims. The new instruments and procedures are available to, and have already been employed by, western business and governments. Not surprisingly, the renaissance of Islamic finance has actually reduced the formerly perceived discord with western finance. This book provides a realisation that the gulf between Islamic and western finance is not as wide as originally thought, and that in fact there is a surprisingly large area of agreement between the two approaches to mutual problems.

Faith, ethics, law and finance

Islamic finance is, of course, inextricably bound with religious thought and teaching. In western business the concepts of religion, law, and ethics only loosely overlap. In Islamic finance, on the other hand, these concepts approach congruency. Without at least a basic knowledge of Islamic faith, a grasp of Islamic finance can only be at best a superficial collection of specific memorised cases. Readers of this book will find that explanations of financial applications are accompanied by explanations of their relationship to Islamic reasoning. It is not necessary to become an Islamic scholar (most Muslim businessmen are not scholars either!), but a working knowledge of the basic thought process behind various financial *fatawa* is necessary to provide perspective and allow extension of the guidelines to similar but different situations. If this seems unfair, realise that for an Islamic scholar an understanding of western financial principles would require a working knowledge of western law and ethics – and of their underlying religious basis. Further, the closeness of religious, legal and ethical bases of Islamic finance often results in a relatively more explicit statement of guidelines. The looser connection of the religious, legal and ethical basis of western finance, on the other hand, results in a less explicit statement of guidelines, unfortunately often assumed or only implied without exact specification. In the United States this is reflected in the recent emphasis in business schools on adding courses in ethics to curricula that already contain courses in business law. Without an appreciation of the differences in the two systems, there is the danger of mistakes resulting from reliance on unconscious habit.

The acceptability of Islamic financial practices and instruments is based on Islamic law. *Shari'a* in turn has three sources. The *Qur'an*, or received word of God, is the most basic source, but usually does not deal directly with commercial problems. A second source is the *Sunnah*, or authenticated sayings and reported actions of the Prophet Mohammed (PBOH), which provides more direct guidance for commercial problems. The third source is *ijtihad*, scholarly interpretation and extension of the *Qur'an* and the *Sunnah*. *Ijtihad* is based on analogical reasoning and takes account of personal preferences, custom, and impact on the welfare of society.

While this may at first seem inflexible to the western mind, the interpretive and extensive nature of *ijtihad* allows innovation and growth in response to the complexity and change of life. Once some understanding of the reasoning is achieved, similarities to more familiar concepts emerge. Many differences from western finance can then be seen as a matter of degree rather than of kind. The religious conditions placed on financial activities have goals that might come from the speeches of captains of industry in the United States or Europe or, for that matter, anywhere in the world. The use of resources for the good of all, a staple in those speeches, is a basic tenet of Islam. *Riba* is not presently strictly forbidden in western finance, but it was forbidden in the past and is at present certainly proscribed and often limited as usury. *Gharar* is certainly reflected in western concepts of the fairness of, and requirements for, a valid legal contract and in consumer protection laws. Both concepts deal with shared problems that are not solely Islamic or solely western, offering solutions that are different but understandable to both groups.

Absolute differences do exist, but in many cases it is not hard for those trained in western finance to understand the nature of the differences when the basic intentions are considered. It is often said that Islamic finance is asset based, while western finance is currency based. The underlying Islamic concept is that money has no value in and of itself, but is only a measure of value. This concept is involved in the prohibition of *riba*, since if money has no intrinsic value there should be no charge for use of money. However, this does not preclude a rate of return on asset-based investments, since those assets do have an intrinsic value. Many find this emphasis on an asset base clumsy, inefficient, and unnecessary. They would argue that money simply reflects a claim on some underlying assets anyway, so that they consider money to be an asset in itself. While this argument is widely accepted, it is interesting to note the repeated references to the 'money illusion' and the associated requirement to 'pierce the veil of money' in the economic and financial analysis found in western texts. Clearly there is some difference between assets and money. Not all would reconcile this difference in the same way.

It would be a mistake to think of Islamic finance as a rigidly prescribed set of dogmatic procedures set by clergy without reference to the realities of business practice. Although Islam does set boundaries and general guidelines for compliance with *Shari'a*, there is great flexibility within those boundaries. There are three ideas that reinforce this flexibility. The first is that those things that are not forbidden are permitted. As long as a procedure or instrument does not constitute a forbidden action, it is acceptable. This leaves wide latitude for the design of instruments, contracts, and procedures. The second idea is that material possessions are the property of God, and that we are but stewards of our possessions who are required to use those possessions in an unselfish manner for the good of all (an idea also professed by many other faiths). This indicates that there is a duty to engage in an ongoing search for better and more efficient methods, within the limits set by *Shari'a*. Development and refinement of Islamic finance, rather then reliance on fixed techniques, is considered a religious obligation. Closely related is the third idea that the intent and emphasis of *ijtihad* is not in limiting or forcing compliance with rules. The intent and emphasis is rather to assist people in seeking a happier life, of making life easier, of removing hardship and obstacles to a better life within the boundaries of *Shari'a*. Extending the consideration of *riba*, for instance, the argument for prohibition of interest is not just that money has no intrinsic value. The extension to prohibition arises because under this viewpoint, interest would result in the lender becoming unfairly enriched without providing anything of value to the borrower. Such unjust enrichment would be a source of conflict and detrimental to society. This indicates that the intent is not to forbid a particular type of contract, but rather to avoid a wrongful action in the interest of the common good.

The reader will find that the emphasis on removing obstacles to a better and happier life gives rise to a practical attitude among Islamic scholars, an attitude that tends to focus less on form or esoteric philosophical arguments and more on substance and impact on daily life. A result of this practical attitude is that some deviations from strict conformance are permitted under *ijtihad*, based on the concepts of *istihsan* (personal preferences), *istislah* (public welfare) and *'urf* (custom). As with Christian theology, necessity may cause certain acts to become permitted, even if discouraged in general or prohibited in other circumstances. As an example, given a lack of alternatives, Muslims are allowed to invest in corporate stock, even though the firm may participate in *riba* through leveraging. The investment is certainly not encouraged, but is permitted as a practical and temporary solution to the lack of acceptable alternatives. This is not, however, a 'free pass.' The permissible amount of corporate borrowing and lending is limited – and the portion of investor return attributable to interest must be purified, usually by donating that amount to charity.

Compatibility

Given the practical nature of Islamic law in the area of finance, it is not surprising that the reader will discover that Islamic methods can be quite compatible with western practices, and the practical result of instruments and procedures is sometimes virtually identical despite what may at first seem to be very different forms. This is to be expected – both systems are dealing with the same practical problems, and the substance of finance is the solution of those problems. Whether a mortgage is currency-based borrowing of money or is an asset-based *musharakah* (roughly, partnership) in which one partner (the purchaser of the home) buys out the other (the financial institution) over time, once we 'pierce the veil of money' we are presented with the same solution to the same problem. The purchaser buys a home through a series of payments, while the provider of capital – the financial institution – receives a rate of return on its investment in the home (remember that *riba* does not preclude a rate of return on assets). The fact that in one case the underlying asset is money, and in the other case is the house, has great religious difference but virtually no financial difference. The underlying philosophical basis may be different in many ways, and the contract may seem strange to western ears and eyes. The two solutions are clearly not identical. Islam and western financiers may disagree about which approach is fairer or more just (or more acceptable in the eyes of God). But in the end, both the mortgage and the *musharakah* contract solve the same problem – and business gets done to the satisfaction and benefit of both parties.

It must be clearly understood that this compatibility and similarity of results is not the result of an effort to circumvent *Shari'a*. Rather, it is an indication of the flexibility and inventiveness of mankind and a reflection of our common problems. To be sure that Islamic principles are not violated, each new project is submitted to a *Shari'a* board. The board is a group of *Shari'a* scholars that will consider whether the project is compatible with Islamic teachings. It is important that the members of the board be widely accepted as scholars in the Islamic religious community. At times the investigation and conclusion of the board may be straightforward, as when the project makes use of previously accepted techniques or instruments. If the project uses new techniques and instruments, or applies a previously accepted solution in a new manner, a deeper investigation of the acceptability of the proposed solution may be required. If an acceptable solution is found and approved by the board, the approval takes the form of a *fatwa*, or declaration of the acceptability of the project.

Compatibility, and the fact that the financial consequences are virtually identical in some cases, is sometimes misinterpreted to mean that there is no substantive difference between Islamic and western financial solutions. The differences are interpreted as definitional 'tricks with words.' The reader should not make this error. For instance, a repurchase agreement – selling an asset while at the same time entering into a contract to repurchase it later at a higher price – is simply a financing device and is construed as *riba*. While differences in allowable or disallowed practices may be subtle, especially to western finance practitioners, they must be substantive in the eyes of the religious community. An identity of financial implications should not be considered as a lack of philosophical differences.

What seems identical to the uninformed may be in fact quite different; what seems different to the uninformed may actually be quite similar. While actual experience in Islamic finance is a necessary teacher, experience can be a hard and incomplete teacher. Anyone who relies solely on experience may well miss subtleties or less visible opportunities or make mistakes that someone who has a background of understanding will be able to use to their advantage.

Shari'a boards and *fatawa*

Mention of *Shari'a* boards sometimes brings forth a criticism of Islamic finance: there does not exist a single, overall authority that sets forth a uniform set of rules. Rather, there are various groups of scholars or schools, and *fatawa* may be issued based on the differing interpretations of these schools. Thus, a *fatwa* in Malaysia might approve of an instrument that would be considered *riba* and not approved in Saudi Arabia. A reaction of those used to western finance may be that this system seems chaotic and inefficient. The process is viewed as one of jumping religious hurdles in a slow and painstaking process, with an uncertain outcome. This results in an apprehension of great risk, which discourages curiosity in Islamic finance. There is also the accusation that a *fatwa* can be obtained for almost anything if only the right set of scholars can be assembled as a *Shari'a* board. In the face of conflicting *fatawa*, how can one proceed, and how is it possible to be sure that an instrument or process will be universally accepted?

This criticism overstates both the difficulties of using Islamic finance and the extent of disagreement. It may be aggravated by the fact that Islamic finance has been recovering from a period of neglect, so that many projects require exploration of new financial ground. Any area of rapid growth will result in differences of opinion that will be worked out over time. While individual projects may be swiftly developed in areas where a body of law is established through widely accepted *fatawa*, development of new law can be a slower process. The process may also seem more cumbersome to western eyes simply due to a lack of familiarity with the process and the underlying legal structure. If we compare the process of dealing with a *Shari'a* board with that of dealing with the Sarbanes-Oxley Act, a problem currently faced by business in the United States, we might get a more realistic picture. The uncertainty of compliance with (and reams of articles on) the Sarbanes-Oxley Act seems to at least parallel (and to judge from the outcry, exceeds) the uncertainty surrounding obtaining a *fatwa*. The objection that a *fatwa* can be obtained for almost anything is exaggerated. A *fatwa* that is not accepted by the body of Islamic scholars will not become an accepted part of *Shari'a*. True, there exist *fatawa* that have not become accepted, and there are differences over the acceptability of other *fatawa*. On the other hand, it is not unusual for a lawyer in the United States to 'shop' for a jurisdiction favourable to a particular type of case – and jury trials often return surprising verdicts! The uncertainty of the present day battle to influence the composition of the United States Supreme Court, and perhaps to reverse prior decisions, is another case in point. One need only look at the diversity of religious thought among Christian denominations for a similar example of differing conclusions on the same topics.

Intellectual curiosity and personal growth

The discussion has established: a) that several of the original questions are simply based on misconceptions, b) that Islamic finance has become a dynamic and practical field that can function well in the modern business world and at the same time serve Islamic society well, and c) that there is a definite need for a book that sums up the state of the art. An understanding of the re-emergence of Islamic finance is, of course, imperative for Muslims who deal with western firms. The importance of the re-emergence is, however, not limited to the points of interaction with western finance. The increasing flexibility and efficiency afforded by new techniques, and the innovative spirit created by new possibilities, is also a driving force for Muslims who wish to see their economies grow and flourish. By spreading an awareness of these new techniques, this book will do much to encourage a dynamic Islamic business culture and continue the process of growth. It is this type of environment that will produce the Islamic entrepreneurs and business leaders of tomorrow. Certainly, this book is important in providing guidance and assistance to those entrepreneurs who wish to remain within the tenets of their Islamic faith.

This, however, explains only part of the need for this book. Why should I be interested in Islamic finance? I am not Muslim, and I do not live in a predominantly Muslim country. What's in it for me?

Perhaps the first motivation to come to mind is that of intellectual curiosity. Islamic finance is intrinsically interesting. It is interesting to learn of different areas of finance even if the area is not of immediate concern. This is my profession, and I should seize the opportunity to increase my knowledge base and encounter new ideas. For those not in the finance area, the intertwining of financial and religious concepts in Islam provides insight and a fuller understanding of Islamic thought. While this does not seem a practical or compelling reason at first consideration, or on an individual level, after a moment's reflection it is clear that, in a broader sense, providing and nurturing such understanding will be one of the most important, if less practical, contributions of this book. Given the strained state of the world today, an increase in understanding among all of us is of major importance.

Closely associated with intellectual curiosity is personal growth. Islamic finance is a change, and change has both challenge and opportunity. Those who do not venture from the confines of the usual are, sadly, likely to realise at some point that they have been bypassed and become obsolete. One often hears that learning does not stop at the schoolhouse door. It is equally true that it does not stop at the edge of today's usual way of doing things. The inspiration that recognises opportunity does not arise from a vacuum; it is what our subconscious does when it struggles to fit new concepts in with existing concepts. Inspiration will not come to us; we must rather seek it out and cultivate it. Genius has been described as the ability to see things differently. Forcing yourself to think 'outside the box' by exploring how others view things is one way of achieving this ability. The re-emergence of Islamic finance as a dynamic force encourages a dialogue with western finance. Those who are aware of the dialogue and are listening to it are the ones who will develop the personal edge that is found in business leadership.

We may not be the one to recognise and seize an opportunity, but someone eventually will. We may not be at the start of the wave, but we certainly do not want to have it pass us by altogether. The question is not whether it will be us or someone else who will eventually seize the opportunity. The question is whether we will be ready when that happens.

The contributions of this book are not limited to the immediate financial context – they also include the intellectual growth of individuals and of society.

Internationalisation of finance

Beyond intellectual curiosity and growth, there are more practical reasons why an understanding of Islamic finance, and of Islamic thought, will have important benefits. We now live in the interdependent 'global village,' where the impact of what happens in other countries is rapidly transmitted around the globe. As a result, the days of business in general, and finance in particular, as a regional discipline are long gone. Even if I am not Muslim, and even if I do not live in a predominantly Muslim country, I will come into contact with Islam and Islamic finance. This need not be a direct contact. It is estimated that 20 per cent of the world population is Muslim. The economic impact of a group of this size cannot be ignored – it is both an opportunity and a force that affects the entire world. The pool of resources held by Muslims is substantial, and there is a search for outlets to apply those resources to worthwhile projects. Islamic finance is now international in scope, and issues of Islamic instruments now occur throughout the world. Both western firms and western governments offer Islamic instruments (often combined with western instruments in the same offering). The size and number of such offerings will increase as Islamic finance grows in sophistication and offers a wider range of instruments. In short, there is potential to be tapped, and it cannot be tapped without a working understanding of Islamic finance and its underlying concepts.

The impact and importance of Islamic finance extends well beyond those who deal in international undertakings. Although the Muslim population may be concentrated in the Middle East and in southern Asia, it is by no means absent from the rest of the world. Substantial Muslim populations are found throughout the world, and Muslims are no longer unusual neighbours. Within the United States, there is a sizeable Muslim population that is, on average, more affluent, better educated and more sophisticated than the national average. This population has an increasing demand for investment vehicles and for Islamic mortgages and insurance. Interestingly, this has actually resulted in a great deal of the innovation in Islamic finance occurring in the United States, rather than in traditionally Muslim countries. Fully-fledged Islamic banking is now chartered in the United Kingdom, another leader in innovation.

Conclusion

This book, then, does fill a need. My brief discussion should make it clear that Islamic finance is not the esoteric topic it was a decade or so ago. It is not something that will affect us at some time in the future. It is something that is already affecting us, an opportunity that is here now. The impact and the opportunity will continue to grow. Written at a level that avoids oversimplification but is accessible to professionals, this book provides in one source a background on the development of Islamic finance, a comprehensive explanation of the state of the art of both Islamic finance techniques and the underlying Islamic concepts, and a prognosis for the future. It will become a staple for anyone interested in the area: those who make the effort of a careful reading will be well rewarded.

29 June 2005

Introduction: the origins and nature of the Islamic financial market

Abdulkader Thomas, based upon the work of Bryan Kraty, Stella Cox and Lawrence Oliver with Mustafa Hussain[1]

Introduction

The *Qur'an*, the revealed text of Islam, provides general advice about wealth. Not only does the pious Muslim have an obligation to spend wisely, and for the benefit of others, but he finds direction in the *Qur'an* relating to the accumulation of wealth. As the Islamic faith took root in sophisticated cities such as medieval Cairo and Baghdad, the precursors of today's banks took shape. These rules-based intermediaries provided an important source for the modern activity that we now call 'Islamic banking and finance'. Our challenge in this book is to work with these same rules, their modern applications, and cases exemplifying contemporary Islamic commercial contracts.

During the colonial area, the attention of Muslim governments, merchants, scholars and jurists to the particular rules of Islam relating to commerce withered. Only in the 1960s did new thinking about the subject become widespread, leading to multi-state and commercial experiments during the mid 1970s. These experiences have evolved into Islamic financial practice as we understand it today.

Early experiments

Classical Islamic expressions of commerce are found in the juristic and theological literature of the Middle Ages, when Islamic empires led the world in commerce. Yet many of the principles perfected both in the classical period and their modern applications pre-date Prophetic Islam. Chapter 1: Examining the role of Islamic law, looks at the methods applied by Muslims to adapt or modify existing tools and invent new ones in order to engage in commerce. To follow the evolution, we must first understand that the modern, emerging business of Islamic finance began with an experiment in micro-credit in the Nile Delta town of Mit Ghamr. The persistence of the project's primary sponsor, Dr Ahmad Elnaggar, to define key methods of Islamic finance led to the founding of a number of today's leading Islamic institutions including the Islamic Development Bank, Dubai Islamic Bank and the Dar Al Mal group of financial institutions.

Dr Elnaggar's project was ultimately terminated and he went into exile. He endured often hostile public debate in his quest to establish Islamic banking. Nonetheless, Dr Elnaggar was able to forge a consensus for the formalisation of Islamic banking by reaching out to important political, social and

Exhibit 1 **Traditional Islamic construct**

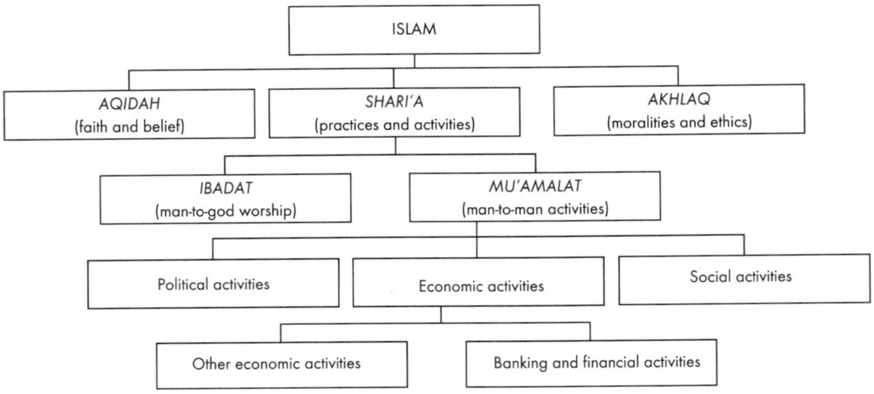

Source: Bahrain Monetary Agency, *Islamic Banking & Finance in the Kingdom of Bahrain* (Bahrain: Bahrain Monetary Agency, 2002), p. 15. *Adapted from Islamic Banking Practice* (Bank Islam Malaysia Berhard, 1415H/1994).

commercial leaders in the Arabian Peninsula and Malaysia. These personalities included King Faisal of Saudi Arabia, Tengku Abdul Rahman of Malaysia, and Saeed Lootah of Dubai.

Dr Elnaggar persuaded these leaders that *riba*, something similar to interest, is explicitly forbidden in the *Qur'an*. If there is no other reason or justification, the devote Muslim must find a way to lead a life free from *riba*. And this means that contract forms, deal substance and approaches to commerce must be adjusted to comply with the injunction against *riba*. Dr Elnaggar's achievement was to raise the consciousness among Muslim opinion leaders and businessmen that modern alternatives to *riba* were feasible and realistic.

Prior to Dr Elnaggar's efforts, most Muslims had ignored the role of *fiqh al mu'amalat*, or the jurisprudence of commerce, in their financial arrangements. The traditional Islamic construct (see Exhibit 1) is to build upon belief and manners with the *Shari'a*, or Islamic law, the way to organise worship and human affairs, in ways that are consistent with the revealed text of Islam and the traditions of the Prophet Mohammed (PBOH).[2] *Fiqh*, which means 'understanding', and *mu'amalat*, which means 'works', combine to define the understanding of Muslims relating to social, political and commercial activities. Although the field has been well honoured in the social sphere, and less so in the political realm, it was widely ignored between the late 1700s and 1960s. When one considers the above classical depiction of the priorities driven by an individual's profession of Islam, it becomes clear why some may consider banking and finance a relatively low priority in the management of one's life. Dr Elnaggar, however, provided a reminder of the severity of the punishment for contracting with *riba* and Islamic scholars and opinion leaders began to view the diagram not as a prioritisation, but as a means of highlighting and organising faith-driven obligations.

The early pioneers of Islamic finance were driven by the overall tenet of sustaining an ethical and equitable mode of conducting financial affairs. Governed by *Shari'a*, Islamic finance derives its principles from the *Qur'an* and *Sunnah*. Although the *Shari'a* prohibits interest and similar forms of income, this does not mean that capital is cost free in an Islamic system. Islam recognises capital as a factor of production, but it does not allow the factor to make a prior or pre-determined claim on the productive surplus in the form of interest.

The core principles of Islamic finance are founded on the 'productive' use of money for community benefit. These will drive us to an asset-based system where money is not a commodity in itself, merely reflecting a value linked to the passage of time, interest, for a return. Because of this, financiers are party to the underlying transactions, which must be transparent with all details ascertainable, if not agreed, in advance with undisputed ownership. Preventable uncertainty, undue risk or systemic speculation is prohibited as well.

This book will show that Islamic finance is very flexible, despite its apparent limitations. When structuring in line with Islamic principles, financing may be provided to: private, public or sovereign entities; Islamic or conventional entities. Funding may come from Islamic or conventional investors. Although funds may be commingled, a point explained in Chapters 1 and 9, no Islamic funds may be used in conventional financings or governed by a contract that is impermissible according to Islamic rules. During the course of this book and its related cases, these points and related elements will be demonstrated.

For a financier to comply with Islamic ethics, the financier is not allowed to finance any activity or entity related to the manufacture, distribution or any facilitation of those things which are explicitly forbidden by Islamic law, namely: alcohol, pork products, illegal and intoxicating drugs, gambling, pornography, arms, and so on. Although business speculation in the ordinary course is understood, undue speculation akin to gambling and 'unjustified enrichment', as we will discuss in the next chapter, are forbidden. Furthermore, a primary value for Muslims is that money is not a 'commodity' and no receipt or payment of interest is allowed.

The growth of the Islamic finance industry

These concept points matter because as much as 20 per cent of the world's population adheres to Islam. The estimated 1.3 billion Muslims are one of the fastest-growing global communities. As we saw above, Islam is one of the most active religions in its efforts to provide comprehensive life guidance to its adherents.

The Islamic finance business is an industry which has known gradual and broadening success. The Islamic banking and finance business is undergoing remarkable growth. Between 2000 and 2004, the number of Islamic banks increased by 70 per cent with a comparable growth in both shareholder equity and assets.[3] Within this universe, money managers estimate that there is an active market for liquid funds looking for quality assets in the range of US$30–50 billion at any given time. This growing, but opaque, market includes trade finance within the Organization of the Islamic Conference (OIC) members, global trade flows, investment activity, and consumer finance and investment.

Geographic dispersion

The growth is driven by an accelerating shift to Islamic finance in all Muslim societies. Retail investors are committed and surveys in Saudi Arabia have shown that as much as 76 per cent of the population desires Islamic banking.[4] Consumers, retail and corporate, are making themselves better informed about Islamic financial opportunities. Conventional bankers, too, are growing their knowledge and competitive position in this business segment. Both conventional bankers and Islamic bankers are improving their cooperation, increasing product offerings and enhancing the drive for improved Islamic finance infrastructure in Muslim countries. Demand is diversified by product and is experiencing geographic dispersion: more than two-thirds of Islamic funds are from the Middle East, with the bulk of the rest from south-east Asia and an emerging number from Africa, North America and Europe.

As much as the modern expression of Islamic values in finance has been centred in the Arabian Peninsula and Malaysia, London has been a global capital market centre for Islamic finance. For example, many transnational Islamic deals are governed by English law. And, with English as an important language for Islamic finance, we find logical expansions of Islamic finance in North America, South Africa and growing comfort with the concepts in a growing number of global jurisdictions. The client universe includes both Muslim consumers and global corporations. Indeed, with the *sukuk* (Islamic bonds, see Chapter 10: Opportunities with *sukuk* and securitisations) issuance by the German state Saxony Anhalt, Islamic financial vehicles are showing themselves to be useful tools for public finance.

This evolution is captured in Exhibit 2 which shows the distribution of institutional establishment of Islamic financial institutions around the globe.

Since the mid-1970s, Islamic finance has followed in the wake of innovations in the global financial services industry. First, this has a strong connection to the importance of London as a global

Exhibit 2 **Evolution of Islamic finance – markets overview**

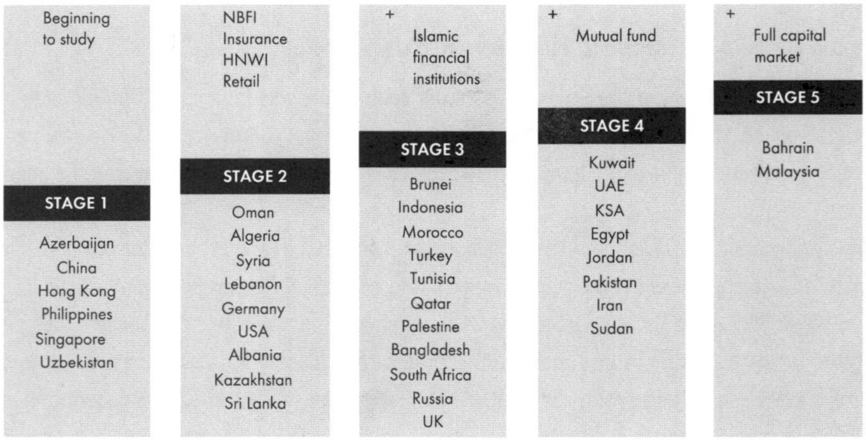

Source: Stella Cox and Lawrence Oliver.

Islamic finance centre. Secondly, global developments have guided the shift among Islamic financial institutions from simple commercial banking products to more sophisticated capital market products with longer tenors. Although London is a premier centre providing capital market services to the global Islamic market, only Malaysia and Bahrain have fully integrated Islamic capital markets which offer virtually all of the capital markets resources found in highly developed conventional markets. Stage 3 and 4 countries are enjoying rapid development and may well be expected to leap rapidly to Stage 5. The number of Stage 1 countries is likely to increase with significant migration to Stage 2.

Curiously, Stage 2 is the most difficult space from which to graduate. Countries such as Algeria, Sri Lanka and the United States have been Stage 2 countries for a number of years and do not look likely to graduate to Stage 3 in the near future. Stage 2 is often the space in which ad hoc accommodations are made from a regulatory perspective. But, the commitment has not been made to formalise or grow specific regulatory regimes that accommodate the evolution of the business domestically.

From a product perspective, the developing Islamic financial markets have shown the following progression (see Exhibit 3).

When Islamic banking took form in the 1970s, the first-generation investors were familiar with such banking role models as Citibank, Barclays, Crédit Lyonnais (now CALYON) and similar commercial banks. The typical chief executive of a new Islamic bank was drawn from such commercial banks or their branches in the Islamic world. Along with the commercial banks, the Islamic banks undertook longer tenors and entered syndicated and project finance in the 1980s. Only in the 1990s did Islamic finance proponents begin to manage a shift to capital markets activities. These have flourished and this book will document the techniques that have been perfected by Islamic banks over these past 40 years, as well as many of the cutting-edge Islamic concepts now gaining a foothold in the Islamic market and its interactions with the global capital markets.

Exhibit 3 **Product timeline**

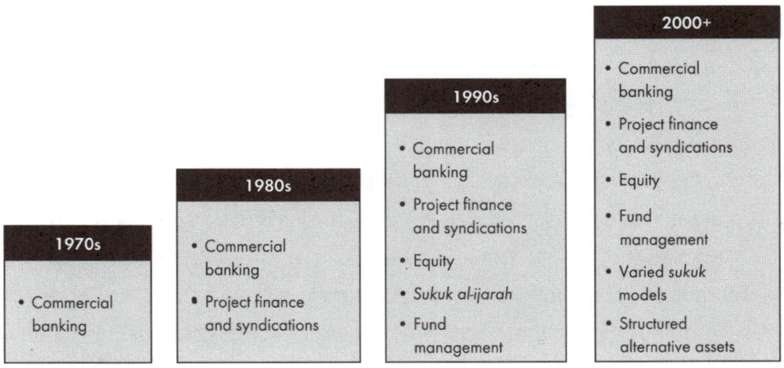

Source: Stella Cox and Lawrence Oliver.

Islamic finance principles

In the emerging business of Islamic finance, Islamic scholars play crucial roles in product development, compliance oversight, and validation of a product's or business' *Shari'a* compliance. A scholar may or may not have a formal degree in a relevant field relating to Islamic finance; or the scholar may have significant experience in the field and attain sufficient respect of others to be accepted as a formal scholar. Although some *Shari'a* scholars believe Islamic finance arrangements relate predominantly to the distribution of wealth,[5] the fact is that the universe of Islamic ideas that governs financial affairs does not fit uniquely into the categories of economic behaviour so well debated in the western academy: capitalism, socialism, communism or mercantilism. In fact, one can reasonably argue within each of these ideas of economic organisation that Islamic ideas might easily be applied. Yet, an examination of two primary precepts of Islam help one to understand better that Islamic finance is more properly a form of 'ethical capitalism'. The first precept is theological: free will. The second is commercial and has a corollary: it is the permission to own private property and the corollary is to freely contract with that property within Islamic confines.

The primary Islamic confine is the prohibition of *riba*, a concept explored in Chapter 1: Examining the role of Islamic law. As we work through the Islamic principles, we will learn that Islamic scholars worry about transactions in which:

> 'the investor has no concern whether the business runs into profit or loss, he automatically gets an interest (Riba) in both outcomes at a fixed rate on his capital. Islam prohibits this kind of trading and the Holy Prophet [sls] enforced the ruling, not in the form of some moral teaching, but as the law of the land.'[6]

With these very basic rules in mind, the primary stipulation of Islamic *Shari'a* is freedom to contract: that is, the parties to an Islamic financial transaction are free to agree any terms they wish, provided those terms are then expressly abided by, and do not conflict with or contradict aspects specifically prohibited under Islamic law.

Core mechanisms

It has been said that: 'In fact, the majority of financial instruments are not revolutionary or new instruments. They are merely combinations of older generation derivatives and/or standard cash market instruments.'[7] Islamic finance is based on the productive use of money for community benefit and is an asset-based system. As such, Islamic products parallel the range of conventional products except for those involving interest unrelated to underlying assets – such as overdrafts, non-inventory-based working capital, general purpose short and medium-term loans and most derivatives. The reason for this parallel existence is that most expertise for financial architecture is in the West and the East is following behind in its tracks. Market forces dictate that to achieve a quicker business success it is easier to tweak conventional models to make them Islamic, or to apply the least-complicated Islamic concepts under conventional regulations, than it is to engineer from scratch new models that can be used bespoke.

In Islam, the owner of capital may profit by sharing risks and rewards in commerce. The range of such activities runs from what one views as being traditional investment management to the partnering in a particular transaction or operating business. The latter may include a true merchant risk with all attendant liabilities or it may mean highly structured funding mechanisms such as those covered in the advanced chapters of this book. Capital may be applied to merchant trading – mark-up governed by contractual pricing or leasing with rentals made fixed or variable according to mutually agreed terms.

Islamic finance instruments

These core mechanisms are the principal groups of trade-related financing instruments. What we mean, and will demonstrate throughout our text, is that these are not 'trade finance' products, even if they may serve that purpose. Rather, the Islamic product universe of financial products is closer to the channels of commerce and trade than traditional debt instruments.

The classical partnership models are explored in Chapter 3: Equity finance vehicles: *mudaraba* and *musharaka*. These methods are finding new and exciting applications in western banks as well as emerging markets corporate finance. For instance, the most widely applied tool of Islamic banking over the past 30 years is the deferred payment sale. When one examines *fiqh al mu'amalat* in the classical texts, the dominant body of literature relates to sales: whether current, deferred or future delivery. These vehicles, including sale of the usufruct or leasing, are covered in Chapter 5: Lease finance and *ijarah*. The widespread acceptance of these applications relates both to the immaturity of the market and the ease with which conventionally trained financiers may adapt to them, easily analogising them to standard loans or leases. Nonetheless, an increasingly informed universe of bankers and consumers is demanding more sophistication as is suitable to more financial risks and challenges.

Complex adaptations of these for working capital, construction and leasing are covered in Chapter 5: Lease finance and *ijarah*, and Chapter 7: Complex transactions: *istisna'a*, pre-export or manufacturing finance working capital and project finance. The extension of these concepts to the management of excess funds is covered in Chapter 11: Liquidity management: developing the Islamic capital market and creating liquidity.

Understanding how equity and contractual arrangements may be reconstituted to generate marketable securities is discussed in Chapter 10: Opportunities with *sukuk* and securitisations, and Chapter 9: Islamic asset management. In this former case, the expanding universe of *sukuk* is transforming how the entire market conceptualises risk management and the transfer of ownership. This has important implications for the future evolution of risk management procedures and other derived instruments as discussed in Chapter 12: Risk management and derivatives. Just five years ago, the white and black boxes in Exhibit 4, along with the least aggressive leasing models, were the primary engines of Islamic financial behaviour.

When we examine the risk–reward distribution of Islamic assets as now deployed in the Islamic market, we see a growing richness. The rapidly expanding range runs from structured commodity trades

Exhibit 4 **Islamic financial assets**

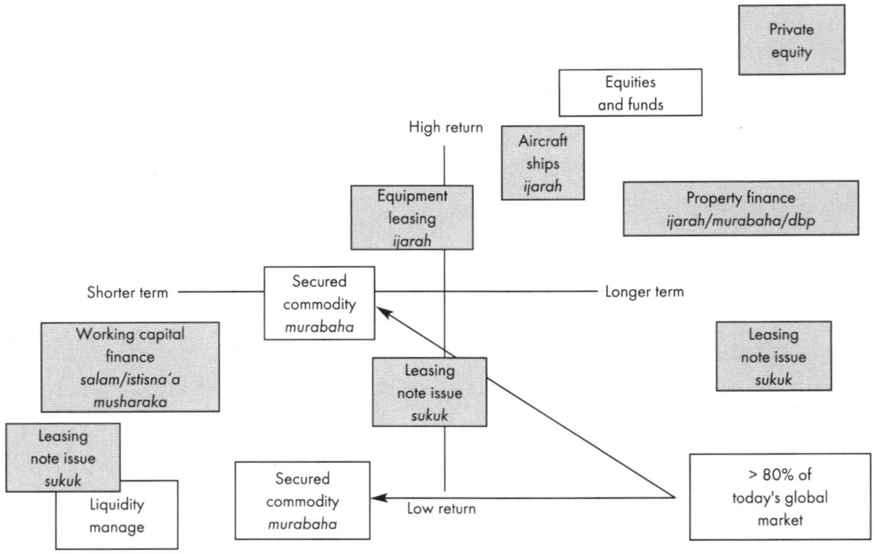

Source: Author's own.

to private equity transactions. The transparent white boxes represent the dominant transaction universes of Islamic banking over the past 35 years; the black boxes are the areas of current rapid growth; and the grey boxes are the evolving areas of Islamic finance most suitable for securitisation and prospectively liquidity management, depending upon the structure of the securities issuance. The focus of this book is to describe the principles that allow one to structure the named transactions in this exhibit and how these are evolving to benefit the global financial markets.

A repeated theme of this book will be that assets and funding have to be structured in accordance with Islamic law. Whether one is serving private, public or sovereign sectors, Islamic or conventional obligors, the assets are subject to what we consider to be the 'sin' screens. Although it may surprise some Muslims, Islamic scholars are agreed that the funds applied may be sourced from Islamic or conventional investors, and their funds commingled, so long as the structure, applications and contracts are compliant with *Shari'a*.

These strictures mean that *Shari'a* authentication is the keystone of this emerging market. *Shari'a* opinions are needed for new products and structures, as well as for the complex documentation associated with syndications in the project and lease financing businesses. Significant work has been made in agreeing standard forms, contracts and structures. As a result, as individual transactions fall into standard or pre-approved structures, then new *Shari'a* authentication is not needed provided the individual transactions contain no alteration to terms of the pre-approved model. Nonetheless, all transactions are open to *Shari'a* audit so long as the provider wishes to retain its certificates (called *fatawa* – plural, or *fatwa* – singular) of *Shari'a* compliance.

What is money?

The classical Islamic scholar Abu Hamid Muhammad Al Ghazali wrote that money:

> '... only reflects the value of goods ... Money should not be created just because its very existence should create a demand for it, but rather it should be used for the procurement of other goods.
>
> '... money has been created so as to be a measure of values and an instrument for exchange. Money itself has no intrinsic value. Had it an intrinsic value, it could not have played its role as money and would have become like other commodities ...
>
> 'Hoarding of money, as well as collecting *riba* on money, means man has turned money into something desirable for its own sake. "*Riba*" denotes that man is trying to "create" money through the medium of money itself, earn more money with less money.'[8]

This classical definition of money is the defining element in Islamic transactions. Each time we cover a specific concept, we will seek to remove money as the object of the contract and return it to its role as our yardstick, measuring the return on our transaction.

What does this mean for banking and finance?

Al Ghazali's concept hearkens directly to the original *Qur'anic* injunction and how the Prophet Mohammed (PBOH) interpreted the *Qur'an* through his judgement or recorded actions. Chapter 1: Examining the role of Islamic law looks at the *fiqhi*, Islamic juristic rulings, the basis for modern Islamic finance. These rulings will provide a specific way of defining a contract, its object and how the contract transacts upon the object with others. We will see that the object itself, not money, is going to limit the ultimate derivations of the transaction. The outcome will be a more restrictive universe of financial arrangements with fewer options for parsing the elements of contract and allowing for a separation of the object, the contract and the cash flow. This asset-dominated family of contractual and transactional processes will have a different impact on the financial system, perhaps reducing the absolute risks to the financial system.

Systemic challenges

Throughout the past 200 years, the evolution of banking has been closely paired to the challenge of managing risks, from consumer and client risks to systemic risks. The unique shocks to the western banking system, particularly the US system, of the Great Depression of the 1930s and the Savings and Loan Collapse of the 1980s, separated by nearly 50 years, have led to well-structured systemic safety nets. In effect, regulated financial institutions are today well supervised, obliged to meet exhausting and improving capital adequacy measures, and must be increasingly transparent in their reporting. As a result, institutional size is less of a concern than institutional inclusion.[9] As we read through this book, we will learn better whether or not Islamic instruments introduce or reduce the prospect of systemic risk as it has been introduced into the US capital markets.

> '... it is worth noting – rather ominously in my view – financial risk is growing rather rapidly outside the regulated institution sector. Enron, Long Term Capital [Management], large private equity operations and even some telecommunications companies are but examples of institutions that today are financial services companies in whole or considerable part but are able to operate totally outside the system of financial services supervision and regulation. In many cases, they compete head-to-head with entities that are regulated, creating a seriously un-level playing field and causing, in my view, regulated institutions to "reach for risk" in order to compete with the cost advantage that comes to institutions that do not have to bear the added burdens that come with being a regulated institution.'[10]

Up until the 1990s, most efforts to systematise and regulate Islamic finance have been ad hoc and sporadic. There were no global *Shari'a* standards, a limited secondary market, and modest integration with conventional banking systems and regulations.

The Islamic banking community is keenly aware of the last point and, through two important collaborative institutions: (1) the Accounting and Auditing Organization for Islamic Financial Institutions (AAOIFI) and (2) the Islamic Financial Services Board (IFSB), has been working closely with the Bank for International Settlements, the International Monetary Fund, the World Bank and global central bankers to ensure that Islamic banking, as a family of methods, is included and that Islamic banks are part of the system. As this book will show, the practices and instruments of Islamic banking may be made to fit, with increasing ease, within the global financial system, and may do so with fewer risks.

AAOIFI, the IFSB and various training institutions have slowly generated a growing consensus relating to *Shari'a* standards, even if the ultimate outcome is likely to be a bi-polar standards set with one polar centring in Bahrain, and the other in Kuala Lumpur: and Gulf and Malaysian standards accommodating

Exhibit 5 **Regulatory infrastructure trends**

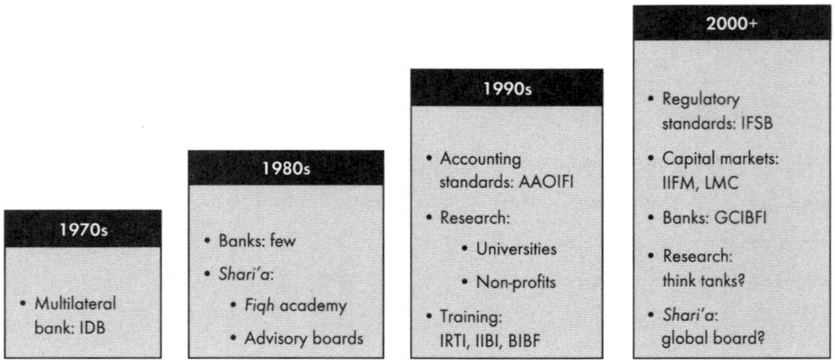

Source: Author's own.

an agreement to disagree about specific rules underlying certain structuring concepts. These tightening, coalescing standards lead to a clear movement to facilitate not only a secondary market for Islamic instruments, but a secondary market that connects to the global capital markets.

The Islamic sector is developing strong vehicles to instill global regulatory confidence in the sector. But what of Muslim consumer confidence[11] and the reputational risk for both institutions and the sector? When one surfs the web, various chat groups provide platforms for consumer and activist complaints about the evolution of the industry, its selection of solutions, and how it is governed. A common refrain in these chat groups is that 'anybody' can give/get a *fatwa* for almost any product. Participants in these chats challenge whether or not there is a system instead of some businesses with Islamic labels. These queries raise a direct question as to whether or not there is an Islamic legal order that plugs into the larger legal and financial order with rules that allow confidence in Islamic products and providers to be protected. Although the Islamic Development Bank (IDB) was designed to be a central bank for Islamic banking,[12] it has not yet filled this role. Into the gap, the BMA, Bank Negara Malaysia and a growing list of central banks have been providing international basis, through bodies such as AAOIFI and the IFSB, for building a global Islamic regulatory approach based on increasingly clear Islamic standards. Such emerging standards are also leading to a tightening of variances between *Shari'a* approaches. This book works through the structures that most closely comply with the core consensus among Islamic scholars and these leading regulators.

The emerging Islamic regulatory framework, however, still does not allow for the prospect of providing liquidity during a crisis. Although certain Islamic banks faced liquidity crises during the first Gulf War of 1990 and 1991, this liquefaction risk was addressed ad hoc when specific central banks elected to step in and make funds available to Islamic institutions. Thus, the question of confidence comes full circle to the question of whether or not there is an institutional commitment backed by means to protect the emerging Islamic financial system from shocks.

Notes about the book

Until the revival of Islamic rules applied to commerce, there seemed to be little basis for collaboration between banking and *Shari'a*.[13] As we work through this book, we will learn that the progress in Islamic finance has created the impression that there are conflicts among *Shari'a* scholars in their analysis or that the *Shari'a* itself is not systematic. However, it should be pointed out that when the field began its revival, 'the handful of scholars that had published on related subjects were without practical experience, having had no exposure whatsoever to modern banks and financial markets.'[14] This is no longer the case, and a growing global universe of *Shari'a* scholars has very practical capital markets' experience.

This book is designed to demonstrate the systematic guidance and structure that the *Shari'a* provides to the fields of commerce and finance. The book, particularly in the formative chapters, draws on a diverse universe of sources. Foremost, you will find that many of these are in English and often easily accessible. This is deliberate and meant to allow you to develop your own library and expand your research. In addition, we have offered a mix of classical and modern sources, some well known and some less so, strict *madhhab*-oriented, and apparently less strict more spiritual *sufi*-oriented.[15] The point is to demonstrate the unity in financial matters that comes from the diversity of thought in the Islamic scholarly and juristic traditions. There is no emphasis or priority on the stricter schools of thought; instead the book focuses on the actual practices according to the evolving consensus of modern scholars and the leading regulators.

---

1 Key elements of this chapter are derived from Kraty, Bryan and Abdelhaq Kafsi, *Islamic Finance & Mechanics* (Bahrain: unpublished manuscript, November 2004), as well as presentations developed by Stella Cox, Lawrence Oliver, Bryan Kraty and Abdulkader Thomas for the pre-conference workshops at the annual Euromoney Islamic Finance Summits in London from 2003 to 2005.

2 In the Islamic theological tradition all prophets before Prophet Mohammed (PBOH) are deemed to be 'Muslim', carrying the same message. Prophet Mohammed (PBOH) is the final prophet according to Muslims.

3 Ayyan Leasing & Investment Co., 'The Work of Islamic Banking & Investment Companies in the Gulf Cooperation Council', *Al-Mustathmiroon Magazine*, no. 37, April 2005, pp. 100–103.

4 State of the US Islamic Home Finance Market, unpublished report, AJIF.org, March 2005, also see Kraty and Kafsi, *op. cit.*

5 Usmani, Muhammad Imran Ashraf, *Meezan Bank's Guide to Islamic Banking* (Karachi: Darul Ishaat, 2002). See Chapter 2. Also see Thomas, Abdulkader, *What is Permissible Now!?* (Singapore: Muslim Converts's Association of Singapore, 1994).

6 Usmani, M.I.A., *Meezan Bank's Guide to Islamic Banking, op. cit.*, p. 13.

7 Edwardes, Warren, *Key Financial Instruments: Understanding & Innovating in the World of Derivatives* (London: Pearson Education, 2000), p. 8.

8 Shirazi, Habib, ed., *Islamic Banking* (London: Butterworth & Co., 1990), pp. 12–13: Quoting Murtadha Mutahhari's Persian translation of Imam Al Ghazali's *The Renaissance of Religious Knowledge*.

9 Lugwig, Eugene, *Systemic Risk: A Regulator's Perspective in Housing Matters: Issues in American Housing Policy* (Washington, D.C.: Fannie Mae, 2004), p. 175.

10 *Ibid*, p. 187. Also see Wirtz, Ronald, A., *Community Banks Full of Change*, (Minneapolis: 9th District Fed Gazette, January 2005).

11 *Ibid*, pp. 176, 177.

12 Thomas, Abdulkader, tr. of Elnaggar, Ahmed, *Memoirs* (unpublished 1995).

13 DeLorenzo, Yusuf, 'Shari'a Boards and Modern Islamic Finance: From Jurisprudence of Transformation and Adaptation', paper presented at IFSB, London, May 2004.

14 DeLorenzo, *op. cit.*, citing Dr Muhammad Abd al-Ghaffar al-Sharif, 'The Shari'a Supervision of Islamic Banks', presented at the First Conference of *Shari'a* Supervisory Boards for Islamic Financial Institutions, organised by the Accounting and Auditing Organization for Islamic Financial Institutions, October 2001.

15 A *madhhab* is one of the primary Islamic schools of juristic thought. There are four major *Sunni* schools and one primary *Shia'a* school which have strong views informing financial transactions. *Sufi* tends to refer to a form of spiritualism that is not specifically legalist or tied to a particular school.

Examining the role of Islamic law

1

Abdulkader Thomas

Introduction

The field of Islamic finance is the revival of a classical approach to commercial transactions. The efforts of a relatively small group of Muslim activists in the 1950s and 1960s began a revival among modern Muslims seeking to organise their financial affairs without *riba*. Their work reflected the view among Muslims that Islam is a complete way of life and is not separated from commerce. The revival was embarked upon in the absence of continuous transacting and litigating in the field of commerce under Islamic rules and applying Islamic concepts. The notable early concepts were tested by economists such as Dr Ahmed Elnaggar or merchants such as Saeed Al Lootah.[1] These first endeavours in Mit Ghamr, Egypt, and Dubai had to struggle against adverse political trends and often had limited *Shari'a* research to support them.

Forty years later, the field of Islamic finance is globally accessible. Islamic institutions and consultants offer solutions and alternatives to consumers in both emerging and developed markets. Yet, many Muslims question the efficacy of many Islamic institutions or financial instruments. Certainly, there are important issues with regard to specific offerings and approaches to developing *riba*-free systems and instruments.

The fact that we are reviving a specific values-based approach to finance means that we must engage in significant historical research. This research is not carried out in a vacuum. 'New research should seek to meet the needs of contemporary life in a light of critical evaluation of modern experience.'[2] For instance, the *Shari'a* does not endow the corporation with a personality, meaning, rights and duties, similar to a natural person, but almost all western laws do. This, and a variety of other legal and organisational matters, are pertinent to the changes in global commerce and communications that require high-quality research into authentic Islamic resources in order to define truly permissible commercial outcomes for the devote Muslim with respect to relevant and fair-priced transactions and structures.

In this book, we work with the consensus of modern Islamic scholars on the core methods of commerce now practised in the field of Islamic finance. We will work through relevant examples of concepts and transactions and analyse the components that make them permissible. But, first, we will look at the underlying framework that is the *Shari'a*. In the next two chapters, we expand upon these principles to discuss their application to permissible commercial practices and contracts as accepted most widely by today's active *Shari'a* scholars.

Maqasid al Shari'a

'The aim of *Shari'a* is to make people happier in this world and the Hereafter.'[3] This is seen to lead to the concept of *taysir*, or making things easy. This relates closely to *raf' al haraj* or the removal of hardship. Such important objectives of *Shari'a* are meant to assure that there is no hardship in religion. The compiler of *hadith*, Tirmidhi, reported: 'You have been sent in order to make things easy, not as ones who make them difficult.'[4] Ultimately, these are meant to lead to the achievement of the public good or *maslahah*.

Often, a survey of bankers and lawyers active in the field of Islamic finance will throw up two firmly rooted replies to a primary query about their understanding of *Shari'a*. The first is to indicate that one is merely an order-taker and that it is the Muslim consumer (banker or otherwise) who defines the *Shari'a* parameters. The second is to retreat behind the defence that one is not Muslim and not obliged to know more than fundamental transaction-structuring rules that have been proven in the market. Neither is an objectionable reply, but neither reply will guide one to the sound basis of structuring a platform for the sound and logical growth of Islamic financial business.

Anyone who will contribute to the field's evolution must have a rudimentary understanding of the theological and philosophical underpinnings of *Shari'a*. The first principle of Islamic theology is *tawhid*. This is the most stringent approach to monotheism and constitutes the fundamental *Qur'anic* message. Adherence to *tawhidic* theology means that the Muslim accepts the concrete rules established by God and His Messenger, the Prophet Mohammed (PBOH). These rules seek to define the *tawhidic* lifestyle and achieve a very clear set of values relating to this life, namely: human life, human intellect, property, honour and conscience.[5] The safeguarding, in order of priority, of these five values should allow each human to live a quality life in which he or she is free to exercise his or her conscience and worship God in the most uninhibited and loving manner.

The protection of these five values leads to two clear principles that will become repetitive themes of this book. Foremost, within the specific framework of the *Shari'a*, there is substantial freedom of choice in almost every aspect of life, including commerce. Second, property may be freely held or traded. (This is independent from a separate theological argument that all worldly property is held by human beings in trust for its factual owner God; or that human beings are merely the caretakers of this world and its contents.) With these tools, we are able to have clarity as to the ends or goals of the *Shari'a*, its *maqasid*.

An understanding of the *maqasid* allows for comfort with *ibaha* or permissibility. This is a defining principle of *mu'amalat* or commerce in Islamic legal terminology. Ibn Taymiyyah wrote that 'Unless God and His Messenger have decreed them to be forbidden. But, God the most High never prohibited a contract in which there is a benefit for the Muslims and does not inflict any harm upon them.'[6] Kamali expands on the quoted approach that it is not sufficient to presume that a contract is forbidden if it is not explicitly forbidden. Therefore, according to Kamali, there is no need to search for affirmative evidence in the original sources to declare a transaction valid.[7]

These freedoms, however, do not exist in a vacuum. The role of humans as defined in the *Qur'an* is as *khulafa'a* or stewards, wardens of this created world. As a result, the *Shari'a* is applied to protect that which is created. Within rules of protection, not only are the five ends to be protected; but all that is created. Among the principles to be applied are the prevention of waste,[8] *israf.* The human inclination is often to be excessive in all things, and the *Qur'an* prescribes a cure in *Zakah.* These purifying dues are a balancing feature that reminds the Muslim of his role as a custodian or steward. Wealth and ownership bestowed upon us for a temporary time oblige its management in a way that is beneficial to all, without causing harm.[9] *Zakah,* which is not a prominent topic in this book, provides an indirect outlet for wealth accumulated in any one place to provide help to others. Another outlet for wealth to be driven to help others is the charitable trust or *waqf,* which is outlined in Chapter 3.[10]

Although man is limited to his destiny or *qadr,* beyond a certain point, the free will of humans is constrained by divine providence. In this book, we emphasise the realm of commerce and finance within the freely chosen acts of humans, as freely chosen to be circumscribed by the *Shari'a.* Certain accompanying principles including *israf* and *qadr* are not expounded upon further as they travel beyond the realm of theologically governed commerce into other aspects of theologically shaped, but not specifically commercial, life.

Sources of law

Qur'an and *Sunnah*

If the concrete rules of *Shari'a* are those established by God and His Messenger, then they must be found in specific places. The *Qur'an,* which Muslims believe as the immutable and final revelation of God, is the primary source of law and contains the rules explicitly established by God. *Qur'anic* verses making precise injunctions and offering specific guidance are called the *ayat al-ahkam.* When it comes to commerce, there are only three clear rules that are established among the *ayat al-ahkam:* the forbidding of *riba;* the admonition to avoid consuming one another's wealth inappropriately; and to engage in commerce through written contracts.[11]

The paucity of explicit *Qur'anic* legislation on commerce drives the Muslim to the authentic sayings and reported actions of the Prophet Mohammed (PBOH). Collectively, these are termed the *Sunnah.* The origin of the term is a *hadith*[12] of the Prophet: 'Follow my Sunnah... and that of the rightly guided caliphs who would succeed me; hold onto it firmly and guard yourself against innovations, for every innovation is a mischief.'[13] Often, this *hadith* is taken as proof that Islam is against any form of innovation. In fact, the specific reference is to innovation in the defined beliefs and practices of Islam. Muslims have, over history, notably in the early centuries of the spread of Islam, clearly understood that this term relates to matters of belief and worship, not science and commerce.

The early Muslims developed an analytical method for qualifying the reliability of *hadith*, a method which is similar to what we now call the scientific method:

> 'Since the *hadith* was passed verbally from one generation to another, the science of *rijal* was developed for the critical examination of the life-histories and the trustworthiness of the *hadith* transmitters. The narrator of a *hadith*, for instance, ought to state his source. If the source was not an original companion of the Prophet, the narrator had to state the secondary source from which he received the *hadith*. Each *hadith*, therefore, had to be prefixed by a chain of narrators of authorities, *sanad*, that went back to the original narrator. This process was called *isnad* (unbroken chain of transmission).
>
> 'The method of criticism which the scholars of *hadith* followed helped them in discovering the degree of accuracy of a particular transmitter of a particular *hadith*. Jurisprudentially speaking, there are many restrictions for considering a *hadith* suitable to furnish the ground for a legal precept. Jurists categorised *Sunnah* into two major categories: *maqbul* (accepted) and *mardud* (rejected). The accepted *Sunnah* is divided into two groups: *sahih* (authentic) and *hassan* (agreeable). The vast majority of jurists regard the first category as the only valid part of the *Sunnah* for serving legitimate grounds for law.'[14]

Although some people believe that the *hadith* are subject to controversy, the rigour of *hadith* analysis has meant that the *Sunnah* has been free from controversy since the ninth century of the common era. Within the *Sunnah*, matters of worship are highly detailed and matters of commerce or *mu'amalat* are subject to varying degrees of emphasis.[15]

Subsidiary to the *hadith* are the *athar* or sayings of the companions and immediate generation following the life of the Prophet. The *athar* are accepted as illumination of the *hadith* or evidence of a particular practice observed or tolerated during the Prophet Mohammed (PBOH)'s lifetime.

Means of legislation: *ijm'a, qiyas* and *ijtihad*

Fiqh, according to Dr Mohamad Adam El-Sheikh is the exercise of intelligence in the absence of command from the *Qur'an* and *Sunnah*, requiring intelligence and independent judgement.[16] Whereas the *Qur'an* and *Sunnah* are the sources of law, *ijm'a*, *qiyas*, and *ijtihad* are means of legislation.[17] Yet this human exercise is limited:

> 'Divine law is an objective transcendent reality, by which man and his actions are judged, not vice versa... To attempt to shape the Divine law to the "times" is, therefore, no less

than spiritual suicide because it removes the very criteria by which the real value of human life and action can be objectively judged and thus surrenders man to the most infernal impulses of his lower nature.'[18]

Nonetheless:

'legal rules in the *Quran* and *sunna* are limited in number, although they cover extensive areas of life. Many of these rules offer general principles and guidelines. Justice is ordained for essentially all human activities: in family, in business, in the whole society, between rulers and the ruled, and in all universal relations in general. In the field of transactions, for example, the *Quran* and *sunna* emphasize the essential requirements for mutual consent for any contract and the prohibition of exploitation, fraud and usury.'[19]

Typically, most analysts of *Shari'a* write that *ijm'a* is the third source of legislation. In reality it is *ijtihad*. One may consider *ijtihad* to be the third source because this is the result of either individual scholarly effort[20] or collective scholarly and juristic analysis. The latter, or collective, *ijtihad* is *ijm'a*. The areas which comprise *ijtihad* include: *qiyas, istihsan, istislah* and *'urf*.

Qiyas[21] *– analogical reasoning*

Many Islamic scholars feel that the application of the principles of the *salam* contract to manufacturing is a clear case of analogical reasoning. *Qiyas* is sometimes rejected by modern factions as a means of determining legal precepts. Yet, an authentic *hadith* of the Prophet Mohammed (PBOH) reports the verbal instructions of the Prophet to Muadh ibn Jabal, may God be pleased with him, when he was posted as governor of Yemen. The Prophet asked how he would determine matters. He replied that he would first turn to the *Book of God;* if he could not find the answer there, he would apply the *Sunnah* of the Prophet; and if he could not find an answer there, then 'I shall decide according to my own opinion.' The Prophet was pleased with his process, for indeed, it would be an informed opinion, and Muadh's appointment was confirmed and with it the acceptance of *qiyas* as a means of legislating practical matters.[22]

'It is the nature of Islamic jurisprudence itself to insist on the freedom of qualified jurists to formulate and hold their own opinions. In fact, the inner dynamic for renewal known as *ijtihad* ensures the relevance of Islamic law to changing circumstances by empowering jurists to constantly revisit points of law and to improve upon them when and where necessary.'[23]

Istihsan – personal preference

Certain forms of contract do not, in general, conform to the accepted principles of contract in *Shari'a*. Yet, it is a personal preference, giving way over time to consensus, that such contracts are permitted.[24]

For instance, some Islamic scholars worry about the lack of commercial morality among obligors and allow for the collection of penalty interest so long as it is given to charity.

Istislah – public welfare

In the United States, primary mortgages generate a tax deduction for the consumer equal to the interest paid. Most Muslim scholars have agreed that non-interest bearing Islamic mortgage alternatives may generate the same deduction, even though the payment is not *riba* or interest from an Islamic perspective on the ground that this is a public good.

'Urf – custom

'Urf is accepted 'as a basis for rulings and judgements, provided it does not contravene or contradict Islamic values and principles.'[25] For instance, when we examine Islamic mortgage alternatives, we will learn that one provider has secured a ruling allowing a consumer to pay real estate taxes, even though she or he is not the primary or majority owner of property. This is consistent with local public (as opposed to private which the *Shari'a* scholars are also willing to examine) custom and justified in that the real estate taxes are inure almost exclusively to the benefit of the consumer.

> 'In the classical system, custom (*'urf*) played an important role. The legal maxim that "all transactions are to be considered lawful as long as they include nothing that is prohibited" went hand in hand with custom and mercantile practice in clearing the way for innovation in trade and commerce. However, when the Shariah boards of the modern Islamic banks began their work in the 70s, there was no significant Shariah-compliant trade taking place, and thus no customary practice in regard to it.'[26]

The conditions for *ijtihad* include making life easier within the permissible, protecting the public interest, eliminating a hardship, or necessity in the context of meeting the objectives of the *Shari'a.*[27] In matters of *ijtihad,* once the collective of Muslim scholars or *ulema* have formed a consensus about the soundness of an exercise of *ijtihad,* the differing opinion of one or a few scholars is not sufficient to overturn or invalidate the ruling.[28]

Ijtihad is a powerful tool available to Muslims for their continuous reinterpretation of authentic texts.[29] Nonetheless, *ijtihad* does not comprise either a permanent or mandatory principle of *Shari'a*. *Ijtihad* is susceptible to modification or replacement by a future derivation.[30]

Ijm'a is as much an outcome as a source of juristic principle. Once the community of jurists are in broad agreement about the *ijtihad* of one or more of their members; the *qiyas* of a qualified scholar; the public benefit that comes from an action or application of a rule; or the validity of a custom; then their common commitment constitutes consensus or *ijm'a*. Nonetheless, one is cautioned that often Muslim masses have confused *ijm'a* with their customs, which may or may not have a basis in the core sources of *Shari'a*, even introducing innovations which are contrary to precepts enshrined in the primary sources of *Shari'a*.[31] Nonetheless, *ijm'a* has been a fundamental tool of Islamic jurisprudence and points towards *shura* or consultation between scholars, jurists, various experts and the people as a whole.

Collectively, these methods are referred to as *usul al-fiqh* or the origins and roots of Islamic jurisprudence. Despite widespread scholarly consensus, there are always minority opinions which may not even look at the same source material and draw parallel conclusions.[32] They provide the methods whereby Muslims are able to extrapolate guidance for everyday life in accordance with the *Qur'an* and *Sunnah*. Historically, the approach of Muslim scholars has been to avoid codification and the evolution of *fiqh* interpretations parallels closely Anglo-American Common Law in the building of judicial consensus upon the interpretive endeavours of individual judges.[33]

For the Muslim, a simple understanding of *fiqh* allows the individual to distinguish between five categories of activity:

- *Fard or wajib* – obligatory actions that are required for the faithful to practise their religion;
- *Haram or mamnua'a* – forbidden activities which constitute major sins for the believer;
- *Mandub* – acts which are recommended, but not required of the faithful;
- *Makruh* – behaviour which is discouraged for the believers, but not explicitly forbidden; and
- *Mubah* – all acts about which the *Shari'a* is neutral and, quite possibly, the preponderance of commercial behaviour.

Islamic schools of law

The argument that Islamic law has ossified into four primary *Sunni* schools of law (Shafi'i, Maliki, Hanbali and Hanafi), the Jafari (*Shia'a*) and one or two less well-known, yet active, schools is based upon the view that *ijtihad* has ceased to inform the juristic process and development. In reality, the primary schools, called *madhahhib* (ways of proceeding on a path, *madhhab* is the singular) have two points that are each based on a body of texts and has a methodical approach to juristic analysis. Clerics and scholars trained in a particular school have a clear approach to problem-solving and legal decision-making, based on the school's approach to *usul al-fiqh*. Generally, a modern review of the rulings and behaviour of scholars indicates that *ijtihad* remains a viable and lively tool, applied with great care because, unlike the secular ruling, the outcome affects one's eternal soul. A Muslim jurist engaging in *ijtihad* perceives that an error in judgement may change the balance for millions of souls. Thus, the pursuit of *ijtihad* and conclusion of a ruling is a matter pursued with great care. In Islam, the role of the *mufti*, a person eligible to issue *fatawa*, is fundamentally the marriage of the spiritual and the legal.[34] Who, then, is eligible to act as a *mufti*?

> 'The pre-requisites for being a *mufti* are that a person be knowledgeable of the law with regard to primary rules, secondary rules, disagreements, and [legal] schools; that he

> possess the tools of independent reasoning (*ijtihad*) in their entirety; and that he be familiar with whatever he needs in order to derive judgements, namely, grammar, biographical information, and commentary on the verses that are revealed with respect to the laws and the narratives in them.'[35]

The second point is that, in matters of *mu'amalat* or commerce, the views of each of the active schools of Islamic law are much closer than in almost any other area.

The concerns of *Shari'a*

Muslims view as non-secular the secular disciplines of sociology, politics, economics and law. In other words, all sciences are fully interdependent under the *Shari'a*. In commerce the starting point for this interdependence is the belief that wealth is a trust given to mankind. Foremost, one does not transact with one's absolute personal property, rather one transacts with property placed in one's control for the duration of this life. This theory means that the law necessarily interferes in the dynamics of contract to ensure that each party is treated justly.

The dynamics most likely to cause injustice in contracts are, according to the *Shari'a*, *riba*, *gharar*, errors in possession or incorrect contract structures.

Riba

The *Qur'an* has four primary references to the word '*riba*' and each of these *Qur'anic* verses provides clarity as to the absolute nature of the prohibition, but without specifying the nature of the offensive behaviour. In order of revelation, these verses are:

> 'That which you give as interest to increase the people's wealth increases not with God; but that which you give in charity, seeking the goodwill of God, multiplies manifold.' Surat Al Rum verse 39.
>
> 'And, for their taking interest, even though it was forbidden for them, and their wrongful appropriation of other people's property. We have prepared for those among them who reject faith a grievous punishment.' Surat Al Nisa' verse 161.
>
> 'O' Believers, take not doubled and redoubled interest, and fear God so that you may prosper. Fear the fire which has been prepared for those who reject faith, and obey God and the Prophet so that you may receive mercy.' Surat Imran verse 130.
>
> 'Those who benefit from interest shall be raised like those who have been driven to madness by the touch of the devil; this is because they say that "trade is like interest" while

God has permitted trade and forbidden interest. Hence, those who have received the admonition from their Lord and desist, may keep their previous gains, their case being entrusted to God; but those who revert shall be the inhabitants of the fire and abide therein forever.' Surat Al Baqara verse 274.

Finally, the revelation in Surat Al Baqara continues to warn the reader that those who are involved with *riba* face, on the Day of Judgement, a war from God and His Messenger.

As if it were not enough that one faced such condemnation for engaging in *riba*, the *hadith* provide an aggressive reminder of the seriousness of the sin. According to Abu Hurayrah, as reported in the *hadith* collection of Ibn Majah, the Prophet Mohammed (PBOH) said that '*Riba* has seventy segments, the least serious being equivalent to a man committing adultery with his own mother.'[36]

These emphases on the extreme nature of the sin connected with *riba* means that the active believer is deeply worried about how to live free from *riba*. Such is the scale of the problem, that many Muslims involved with Islamic financial institutions, as customers or bankers, see this as a matter of eternal life and death.

Beyond the *Qur'anic* citations, there are just the six *hadith*,[37] not including the Prophet's Farewell Sermon, which cover the general issues of *riba*. As a result, understanding the meaning requires a clear interpretation of these *hadith*. Historically, Muslims have viewed these *hadith* as characterising *riba* in two categories: credit or *riba al-nasiyah* and exchange or *riba al-fadl*.

Riba al-nasiyah

Usamah ibn Zayd reported that the Prophet Mohammed (PBOH) said that, 'There is no *riba* except in *nasiyah* (waiting).'[38] This appears in Bukhari's Book of Sales and is complemented by the following report.

> 'Ali, may God be pleased with him, said that the Prophet, peace be upon him, said that "every loan that draws interest is *riba*."'[39]

Anas ibn Malik, as recorded in the Book of Sales in the Sunan of Bayhaqi, reported that the Prophet, peace be upon him, said:

> 'When one of you grants a loan and the borrower offers him a dish, he should not accept it; and if the borrower offers a ride on an animal, he should not ride, unless the two of them have been previously accustomed to exchanging such favours mutually.'[40]

The parallel to a loan of money at interest is intended and seen by Muslim commentators over the ages. As a result, the waiting of the first *hadith* means the waiting for a return of monies borrowed.

Riba al-fadl

The query for Muslim commentators then became how to know precisely what is the monetary commodity susceptible to *riba*. Abu Said Al Khudri reported that the Prophet, peace be upon him, said:

> 'Gold is to be paid for by gold, silver by silver, wheat by wheat, barley by barley, dates by dates and salt by salt, like for like and equal for equal, payment made hand to hand. He who makes an addition to it or asks for an addition, deals in *riba*. The receiver and the giver are equally guilty.'[41]

In this specific *hadith*, the circumstances relate strictly to the commodities used by the Arabian peoples as money.

Fadala bin Ubaid reported:

> 'we were in the company of Allah's messenger on the day of Khaibar, and mad transactions with the Jews for the *uqiya* of gold for the dinars or three [gold coins], whereupon God's messenger said, "Do not sell gold for gold, but for equal weight."'[42]

> 'Abu Said reported that Bilal came with fine quality dates. God's messenger asked him, "where did you buy them?" Bilal replied, "We had inferior quality dates and I exchanged two measures of the inferior for one measure of the superior as food for God's Messenger." The Prophet, peace be upon him, replied, "Beware, that is in fact *riba*, don't do it. When you intend to buy good quality dates, sell the inferior in a separate deal and then buy the superior."'[43]

The classical interpretation of these authentic instructions is that there are two forms of *riba*: *riba al-nasiyah* which is the *riba* of delay or interest on a loan; and *riba al-fadl*, which is the *riba* of excess when monetary commodities are traded.[44] When we examine these dicta from the *Qur'an* and the *Sunnah*, we understand clearly that the trading of money for money, whether hand to hand or over time is not meant to be a business per se in the *Shari'a*. Money is not a 'commodity' in itself, merely reflecting a 'time value' for a return. Rather, money is a measuring tool and value determinant, devoid of its own integral value.

At different times in history, some Muslims have tried to limit the rules of *riba* to the six commodities used as money by the Arabians during the time of the Prophet Mohammed (PBOH). Yet, the consensus of Islamic scholars has always been that anything which has the genus of money in a particular society is governed by these rules, whether it is paper money, cowry shells, electronic chits, leather strips or items and concepts as yet unimagined by inventive people.

As a result, interest mirrors the condition of *riba*. This requires the financier to be linked to the underlying transaction in a way that is not the same as a traditional interest-bearing loan. The implications for modern financial businesses are quite broad. For instance, receivables are deemed to be money, as are guarantees. As money, they are necessarily subject to the rules of *riba*.

Gharar

Abu Huraira reported that the Prophet Mohammed (PBOH) said, 'Do not meet the merchant in the way and enter into business with him, and whomever meets him and buys from him, then should the merchant [find a better price] in the market when he arrives, has the option [to rescind the original transaction].'[45]

According to Kamali, the majority of Islamic scholars view *gharar* as 'both ignorance of the material attributes of the subject matter of a sale, and also uncertainty regarding its availability and existence.'[46] As a general principle, *gharar* is prevented when transactions are transparent with all details agreed in advance and ownership undisputed, preventing one party from improperly consuming the wealth of another. The above *hadith* indicates the first of two primary components of *gharar*, namely that transactions must be transparent to the mutual advantage of both parties. *Gharar* is derived from the root concept meaning 'deception'; there is no basis in *fiqh* or linguistics to consider *gharar* as 'trading in risks' as contended by some western scholars. As a general principle, *gharar* is defined as 'preventable ambiguity or uncertainty.'

In *Shari'a*, for *gharar* to invalidate a contract, it must not be trivial, it must be relating to the object of the contract, and it must specifically prove in conflict with custom. Either non-trivial or excessive *gharar* may, in the view of many jurists, be tolerated if there is an overriding *maslahah* or 'public benefit.'[47] This causes Kamali to point out a matter of significant importance for this book, that such tolerance allows the Islamic contracts of *salam* and *istisna'a*. Preventable uncertainty is the definition preferred in this work, as some degree of *gharar*, in its expansive meaning, is present in any contract subject to risks in the ordinary course of business.[48]

For instance, Uqba bin Amir said, 'It is illegal for one to sell a thing if one knows that it has a defect, unless one informs the buyer of that defect.'[49] The case raised here is that disclosure in advance cures many otherwise problematic issues in a sales or other relationship.

The prevention of *gharar* is similar to modern western market and consumer protections. As a result, many Islamic scholars find comfort in the forms of disclosure used in highly regulated consumer lending and securities markets and encourage the adaptations of such disclosures to protect consumers of Islamic products and services.

Contracts

> 'Do not consume one another's wealth unjustly, and be aware that lawful gain should be only through business based on mutual consent among you, and to not destroy one another.' *Qur'an* Sura 4 verse 29.

The concept of 'contract' in Arabic has parallels to contract in most western legal systems. The Islamic approach is significantly more narrow than the Anglo-Saxon view of contract. The Islamic view distinguishes between contracts, promises, commitment, disposition, and expressed intentions.[50] When these actions have legal impact, they are the objects of law and subject to specific rules in the *Shari'a*. The precision is from the word for contract *'aqd* which means to bind or tie tightly.[51] The strength of binding defined by this word is given in its *Qur'anic* usages.[52]

For *Shari'a* purposes, a contract (in this book, we only mean *'aqd* when using the English word contract) is the freely made mutual binding of two legally competent parties and typically relates to property or money (*mal*).[53] The parties to a contract are obliged to fulfill their stated obligations so long as these are not repugnant to the *Shari'a*. Ibn Umar reported that the Prophet Mohammed (PBOH) said, 'There is no transaction between two persons entering a transaction until they separate, but only when there is an option to annul it.'[54] If one party fails, it is subject to punishment or losses. Even unwritten contracts have very specific rules that must be observed in order for a contract to be validly executed.

Rights and freedoms of contracting parties

These are extensive under *Shari'a*. But, scholars agree that any stipulation among the contracting parties should not frustrate the nature and purpose of the contract itself.[55] For instance, elements of a contract may be deferred so long as they are recorded and witnessed.[56] There are subtle distinctions relating to these freedoms and underlying conditions in the main schools of Islamic thought that are not the object of this book. As a general principle, whenever a *Shari'a* scholar finds invalid stipulations in a contract, like most western law judges, he or she will only require the removal of the invalid *shart* or stipulation.

A commitment is a specific unidirectional judicial condition by one party to do or refrain from a specific thing. A contract contains two commitments which are specific in nature.

A promise (*wa'ad*) is a unilateral expression of obligation to perform an act, transfer a right or refrain from something. A promise is one party's commitment, for which that party may suffer specific consequences including being obliged to pay compensation to the promisee.[57] But, a promise, no matter how specific, is not a contract due to its unilateral nature. Whereas a contract is a legal and a moral duty, the *Shari'a* views a promise solely as a moral obligation.[58] Nonetheless, according to Usmani, a promise may be enforced or made the subject of punishment.[59]

Disposition is a general state that includes expressed intention. But neither is necessarily specific. Thus, a promise or commitment is a form of disposition, yet a disposition may be more general and not have legal effect in *Shari'a* parlance.

Conditions of contract

A contract is built on the pillars of offer (*ijab*) and acceptance (*qabul*). Once *ijab* and *qabul* are married through statements using the past tense such as 'I bought' and 'I sold', the contracting parties are liable for execution of their parts under the contract.[60] A valid contract in *Shari'a*, however, requires three primary conditions:

1. The object of the contract must be permissible under *Shari'a*;
2. The object should be specific and free from *gharar* (preventable ambiguity or uncertainty); and
3. Generally, the object should exist (certain contracts such as *salam* or *istisna'a* relate to objects which may not exist yet, or are to be produced).

Dr. Kharoufa cites Surat al Nahl, verse 90 of the *Qur'an* to demonstrate that the Islamic law of contract admits a theory of modification due to contingencies. Such a theory of contingencies is based on a core concept of equity and justice at the centre of the *Shari'a*.[61] Likewise, certain options allow contracting parties to validate the offer and acceptance of their proposed counterparties.

The theory of contracts in *Shari'a* is, as a general principle, built upon specifying quantity, quality and number, even though some jurists are willing to be more flexible than others.[62] Also called 'stipulation', there is a wealth of *hadith* discussing complex stipulations; for instance, according to Ibn Umar, 'Whoever pollinates date palms and then sells them, the fruits will belong to him unless the buyer stipulates that the fruits should belong to him [and the seller agrees].'[63]

As noted above, a contract is not necessarily void if it has a condition that is impermissible.[64] In certain cases, the invalid condition may be removed in and of itself, or the entire contract may be rendered void. The circumstance is subject to review on a contract-by-contract basis.

The preponderance of Islamic commercial law literature covers the law of sale and what constitutes the valid conditions of a sales contract. Although banking existed in Baghdad prior to the Crusades,[65] it facilitated the long-distance sales of international trade and safekeeping of monies. Partnership, renting and other activities which we today view as financial are developed in *Shari'a*, but not in the same manner as they have evolved in the West and this is why we must return to the question of *ijtihad.*

> '... even if the nominate contracts were based on earlier models, their real value was that they were widely known and accepted. By insisting that Muslims transact by means of a specific set of well-defined contracts, the Shariah ensures that all parties have every opportunity to understand what they are getting themselves into when they transact. The classical Islamic system of *mu`amalat* (transactions) is so highly articulated for precisely this reason. While the scriptural foundations of that system may be abbreviated, owing to their delineation of principles rather than specifics, the dynamic of ijtihad inherent to fiqh has ensured that Muslim jurists, and especially Shariah boards continue to comment and build upon the theoretical constructs.'[66]

Finally, a contract will entail one party appointing a third to fulfill his or her obligations as an agent. This gives risk to the broad concept of *wakala* or agency. Muslim jurists have granted substantial liberty for the parties contracting to appoint one or another as agent to complete a transaction. This might even include a seller appointing the buyer as an agent to source goods for sale to the buyer as the seller's agent.[67] As is explained later, this liberal approach to agency will prove extremely important to pursue a large number of the transactions described in this book.

The rule of possession (*qabd*)

The right to sell things is subject to properly coming into possession. Wrongful possession is a matter that is subject to punishment after death in an obvious and painful way: 'He who wrongly took a span of land would be made to wear it around his neck ... on the Day of Judgment...'[68]

The fundamental principle underlying the rule of possession is that wealth, in every conceivable form, is created by God and is His 'property.'[69] This is derived from the following respective *Qur'anic* instruction and observation: 'Give to them from the property of Allah which He has bestowed upon you.' (24:33) and, 'Have they not seen that, among the things made by our own hands, We have created cattle for them, and thus they acquired the right of property over them?' (36:71). Such rights are not arbitrary, but subject to divine injunction and guidance.[70]

Ibn Abbas reported that the Prophet Mohammed (PBOH) said, 'He who buys food grain should not sell it, until he has weighed it [and then taken possession of it].' And Ibn Umar reported that He said, 'He who buys food grain should not sell it until he has taken full possession of it.'[71] The rules of possession for grain and money are distinct, more restrictive, from non-foodstuffs as these are explicitly cited in the *hadith* governing *riba*. The *hadith* 'Sell not what is not with you', according to Kamali, is not in Bukhari and Muslim, and has transmission issues elsewhere.[72] As we shall see in our chapter on derivatives, this point will be critical.

Forms of possession: *haqiq* and *hukm*

There are two forms of possession in *Shari'a*: physical (*haqiq*) and constructive (*hukm*). The former is self-evident, the latter means that the physical has not been realised, but an object is within the control of a party with all attendant rights and liabilities.[73] Possession, whether physical or constructive means that one has the capacity to deliver. Historically, Islamic courts have been willing to vouch for contracts of sale, no matter the distance, so long as the capacity of the seller to deliver could be validated.[74]

Possession is not a requirement for items that the seller did not buy or does not have to buy (bequests or gifts).[75] The Fiqh Academy ruled that the cause for this ruling is to avoid *gharar* as to the origins or delivery of the object of sale. Therefore, it is not a requirement, but a subsidiary condition, according to Kamali. One of the differences among scholars and schools of *fiqh* is that the ruling of *qabd* is only required with respect to the foodstuffs mentioned in the *hadith* about *riba*. This necessarily means that commerce should flow freely.[76]

As pointed out, *qabd* traditionally, in the view of many scholars, hinges on the existence of the object to be contracted. Yet, Ibn Qayyim pointed out that the seeming prohibition of the sale of non-existent objects is meant to be a prohibition of those things that are subject to excessive or non-trivial *gharar*. (The general rule, however, will not apply in key nominative contracts such as *salam* and *istisna'a*.)[77] Nonetheless, as a general principle for key contractual forms 'existence' is a test that will be applied in conjunction with the analysis of the object's capacity to be inspected and possessed. However, *qabd* is not required for certain contracts, as we shall discuss in this book.

Forbidden contracts and accountability

On the surface, the only forbidden contracts are either those that are explicitly forbidden or those centred on a forbidden object or purpose. In our case, we are mostly concerned about those contracts called *hila* and are meant to disguise a forbidden transaction as if it were permissible. The most common of these is called *ina Inah* which is the sale of the same object between the same buyer and seller in such a way to synthesise a forbidden loan at interest without drawing scrutiny. Curiously, this is the object of disagreement between Malaysian scholars who follow the ruling of Imam Shafi'i that each sale is a valid sale on its own merits, even if the combined act is the forbidden loan. This view is supported by a solitary *hadith* that is rejected by most others. As a general principle, the transactions described in this book are not meant to incorporate features that would draw them into the universe of *hila* structures. Nonetheless, one case will examine the use of *bai' al-'inah* as practised in Malaysia today.

Sh. Yusuf Al-Qaradawi interpreted the *hadith* of the Prophet Mohammed (PBOH) as follows:

> '"If people are left alone, Allah will give them provision from one another" establishes the principle in the field of commerce: that the market, its prices and sales, should be left free to respond to internal economic forces and natural competition without manipulation.'[78]

This last point leads us to understand clearly that merchants are accountable and governments have a responsibility to oversee the markets as fair, level fields of competition. In the case of Islamic transacting, there is an expectation that the government will prevent *hila* to the best of its ability.

Conclusion

Each element of structuring that we will describe harkens back to the principles outlined in this chapter.

In the relatively unsophisticated environments of many emerging markets, asset-backed finance and complex securities have not yet been introduced; if introduced, they are not yet widely accepted. This is typically an issue of local laws. Islamic finance, as we have discussed in this chapter, requires both a modern asset-based finance framework and updated analysis of the applicability of Islamic law and codes through *ijtihad*. Therefore, the methods with which successful bankers in emerging markets are familiar are often distinct from the latest asset-oriented developments in the developed capital markets. The application of Islamic rules will demonstrate strong parallels to some cutting edge practices in the developed markets, but with significant limitations on the derivation of non-asset-linked instruments and the geometric growth of debt. We will examine some simple concepts in the next chapter to understand the distinctions between an asset-linked debt in Islamic finance and the derivation of these rules in Malaysia. When we have completed that review, we will have substantial clarity about why, mathematical similarities aside, Islamic financial contracts are guiding the participants along a distinct path in contrast to traditional lending.

In contrast to the caustic criticism of one professor that the modern effort in Islamic finance is 'bad 14th century economics' with 'jurists developing rules themselves,'[79] one finds that the methods and tools are competitive 21st century economics with jurists and bankers following rigorous rules.

---

[1] Thomas, Abdulkader, tr. of Elnaggar, Ahmed, *Memoirs* (unpublished 1995).

[2] El-Sheikh, Mohamad Adam, 'The Applicability of Islamic Penal Law (Qisas and Diyah) in the Sudan', (Philadelphia: Temple University unpublished Ph.D. Thesis, Department of Religion, 1986), p. xviii.

[3] Doi, Abdur Rahman, *Shariah: The Islamic Law*, (London: Ta Ha Publishers, 1984), p. 449.

[4] Kamali, Mohammad Hashimj, *Islamic Commercial Laws: An Analysis of Futures and Options* (Selangor, Malaysia: IlM.I.A.h Publishers, 2002), p. 73.

[5] El-Sheikh, *op. cit.*, pp. 15–18.

[6] Kamali, *op. cit.*, p. 67.

[7] *Ibid*, p. 69.

[8] O'Barret Lakhdar, 'Towards a Green Planet: Why Islam holds the keys to a sustainable world', *Al Jumuah* vol. 16, issue 12, Thuls Hijjah 1425 (March 2005) p. 34.

[9] Esposito, John L. and John O. Voll, 'Khurshid Ahmad: Muslim Activist-Economist' in Abu-Rabi, Ibrahim M., ed. *Islamic Resurgence* (Islamabad: Institute of Policy Studies, 2000), p. 50. For an exhaustive discussion of *Zakah*, see, Al-Qaradawi, Yusuf, *Zakat* (London: Dar Al Taqwa, 1996).

[10] A useful resource on *waqf* is Al-Fadhli, Dahi with Thomas, Abdulkader, 'Characteristics of the Historical Formation of Awqaf' available at www.ajif.org.

[11] Ramadan, Said, *Islamic Law: Its Scope and Equity* (Kuala Lumpur: Muslim Youth Movement of Malaysia, 1992), p. 43. He indicates that there are 10 specific economic and financial injunctions, which I further reduce to these three primary categories.

[12] Individual sayings and reports are called *hadith* (plural: *ahadith*).

[13] Ibn Majah, *Sunnan Ibn Majah* (Cairo: Issa Al Halabi Press, 1952). p. 42–43. Variably, the term '*sunnah*' means 'method' (Ramadan, *op. cit.*, p. 45) or 'path' see DeLorenzo, Yusuf, 'Shariah Boards and Modern Islamic Finance: From the Jurisprudence of Revival and Recovery to the Jurisprudence of Transformation and Adaptation' presented to International Islamic Financial Standards Board, May 2004, London.

[14] El-Sheikh, *op. cit.*, pp. 41, 42. Also see Motziki, Harald, *The Origins of Islamic Jurisprudence: Meccan Fiqh before the Classical Period*, (Leiden: E.J. Brill, 2002).

[15] Ibid, p. 39. Often the rules governing Islamic finance are called *fiqh al-mu'amalat* or the 'jurisprudence of works'.

[16] Ibid, p. 1.

[17] Ibid, p. 58.

[18] Nasr, Seyyed Hossein, *Islamic Life and Thought* (London: George Allen & Unwin, 1981), p. 26.

[19] Osman, Fathi, *Sharia in Contemporary Society: The Dynamics of Change in the Islamic Law* (Los Angeles: Multimedia Vera International, 1994), p. 19.

[20] Ramadan, *op. cit.*, p. 33. Dr. Ramadan notes that the traditional order is not immutable. The root of *ijtihad* is *jhd* which means to strive or make a strenuous effort. Ijtihad is the VIIIth form intensification of this root which also gives us the IIIrd form *jihad* or defensive effort.

[21] Often referred to as one of the four main sources of legislation open to Muslims. Classically, the four sources are listed as the *Qur'an*, the *Sunnah*, *ijm'a* and *qiyas*.

[22] Al-Ashqar, Umar S., *Al-Qiyas* (Kuwait: Dar as Salafiyah, 1979), pp. 44, 45.

[23] DeLorenzo, *op. cit.*

[24] Kamali, *op. cit.*, p. 99.

[25] Hakim, Besim S., *The Role of 'Urf in Shaping the Traditional Islamic City*, in Mallat, *op. cit.*, p. 141. Hakim further links *urf* as a subset of *ada* (habit) and the basis for not overthrowing a people's live habit in the analysis of the early Muslim jurists, p. 144. Also see Kamali, *op. cit.*, pp. 79–81.

[26] DeLorenzo, Yusuf, 'Shariah Boards and Modern Islamic Finance: From the Jurisprudence of Revival and Recovery to the Jurisprudence of Transformation and Adaptation', presented to International Islamic Financial Standards Board, May 2004, London.

[27] Al-Omar Fuad and Munawar Iqbal, 'Some Strategic Suggestions for Islamic Banking in the 21st Century', in *Review of Islamic Economics*, no. 9, (2000) p. 49.

[28] Kamali in Mallat, *op. cit.*, p. 65. Kamali goes on to exposit cases from both authentic texts and classical scholars which indicate that a judgment need not build on prior cases, but invite fresh ijtihad to assure that a matter is addressed with proper equity.

[29] El-Sheikh, *op. cit.*, p. 28. Yet, as we shall see in this discussion, *ijtihad* requires significant training, and established religious authorities have been at points to point out that modern rejectionists like Al Qaida's Egyptian predecessors have no right to apply *ijtihad* based on their relatively limited learning and their narrow political aims, see Botiveau, *op. cit.* p. 274.

[30] Osman, *op. cit.*, p. 23. Osman goes on to propose that the role of *ijtihad* may result in distinct rulings applicable in Muslim majority societies as compared with Muslim minority communities in the West, p. 26.

[31] El-Sheikh, *op. cit.* p. 49.

[32] Cornell, Vincent J., ed. and trans., *The Way of Abu Madyan* (Cambridge: The Islamic Texts Society, 1996), p. 17. Elsewhere, see Motziki, Harald, *op. cit.*

[33] DeLorenzo, *op. cit.*

[34] Johansen in Mallat, *op. cit.*, p. 35.

[35] Powers, David S., *Legal Consultation (Futya) in Medieval Spain and North Africa*, in Mallat, *op. cit.*, p. 89, citing Abu al-Abbas Ahmad b. Yahya al Wansharisi (d. 1508) *al Mi'yar al Mughrib wa jami al Mu'rib al Fawai Ahl Ifriqiya wal Maghrib* (13 volumes, Rabat 1981 - 1983), vol. 10, p. 31.

[36] Ibid, p. 40.

[37] Usmani, M.I.A., *Meezan Bank's Guide to Islamic Banking* (Karachi: Darul Ishaat, 2002). pp. 39-44.

[38] Khan, Dr. Muhammad Muhsin, tr., Sahih Al-Bukhari, Vol. III (Beirut: Dar Al Arabia, undated), p. 210. Siddiqi, Abdul Hamid, tr. Sahih Muslim, Vol. III (Lahore: Sh. Muhammad Ashraf, 1992), p. 834. Also see Bukhari, *op. cit.*, pp 210-214 for a comprehensive listing of *hadith* relating to *riba*.

[39] Usmani, M.I.A., *op. cit.*, p. 47.

[40] *Ibid*, p. 41.

[41] Sahih Muslim, *op. cit.*, p. 834. Also see Bukhari, *op. cit.*, pp. 210-214 for a comprehensive listing of *hadith* relating to *riba*.

[42] Sahih Muslim, *op. cit.*, p. 836.

[43] *Ibid*, p. 837.

[44] Thomas, Abdulkader, ed., *Understanding Riba* (London: Routledge, forthcoming).

[45] Sahih Muslim, op.cit., p. 800. Also Sahih Bukhari, *op. cit.*, p. 199. In Bukhari, the concept of *gharar* is characterised as the sale of that which is not present. But, juristically, the concept has evolved over time as described herein.

[46] Kamali, *op. cit.*, p. 85.

[47] *Ibid*, p. 85.

[48] *Ibid*, p. 88.

[49] Bukhari, *op. cit.*, p. 166.

[50] Kharofa, Ala' Eddin, *Transactions in Islamic Law* (Kuala Lumpur: A.S. Noordeen, 1997), p. 7.

[51] *Ibid*, p. 1.

[52] Al Maidah, verse 1 and Al Bakara verse 278. These are two of the keystone references to *'aqd* or its plural *'uqud*. It is used repeatedly in the *Qur'an* to refer to the highest order of mutual binding, whether between believers and God or two human beings.

[53] Doi, *op. cit.* p. 356.

[54] Siddiqi, A.H., p. 804.

[55] Kamali, *op. cit.*, p. 131 and p. 76.

[56] *Ibid*, p. 142. The interpretation derives from a variety of interpretations of the *Qur'anic* verse 2:276.

[57] Yaquby, Nizam, Shari'a Panel, 4th Annual Euromoney Islamic Finance Summit, London, 23 February 2005. Also Dr. Mohammed Elgari in the same panel noted that the western law interpretation may treat a promise differently than *Shari'a*, but as a general principle, *Shari'a* scholars will not go beyond the *Shari'a*.

[58] Kharoufa, *op. cit.*, p. 23.

[59] See Usmani, M.I.A., *op. cit.*, p. 119 and M.T. Usmani, *An Introduction to Islamic Finance*, (Karachi: Idaratul Ma'arif , 1998), p. 88.

[60] Kharoufa, *op. cit.*, p. 12.

[61] *Ibid*, pp. 42, 43.

[62] Kamali, *op. cit.*, p. 93.
[63] Bukhari, *op. cit.*, p. 223.
[64] Usmani, M.I.A., *op. cit.*, p. 72.
[65] Maalouf, Amin, *Les croisades vue par les Arabes* (Paris: JCLattes, 1983), p. 70.
[66] DeLorenzo, *op. cit.*
[67] *Mejelle*, *op. cit.*, pp. 239-254.
[68] Sahih Muslim, *op. cit.*, pp. 847, 848.
[69] Usmani, M.I.A., *Meezan Bank's Guide to Islamic Banking*, *op. cit.*, p. 17.
[70] *Ibid*, p. 18.
[71] Sahih Muslim., *op. cit.*, p. 802. Also see Bukhari, *op. cit.*, p. 192-195.
[72] Kamali, *op. cit.*, pp. 110, 111. On p. 118, Kamali notes that Ibn Abbass uniquely expands the concept to other items than foodstuffs by conjecture.
[73] Usmani, M.I.A., *op. cit.*, p. 79.
[74] Hanna, Nelly, *Making Big Money in 1600: The Life and Times of Isma'il Abu Taqiyya, Egyptian Merchant* (Syracuse, NY: Syracuse University Press, 1998), p. 51.
[75] Kamali, *op. cit.*, p. 119.
[76] *Ibid*, p. 120.
[77] *Ibid*, p. 100.
[78] El-Helbawy, Kamal et al, tr., Al-Qaradawi, Yusuf, *The Lawful and the Prohibited in Islam* (Indianapolis: American Trust Publications, undated), pp. 258, 259.
[79] Elgamal, Mahmoud, remarks at the Fifth Harvard Islamic Finance Forum, Cambridge, MA, 9 April, 2004.

2 Understanding the *Shari'a* process

Abdulkader Thomas

Introduction

Shari'a scholars have played a highly visible and critical role in the development of modern commercial and financial services that comply with Islamic precepts. Often business people, including bankers, lawyers and beneficiaries, as well as regulators have found the *Shari'a* process daunting. Some feel it to be a non-systemic approach to law driven by personal whim. Many have failed to understand that the modern application of Islamic principles is actually taking place in a legal vacuum. Therefore, *Shari'a* scholars are as much engaged in product development, legal analysis and compliance oversight. As the scholars have worked hard for more than 20 years to build consensus on the primary products of the industry, business people impatient for results have chaffed. Yet, there are often challenges merging the *Shari'a*-engineered product into a financial regulatory environment that does not accommodate the fine points of *Shari'a* structures when shoehorned into the operations of banks.

Today there are three primary centres for thought on Islamic matters: Cairo, the Arabian Gulf–Indian Sub-continent axis and Malaysia. In the matters of Islamic finance, Cairo has taken a backseat, although Egyptians are engaged and active in the field in the two leading centres. Within the Arabian Gulf and Sub-continent regions the guidelines have tended to be stricter than Malaysia, relating in part to a strongly different view on the question of trading and discounting debt. Except in these two matters, the areas of convergence are wide and inclusive across the regions.

> 'It is the nature of Islamic jurisprudence to insist on the freedom of qualified jurists to formulate and hold their own opinions. In fact, the inner dynamic for renewal known as *ijtihad* ensures the relevance of Islamic law to changing circumstances by empowering jurists to constantly revisit points of law and to improve upon them when and where necessary.'[1]

Shari'a boards

Composition

There have been two distinctive approaches to the formation of *Shari'a* advisory boards with a third emerging. The first has been an effort of banking institutions to secure the membership of prominent and well-known Islamic scholars. Whenever the appointing body is an Islamic bank, the panel is normally appointed by the general assembly or board of directors. As such, the panel is independent of the management of the company and reports directly to the owners or their representatives. Often the appointing party will seek for the panel to include scholars who are well known within their home markets. Sadly, the universe of well-known scholars across borders who are multi-lingual is very small; perhaps only a dozen scholars are thus recognised. Many of these scholars are known as the 'Wall Street Sheikhs' due to their membership on the *Shari'a* advisory panel of the Dow Jones Islamic Market Indexes.

The second approach has been for a panel to include one or more of the well-known scholars as well as one or more that are less well known. The latter may be popular or respected in local markets. In addition, the latter may be viewed as candidates for membership in the more exclusive global universe of leading scholars.

Duties

Shari'a boards will normally deliver an annual letter of audited *Shari'a* compliance to be included in an Islamic institution's annual report and addressed to the shareholders, directors and public. The boards may also deliver a letter or *fatwa* relating to specific activities, transactions, or products to be posted or circulated as appropriate for the purpose of the *fatwa*. In the latter case, such letters may be addressed internally as guidance or externally as approval. It is not uncommon for scholars to view themselves as an additional layer of independent compliance oversight and audit for a business.

The evolving trend in several markets including Pakistan and Malaysia is for the central bank or other national authority to establish a national panel and require institutions to have in-house scholars. The former set either hard and universal rules or establish broad guidelines. The latter assist in the process of product development and implementation, assuring adherence to the rules or transacting within the guidelines.

Often, external observers fail to understand that the typical *Shari'a* board is an independent body. Although a panel may be compensated very well, the members are compensated whether or not they meet, issue a *fatwa* or prove favourable to the institution appointing them.

The vast majority of *Shari'a* scholars hold one or more of three main qualifications. Many hold an *ijaza* or licence from a traditional institution or noted scholar of authority in the appropriate branch of *fiqh*. Others are recent graduates with western-style degrees from specific degree-granting institutions in various Islamic countries. Examples of these include the International Islamic University in Malaysia or Al Azhar University in Cairo. A small number of active scholars are self-taught and have gained the respect of their formally educated peers and are admitted as colleagues by accepted Islamic scholars on the merits of their demonstrated expertise.

What is a *fatwa*?

A *fatwa* (plural: *fatawa*) is a certificate representing the opinion of its issuer, a *mufti*. In certain countries, the *mufti* is a formal judge with the power to adjudicate disputes and issue rulings of law which must be followed. In Islamic finance, the majority of scholars issuing *fatawa* are advising believers that they have formally examined the product, business, service or process and found it to comply with the rulings of *Shari'a*. Such a *fatwa* is non-binding, but a company would lose its *Shari'a* advisers (they would resign) and run significant reputational risk if it failed to comply with the terms of a *fatwa*.

The elements of research and approach are best described by one leading scholar:

> 'All Sharia Boards I know of, including ours at (The International Investor Co., Kuwait), and the International Fiqh Academy of OIC, Jeddah, do not restrict their fatwas [sic] in financial transactions to the rulings of any particular school of fiqh. They have the capacity and authority to choose a prior fiqh ruling from one school or the other, or exercise fresh ijtihad (original juristic ruling) not bound by the prior fiqh rulings of any school. This gives rise to Multiplicity and Variance.'[2]

Although confusing to outsiders and those unfamiliar with the *Shari'a* decision process, most Islamic scholars are comfortable with variability in *fatawa* and the periodic, apparent contradictions that may arise. This is because they retain, like any reasonable common law judge, the right to analyse the particulars of specific situations and local conditions in order to arrive at the best rulings that allow people of different circumstances to comply with the *Shari'a*. Likewise, so long as the impermissible is not incidentally embraced, the scholars generally wish to encourage innovation.[3]

The vast majority of *fatawa* surprise their readers with their simplicity. Islamic scholars do not believe that they have an obligation to do more than certify the correctness of a product or process when it is treading ground already well covered. For instance, a bank wishing to use the well-established *murabaha* or *ijarah* methods in consumer mortgaging, now well developed in the field of Islamic finance, may find that their *fatwa* comprises one or two paragraphs. However, *fatawa* relating to complex products often mirror the complexity of the product. For instance, a profit-sharing deposit at a US bank may have a primary *fatwa* for internal guidance running five or six pages and covering certain issues in depth. That same bank may have a shorter *fatwa* for public display as well. Or, a *fatwa* for a hedge fund complying with *Shari'a* may stretch to more than 50 pages.

Dr Zarka offers an important warning relating to the understanding of Islamic certificates or *fatwa*:

> 'Fatwas are not created equal! Those who have sufficient financial and fiqh background have a moral duty to look critically at different fatwas and be forthright in their well

reasoned approval or disapproval. Shariah scholars have a binding religious duty to retract an erroneous fatwa or correct it. We can help them in this by critically examining fatwas and their implications.'[4]

Preparing for the process

The best preparation for securing a *fatwa* is a detailed schematic of the product or process that is the object of debate. The schematic needs a clear legal analysis for the product, identification of tax issues, and logical flow of how the product or process works or is crafted. Diagrams supporting the text are helpful. If there are specific Islamic references or particularly relevant matters of *'urf* known to the bankers, these should be highlighted clearly. This schematic is the first step in what is almost always an iterative process with Islamic advisers.

There are several elements to the *fatwa* process. The scholars will have looked at a concept and rooted their analysis with the core sources of *Shari'a*. The primary meaning of *Shari'a* is the *path* (to truth, to pure water). This path of analysis will take general principles from the *Qur'an*, then look to the *hadith*, then the *athar*. Judgements, historical and recent are examined for applicable principles. The factors raised in the previous chapter will inform the process. The depth to which the *Shari'a* scholars will look into these resources will depend upon the novelty of the suggestion. For instance, the adaptation of a *murabaha* contract to a new jurisdiction will require less complex analysis than the determination of whether or not a hedging strategy is permissible or is tainted by impermissible instruments or processes.

Historically, the approach of the scholars was to pursue the strict methodology of one of the primary schools of *fiqh*: Hanafi, Hanbali, Maliki, Shafi'i or Jafaari. Yet, the complexity of modern commerce and finance has caused scholars trained in the unique disciplines of each school to work across disciplines. Increasingly, this inter-disciplinary approach is prevailing among the most active scholars as they manage new innovations and oversee ever more complex financial institutions. Islamic scholars do not follow a uniform code and are not obliged to follow legal precedent, as are Anglo-American judges; they have considerable flexibility within the law.[5] Nonetheless, the Muslim scholar finds that the nature of contracts within the *Shari'a* ambit is well defined, meaning that interpretive flexibility is limited with respect to the core of transactions as discussed in later chapters on *mudaraba* and *musharaka*, *murabaha*, *salam* and *istisna'a*, and *ijarah*. Interpretation becomes more critical on the margins, driving scholarly analysis into high gear with respect to novel transactions.

What will often frustrate bankers is that the well-known nominative contracts *mudaraba* and *musharaka*, *murabaha*, *salam* and *istisna'a*, and *ijarah* are traditionally practised as commercial contracts. Therefore, their application to finance is an adaptation that does not cause these contracts to shed their nature. This will cause new costs or challenges to arise in structuring a transaction that may not be present in the writing of a traditional banking transaction.

Another challenge for bankers is that there are variances between rulings at different Islamic institutions. Such differences often involve the same scholars. The implications of these differences include accounting, tax and regulatory treatment. Moreover, such distinctions may also make it difficult to compare the principles of *Shari'a* in order to draw conclusions about the development of repetitive processes. As is explained later in Chapter 13: The regulatory constellation and challenges, the Islamic system is evolving its own standards and best practices.

Two case studies: exceptions to the rule

This chapter closes with two case studies that are based on live situations. The parties and locations have been changed to make the actual deals and parties anonymous. Instead of focusing on the good ending or successful product development process, we look first at a situation in which an aggressive product design resulted in a poor marketing decision and an independent, negative *fatwa* against the company and its product. This first case highlights the need to have a clear understanding of *Shari'a* rules applying to one's product ingrained among the staff as well as a disciplined approach to interaction with *Shari'a* scholars, whether on one's own panel or independent.

The second case examines a situation whereby Islamic finance may provide a useful solution to a clear business problem. But, the apparent similarity of Islamic commercial instruments is deceiving. As a result, the seemingly obvious transaction structures and ease of adaptation are trumped by the fundamental changes in the business model required if a *Shari'a*-compliant approach is chosen.

Both cases represent exceptions to the rule, which is why they are helpful. As a rule, *Shari'a* scholars are collegial and unwilling to attack one another's opinions without the most deep and egregious cause.

Most often business decision-makers and *Shari'a* scholars ferret out bad ideas or incompatible processes very quickly. In fact, business planners, bankers and their lawyers often complain not that they are dragged months-long down a path to rejection, but that their 'good' ideas are too quickly dismissed.

Case Study 1: HomeFinCo – the need for a clear and disciplined approach

In early 2002, HomeFinCo was established by a wealthy South Asian with UK nationality and Dubai residence to provide Islamic mortgage alternatives in the UK and European markets with aspirations to follow into the US market. The company formed a panel of distinguished Islamic scholars, including several of the so-called Wall Street Sheikhs.

After extensive product development work with a leading City of London law firm and a major international consulting firm, HomeFinCo established a detailed business plan, retained its *Shari'a* board, and began product development. Ultimately, HomeFinCo designed and prepared for delivery to the

UK market a declining-balance partnership. Internally, the company was driven by its marketing focus as much as a desire to deliver *Shari'a*-compliant products.

The declining-balance partnership product developed by the company is a partnership between the consumer and HomeFinCo. The company's share declines with each monthly payment. Ostensibly there should be a lease, but HomeFinCo's adviser feared that a lease would cause securities investors to refuse to buy the end instrument. Ultimately, the instrument itself was a pool of instruments: an assignment of the partnership agreement, a note and a mortgage.

HomeFinCo secured a *fatwa* based on a highly nuanced understanding of the UK and European regulatory environment. The scholars were also influenced by their concern about specific practices known to be *maslahah*, protecting investors and consumers in poorly regulated countries that have poorly structured, unfair tax regimes. For instance, Muslims are allowed to enter into implicit, unwritten leases in those jurisdictions in which the authorities would penalise them excessively for entering into an explicit, written lease.

Contrary to the instructions of its *Shari'a* board, the company's head of marketing took it upon himself to present the product to a prominent board of local scholars. HomeFinCo's own scholars wanted any such enquiries to be directed to them. But the marketing manager was afraid that the company needed the approval of local scholars. He convened a meeting with a well-known Salafi scholar from Egypt with a significant following in the company's home market.

The scholar asked these questions and received answers as follows.

- As a partnership, will you share in the losses, if any, when the property is sold to anyone other than your partner? If so, what is the formula of profit and loss sharing?
  > HomeFinCo would not lose any sums, and there is no pre-set ratio of profit and loss sharing. [In fact, there was a pre-set ratio, but sales were driven to a procedure that would, in the normal course of business, cause the consumer to take title and negotiate the consumer's own sale to the market independently of the partnership.]
- If you are a partner, what share of taxes, insurance and maintenance do you pay?
  > HomeFinCo will not pay any of these costs and relies on a novel *fatwa* that looks at the benefits derived from such payments. [This *fatwa* relied upon a careful review of local *'urf* and tax policy which demonstrated that the consumer was almost the sole beneficiary from both tax and insurance payments. The manager failed to deliver the analysis to the Egyptian sheikh.]
- What is the object that you sell to the investor?
  > The manager incorrectly stated a mortgage and not a divisible ownership stake in the house.
- What is the basis for determining rent?

> The manager correctly stated Libor.

The following *fatwa* was then issued by the Egyptian scholar.

The fatwa[6]

In the name of God the most Merciful and most Gracious

Final Report Presented to HomeFinCo

To the dear brothers responsible for HomeFinCo: May God's peace and blessings be upon you; and now,

In response to your request for a legal ruling concerning the contract which your company is offering in the market to facilitate homeownership according to the *Shari'a* and following the consultation and opinion of many of the people of [religious] knowledge in this area, we are pleased to present you with the following [conclusions]:

First: Introduction to the Agreement:

We agree with you about the introduction you presented to us relating to the project and which indicates the necessity for a contract which is consistent with the *Shari'a* from one perspective and which is competitive in the marketplace and makes it possible for the consumer to enjoy benefits similar to or close to what he would realise with a *ribawwi* contract from the other perspective. And, this is the *Shari'a* consideration for those who would apply it by God's will.

Second: Observations of the Contract's Features:

The following are our observations about the contract:

This contract is not a valid contract of *sharika* based upon the information shared in our conversations and deliberations. The reasons follow:

- You don't abide by your duties as a partner as set out under *Shari'a*. The simple form of *musharaka* [partnership] includes participation in costs and benefits. For instance, in the event of selling the house, there are obstacles for the buyer and he is unable to leave without bearing the costs. As for the partner [co-owner], he is free from the normal consequences [of selling] and has but to realise his debt and what belongs to him from the selling price. And, you have reported that any profit or loss is solely for the buyer.

- The customer singularly bears the costs of insurance, taxes and maintenance costs as well as any other costs related to ownership, which may be officially required. In spite of being a partner in this house, your portion of ownership is decreased by the consumer's increasing ownership over time. This is not compliant with the *Shari'a* rules of contract.

In summary, you will buy your portion and you ought truly to consider yourselves creditors and not partners. Perhaps your justification for this is that your borrower will buy your portion at the end. And, you considered the value of this portion as a debtor's responsibility and you have organised yourselves on this basis:

- Your capital which represents your portion is not more than in the beginning. And there is no reliable relation between it and the price of the house. The profit is limited from the beginning and it will be collected monthly.
- The risks of ownership stop with the buyer and you cut yourselves off from them in the beginning. In the event that the house is sold for less than what remains of your portion, you will only take as a loss, as you mentioned. The part between the sales price and your debt, what is left, will be covered by insurance. What has been described is known to be corrupting [*fasid*] to a contract as executed in these societies, one in which the buyer in all circumstances carries the burden, and is obliged to increase his portion every month for insurance.
- The result is that you given up the role of a partner by leaving out of the partnership the costs and benefits and obliging the buyer alone to pay the taxes, insurance and maintenance while all that he owns is a small portion.

How can we fix this contract?

What remains is to determine the prospective scenarios to correct this contract as follows.

- First: The formation of a declining balance partnership which ends in ownership with the requirement of corporate responsibility and obligations, and you as partners in the house to the percentage of your portion in it, and all of the requirements relating to the house discharged according to one's portion in it. If the house's price is £100,00 and you own 90% of it, for example, when the house was sold for £90,000, then you will own only 90% of it, or £81,000. And it is possible that you would lease the house. This would be a separate contract. And, what you would take from it is rent based upon a lease, and not profit based upon sale. This is because the basis of rent is leasing the percentage that you own of it [the house] and not your sale of the house. Therefore it is a requirement that you meet the requirement of lessor for the expenses of maintenance and repair, and you have the ability to set the value of the rent to guarantee whatever you believe you should earn from it as a return on the investment of your capital. And, whatever arises as expenses and costs of maintenance, the total will be the rent. In this way, you avoid more expenses that you don't wish to bear. Then as you previously agreed, you may arrange to dispose of the house to the buyer in installments. And, each portion that you own will be the basis of rent until the full ownership is transferred.

- Second: The formation of a contract to sell in installments. If you wished to confirm your sum from the beginning as a creditor, with the buyer indebted, and to turn away from the hazards of partnership, then you might complete the arrangement applying the contract of *murabaha* [installment sale contract] as an arrangement for sale. Upon beginning this question, one proposes in the beginning, without any risks, to sell whatever one owns. If you owned this contract and sold it to your partner according to the agreement, and the installments may be exercised over years, your balance does not change as a debt obligation. The debtor pays the installments over the agreed period, and in this case if the house is sold because of a payment default, you have the right to claim all that is due to you from the price. There is no gravity in this case if you take from your legal guarantees what remains of your rights toward the buyer. This is certainly under the condition of a specific mortgage for the same sale.

But, there remains a risk, when we return to this matter, that it is not permitted to sell this contract to Big Investment Bank. As for the situation of selling according to this contract with a special purpose company, it is the question of the category of selling a debt. The solution of the contract is that it is not allowed as the revenue running from it is *riba*. In this condition, you are selling money on a deferred basis for money received today. If you don't sell the contract, the danger continues in the project in what you began from its basis. And, the outcome is that the contract should be signed from the beginning between the buyer and Big Investment Bank. The role of the special purpose company is that of a middle man or agent or intermediary company and your compensation for this project should be from the special purpose company, not the buyer.

If there were some operational considerations which need more discussion or suggestions to form another or to justify this formation, then please contact us to allow us to understand it.

Finally: We have to assure you of our thanks and the appreciation of your brothers for the idea of this project, and your care for questioning and investigating [the matter]. Nonetheless, we are unable to issue a positive *fatwa*. We hope that you take this view and these suggestions into consideration, and that you agree to stop marketing the project in its present form of mortgage until the contract is corrected and its permissibility validated. As we hope that you correct what you have made with respect to various contracts in the light of these observations. If you would like to answer further questions or convene a meeting to discuss and deliberate our view, we are more than willing to attend, by God's permission, We see that every sincere Islamic exchange is a thankful effort and should be supported. It is necessary to help one's companions and we offer you our respected advice and consideration. You have claims upon us for constructive advice and sincerity. And, God is behind the aspirations [of the believers] and He is the one who guides to the correct way.

Prominent Egyptian Sheikh's Teacher
Fiqh & Economics Expert
Member of the Organization of Islamic States
Fiqh Council

Prominent Egyptian Sheikh
Vice President
United Kingdom Islamic Fiqh Group

Outcome

Not only did the sheikh issue the *fatwa* cited above, but the word went out and interested consumers emailed a popular *mufti* with an online *fatwa* service. The result was similar. Although HomeFinCo developed a robust business, the company found that a significant sub-market refused to deal with it. Whenever the company made public presentations, there was always a buzz in the audience that the company was not truly *Shari'a* compliant and its prominent *Shari'a* scholars had been duped.

Case Study 2: US auto securitisation – differences in instruments are revealed

In late 2004, a significant US Twenty Group[7] organiser was receiving consistent feedback that investment bankers were pressing its members to securitise their car receivables servicing released. In auto dealerships, margins on sales are thin, and consumers lack sufficient means to make outright cash purchases. But, for a dealer to lend money would tie up too much cash. Investment banks had traditionally bought notes from dealer groups, allowing the dealers to retain servicing of the installment credit loans. The value of the servicing was often as much as 50 basis points on the loan balance for a period of up to three years. This residual income exceeded the costs of servicing and was perhaps the most profitable part of the business for the dealers.

One member of the group had been introduced to a Lebanese investment bank that had previously securitised, applying an Islamic method, auto leases in a major Middle Eastern market. He made his case to investigate an Islamic issuance strategy which would allow the group members to initiate Islamic instruments for securitisation, servicing retained.

The group appointed a lead member to engage in dialogue with representatives of the Lebanese investment bank as well as a panel of Islamic scholars headed by one of the Wall Street Sheikhs. Although the Lebanese bank was concerned with volumes and credit quality, the dialogue quickly turned to what instrument should be utilised. Could the standard installment sales contract and resultant note meet Islamic standards or could a standard auto lease meet the needs of Islamic investors and pass *Shari'a* scrutiny?

Complying with Shari'a

In the course of their meetings, the Twenty Group representative learned that neither the *Shari'a* panel with which he was dealing nor the likely Islamic investors organised by the Lebanese bank would accept to buy discounted auto receivables represented by notes, even if the underlying contract was structured to comply with the Islamic rules governing installment contracts. This was problematic, as from the auto dealer's perspective, *murabaha* was ideal. It seemed to be very similar to the type of installment credit loan with which the Twenty Group members were familiar. Title would pass from the dealer to the consumer and the consumer would agree to all obligations of ownership from insurance to maintenance. As a practical matter, the application of *murabaha* principles meant that the dealers could take the uniform installment credit contract and note, make small changes and be done with it. The process was easy and simple. The core concepts of the auto sales process matched nicely to the *murabaha* process:

1. identification of the asset;
2. possession by the dealer;
3. inspection by the consumer;
4. sales offer by the dealer;
5. consumer's acceptance; and
6. delivery to the consumer.

The difference would be that the contract forms would change. The servicing adjustments would be minimal.

But, from a *Shari'a* perspective, the installment credit sales receivable would be classified as 'money'. According to the *Shari'a* advisers, the re-pricing of a pool at any value other than the aggregate capital and mark-up would violate the Islamic rules of *riba*. As a result, the dealers found that they would not be able to securitise a pool comprised solely of *murabaha* receivables.[8] Moreover, the *Shari'a* scholars pointed out that even if eligible for a *Shari'a* securitisation, that is *sukuk* issuance,[9] requirements would make collections practices and late payment fees very different than standardised securitisations would allow. The scholars proposed leases as a preferred alternative.

Examining the documentation

The Twenty Group members were pleased with the result. They were familiar with leasing. Their initial impression was that there would be no significant difference between an Islamic and a conventional lease. The dealers delivered sample lease documents to the *Shari'a* panel. They were enthusiastic. They were comfortable that the cash flow, traditionally the object of western securitisation, may be attached to the asset without too much fuss from an Islamic perspective. Moreover, they liked the flexibility of Islamic leases, which included the independent pricing, pooling and trading of such leased assets.

Following their receipt of the lease documents, the Islamic scholars forwarded the following detailed questions to the Twenty Group representative:

1. How much variation is there from state to state for the lease masters?
2. The leases mentioned a 'prior credit balance': This was the loan or lease termination value from a prior vehicle merged into the value of the new contract. Would this mean that the financial obligation was greater than the value of the car before the car left the dealership?
3. Do you have the text of The Consumer Leasing Act; is it a state or a federal act; and will it prevent us from doing anything that we need to do to produce an Islamic lease?
4. Is the amount due at signing or delivery characterised as a 'deposit'?
5. What are the dealer's conditions triggering a disposition fee (practice and terms)?
6. What is the capitalised cost reduction?
7. Is the refundable security deposit different from the amount due at signing?
8. Reconditioning reserve – how does it work?
9. How is the termination charge determined?
10. What is the purchase option price and how is it priced?
11. What is the gap contract and waiver? Is gap insurance permissible?
12. Who pays the ownership costs: maintenance, taxes and registration fees?
13. How are liability and personal injury insurance handled and what are the state requirements? Are these uniquely related to operator issues?
14. How are funds applied in the event of a repossession?

Suddenly, it was clear to the dealers that an Islamic lease was not a reconstituted loan, but a unique instrument. A number of customs, geared towards facilitating dealer sales, were also likely to be unacceptable from a *Shari'a* perspective. If adopted, an Islamic lease programme would require a new lease form; new leasing practices; and new sales practices.

Outcome

The underlying US auto case led to the actual structuring of both *Shari'a*-compliant leases and installment credit transactions. After the Lebanese bank expended considerable money working on the products, one of the key US investment bankers resumed purchasing auto receivables servicing released, allowing the Twenty Group to cease pursuing the project.

---

1 DeLorenzo, Yusuf, 'Shariah Boards and Modern Islamic Finance: From the Jurisprudence of Revival and Recovery to the Jurisprudence of Transformation and Adaptation', presented at Islamic Financial Services Board Conference, May 2004.

2 Zarka, Dr. Muhammad Anas, 'Schools of Fiqh and Differences in Financial Rulings', posted 26 December 2004 at www.islamic-finance.net

3 Zarka, *op. cit.*

4 *Ibid.*

5 DeLorenzo, *op. cit.*

6 Based upon an actual *fatwa* delivered to an organisation offering an Islamic mortgage alternative to consumers.

7 A Twenty Group is a formal membership body of peer car dealers who share detailed data on a non-disclosed basis through a trusted moderator.

8 The *khulta* is discussed in greater detail in Chapter 9. As a rule, the *khulta* or mixture of sales receivables to asset certificates (non-cash, non-receivables) must be restricted to one third of the securitised assets. As an exception, some scholars have allowed this to be 50 per cent.

9 For more information regarding *sukuk*, see Adam, Nathif J. and Abdulkader Thomas, *Islamic Bonds: Your Guide to Issuing, Structuring and Investing in Sukuk* (London: Euromoney Books, 2004).

Equity finance vehicles: *mudaraba* and *musharaka* 3

Abdulkader Thomas with M. Ikram Thofeek

Introduction

The historical applicability and variety of *shirkah* or partnerships in *Shari'a* is easily traced to the partnership contracts registered by Muslim merchants in local courts.[1] Large numbers of these documents were later adjudicated for disagreements as to the particulars. By and large, the classical contracts represented either direct, unintermediated commercial investment or true peer partnership. These classical contracts provide a basis for the formulae that are applied in modern Islamic finance. Yet, financial intermediation and the emergence of the modern limited liability company with its unique personality both raise significant requirements for *ijtihad* to apply changing the formulae to meet the needs of modern commerce, such as in the case of a large-scale enterprise. Clearly, classical scholars had not contemplated the possibility of modern large-scale commercial enterprises with multiple layers of business complexity.[2]

When considering a choice between *mudaraba* and *musharaka*, the decision often turns on the role that the investor expects to play in the business. When seeking merely to be a capitalist and not be active in the management of a business, then the *mudaraba* is the optimal choice and has been so historically. Its flexibility to serve investors made it a common tool, named the *commenda* in trans-Mediterranean trade. But, *musharaka* allows one a significant freedom to amend the contractual arrangements and adapt to business circumstances as both a capitalist and an active partner or co-director of the operating business.[3] Two of the predominating trends in modern Islamic finance turn on an evolving consensus among Muslim scholars that modern concepts of limited liability and corporate personality may be applied to both the *mudaraba* and *musharaka* concepts. The first of these trends is the successful and widespread application of *mudaraba* to the Islamic funds and commercial finance syndication business. The second is the adoption of a form of *musharaka* to the deposit-taking business. Because *mudaraba* and *musharaka* fundamentally change a firm's ownership structure, they have not yet been widely adopted in emerging markets where they are unappealing to many privately held and family-owned companies. Even within the banking ambit, as is shown in Chapter 13 on the emerging regulatory environment, these forms produce unique challenges for implementation within the global regulatory framework.

Limited liability and corporate personality[4]

The traditional *shirkah* does not have a unique legal personality independent from the legal personalities of its partners.[5] On the one hand, countries in which Islamic courts are active, including Saudi Arabia, Pakistan and Malaysia, have all allowed the modern corporation and limited liability entities without significant challenge. On the other hand, many *Shari'a* scholars who actively work in the field of Islamic commerce and write about it remain uncertain that the concepts are fully applicable.

The prevailing trend is that limited liability provides a public benefit or *maslahah*. Also, that the concept of limited liability is closely related to the concept of corporate person or juridical personality. This point is critical as certain entities exist in Islamic law and tradition which have corporate personality. As a result, Shafi'i scholars, whose school is the leading school in south-east Asia, have ruled that joint stock companies have a *Zakah* obligation at the entity level.

Endowed charity or *waqf*

The classical Islamic form of endowed charity, called *waqf* (plural *awqaf*), has attributes of a natural person. This means that a foundation may enter into commercial transactions and investments on its own account. *Awqaf* have a long and documented history buying and owning real property, with the assumption to the foundation of all attendant property rights and risks. Some Islamic scholars, however, hesitate to draw the full parallel to modern limited liability entities since the *waqf* concept is explicitly charitable. This unease is more clearly understood when the comparison between a *waqf* and an Anglo-American-style trust is made. As much as the attributes are similar, most *Shari'a* jurisdictions do not have any form of indigenous trust law that allows for non-charitable trusts. As we shall see in Chapter 10 on *sukuk*, this causes a number of deal-structuring problems.

During the early period of the Islamic caliphates, a special treasury was established for the distribution of charitable proceeds and the spoils of war. Termed the *baitul mal*, the treasury was administered by the state. Since it often held surplus funds, it too behaved like the *waqf* with the attributes of a natural person in the area of commerce. As a result, the treasury would in and of itself engage in buying and owning property, with the assumption of all attendant property rights and risks. Yet, again, some Muslim scholars have hesitated to accept this as an analogy supporting the acceptance of limited liability commercial entities as the *baitul mal* was fundamentally a state function and not a commercial enterprise.

The concept of inheritance

The next basis for understanding the applicability of limited liability in *Shari'a* and its prospective incorporation into commercial finance is the concept of inheritance in Islamic law. *Shari'a* rules governing inheritance are detailed and expansive. They do comprehend complex cases of a merchant dying intestate and with debts. The dominant view in the case of a deceased indebted person is that the estate has obligations which are uniquely that of the estate. These obligations may not be imposed upon any of the inheritors or any other person. Once the assets of the estate are exhausted, nobody else may be sued for settlement should the creditors of the deceased suffer a shortfall in recovering their claims. This strong argument for non-recourse, limited liability has been taken into account by many Islamic scholars.

Once the concept of limited liability is incorporated into Islamic commerce, its two clear branches are individual transactions and the realm of *shirkah*. The balance of this chapter will look at both the *mudaraba* and *musharaka* concepts almost exclusively in light of their being limited in liability whenever the banking and investment banking businesses adopt them.

> 'Despite the higher profit potential of *mudarabah* financing in principle, the mode could not make much headway in modern Muslim societies. It did blossom as a deposit collecting mechanism with the Islamic financial institutions.... But, these companies could not find business investment opportunities to absorb [the] bulk of the deposits they received.'[6]

Mudaraba

The term *mudaraba* is derived from an interpretation of a *Qur'anic* verse relating to 'walking and traveling the earth' as this is what the *mudarib* will do to seek profitable opportunities.[7] The first true example of the *mudaraba* is given in the example of the Prophet Mohammed (PBOH)'s partnership with his first wife Khadija prior to their marriage. This method of one partner providing capital with profit-sharing for a manager, who in this case would manage a commercial sales trip or caravan, would be adopted by many of the Prophet's companions.[8]

The two primary parties in a *mudaraba* are the managing partner or *mudarib* and the investor or *rabb al-maal* (literally owner of the capital). The *mudarib* is the managing partner of the enterprise of business activity. As such, the *mudarib* alone is empowered to make business decisions. Although the *mudarib* may contribute capital, the *mudarib* typically invests effort and expertise in exchange for a share of any profits and the recovery of certain expenses. When a *mudarib* co-invests his or her own money, many Islamic scholars do not allow any commingling of funds. *Mudaraba*s may have additional parties, subject to the agreement. There may be a *wakil* or agent; an *amin* or trustee (an *adil* in some *Shari'a* jurisdictions); some transactions will have a guarantor or *kafil*.

Restricted and unrestricted *mudaraba*

Classical *fiqh* speaks of two primary forms of *mudaraba*. The first is *mudaraba al muqayyada* or restricted *mudaraba*, which is formed for a specific business or place. A restricted *mudaraba* is contractually limited by time and place, to one kind of trade or counterparty. The second form is *mudaraba al mutlaqa* or unrestricted *mudaraba*, which is formed for general purpose investment. An unrestricted *mudaraba* is unrestricted by time, place, type of permissible trade or counterparty.[9] A *mudaraba* has an independent personality.[10] According to the classical concept, a *mudaraba* is an unlimited liability entity. But, almost all modern *mudaraba*s are structured with limited liability.

Unlike most other *Shari'a* jurisdictions, Iran has codified in its civil code a form of civil partnership, that elsewhere is viewed as a variant of *mudaraba*.[11] This Iranian model, which is more flexible on costs deducted before sharing profits or losses, represents an expected future development in most *Shari'a* jurisdictions whereby local commercial laws and or banking regulations will specifically codify the meaning and practice of *mudaraba*.

Parties to the *mudaraba*

The *rabb al-maal* is the sole party obligated to contribute *ras al-maal* or capital. As a financial investor, the *rabb al-maal* has an expansive right to information and to monitor the business activities. The expansiveness of this right is subject to negotiation and mutual agreement. In a typical *mudaraba*, the *rabb al-maal* has the same rights and obligations as a limited partner, member of a limited liability company, or an investor in a mutual fund company.

The cardinal rule of Islamic equity forms is that investors must share profits and losses proportionately, with the proportion of loss and profit being the same. However, the parties have a number of contractual freedoms. For instance, the allocation of profit and loss may be made from either the business's gross operating profit or loss or the net operating profit or loss.[12] This is particularly applicable for complex businesses or businesses laden with large numbers of fixed assets. Furthermore, such profit-sharing spares the investor arguments relating to business expenses, costs of goods, intangibles such as depreciation, and other areas subject to management allocation or audit valuation risks. The allocation of sharing at the gross profit/loss line is meant to reduce the risk of moral hazard that many Islamic scholars worry plagues the business environment in many emerging markets.

The *mudarib* may elect and so indicate a limit to the profits that the *mudarib* will realise. A *mudarib* may also hold reserves that allow the *mudarib* to smooth income across reporting periods so as to generate a certain level of profitability for investors. Such income smoothing is not forbidden across business lines in the same business investment. These latter two points are of pivotal importance to the use of *mudaraba* in Islamic banks and apply equally to *musharaka*.

The termination of a *mudaraba* is defined according to time or notice and is subject to the liquidation of any remainder assets (if non-cash) at the termination of the enterprise. There is broad consensus among Islamic scholars that the measuring of a net asset value may be pursued as a means to determine the sale or buyback of units in a *mudaraba*. As a result of its flexibility, the concept of *mudaraba* has become a key organising principle of Islamic banking and asset management.

Syndication by *mudaraba*

Early on in the development of Islamic banking, the concept of *mudaraba* was grasped as an important tool for organising capital (see Exhibit 3.1). There have been three primary approaches: syndication of *murabaha* and commercial transactions; retail funds collection as deposits, unit trusts and mutual funds; and aggregation of capital in a non-bank financial institution.

Exhibit 3.1 ***Mudaraba* inbound fund structure**

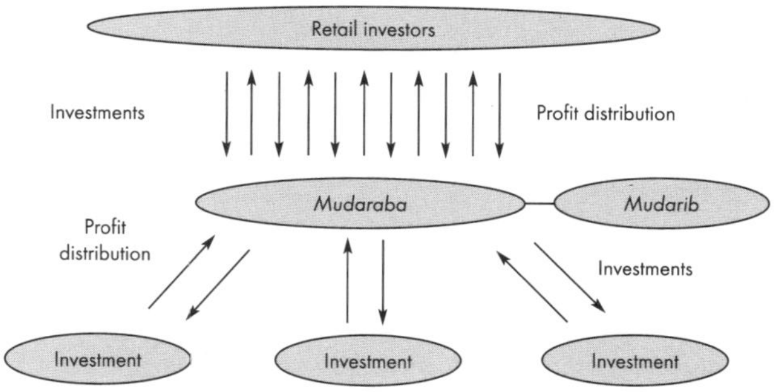

Source: Stella Cox and Lawrence Oliver.

The syndicated transaction case is very straightforward and may be examined in two examples below. The primary principle is that the *mudarib* is a licensed financial intermediary and collects retail or other funds into the *mudaraba*. Once aggregated, the investors hold *mudaraba* certificates and the funds are deployed in permissible investments. Certificate holders earn or lose proportionately to their cash investment and the terms of the *mudaraba* agreement. The *mudarib* earns its proportionate share of any profit and loses its effort and set up expense funds if there is no profit. A plurality of Islamic scholars allows the *mudarib* to be compensated for certain expenses relating to the operation of the *mudaraba*. This method is equally applicable to both retail and commercial funds aggregation.

Although a syndication may engage in a purchase of goods followed by an installment credit sale, the general principle is that *murabaha* debts may not be subsequently securitised or sold at other than par. But, a blended portfolio including *murabaha* debts from an active portfolio in which these are not the majority may be part of a traded portfolio.[13] Ideally, such a mixture would only be 30 per cent receivables.

Example 1: Islamic Global Bank (IGB) and retail aggregation

In the mid-1990s, IGB initiated a private equity business in the United States. The firm had restricted capital and sought to apply its capital to the initial acquisition of target companies and then to sell down the combined acquisition to a *mudaraba* formed by IGB in the Cayman Islands.

IGB acquired three family-held sporting goods manufacturers that specialised in the same consumer product which enjoyed an attractive, recession-proof niche. During the acquisition phase, IGB negotiated *ijarah* and *murabaha* facilities from a global bank headquartered in the United States, and one in the United Kingdom. These allowed IGB to leverage its equity in a manner consistent with *Shari'a*.

Once the acquisitions were completed and the companies merged into one with a unique brand identity, IGB launched its *mudaraba* and raised funds from GCC-based investors. The *mudaraba* agreed upon a price with IGB, which also acted as *mudarib*, and acquired the merged company. Investors agreed to take the operating business risk of the US company as well as the tax and other risks. IGB used state-of-the-art tax planning to assure that the entity would face minimal tax charges for transfers of profits back to the *mudaraba* members.

IGB later returned to the market with further, larger prospective offerings to follow the private equity model in the US, European and east Asian markets. In all three cases, the modulation was that IGB secured the investors and funds for the *mudaraba* prior to making acquisitions.

Example 2: Global Telecoms and syndicated *murabaha*

In the late 1990s US telecoms provider Global Telecoms was faced with a very clear dilemma. Its market position meant that it should be a favoured provider of internet services in the United States. But, a shrinkage of some of its non-core businesses and a recent management crisis meant that the company had suffered a credit-rating downgrade. As a result, the company found that its access to the US and UK capital markets was unfavourable, and its margin on banking loans increased above the company's target hurdle. Uncertain as to the potential profits in the internet business, the company was unwilling to over-leverage itself (in fact, the ratings agencies felt that it was over-leveraged) at unfavourable rates to bet on the rate of internet subscription uptake.

One of Global Telecoms' investment bankers' NY Bros., however, had a unique proposition: Global Telecoms participated in a tax-advantaged minority supplier programme. The financial dynamics of the programme meant that Global Telecoms might pay more for a particular supply, but that it would earn a tax benefit with a value greater than the price disadvantage. NY Bros. had advised a limited number of Islamic banking transactions and pitched the concept to United Qatar Bank (UQB) in London. The idea was that UQB would form a joint venture with one of Global Telecom's minority suppliers, and the joint venture would act as *mudarib* to a *mudaraba* composed of GCC-based Islamic banks and investors.

UQB agreed and one of Global Telecoms' leading minority suppliers also agreed. Global Telecoms agreed, subject to the continued utilisation of the company's standard purchase order format and no disruption to its chain of supply and standard shipping and receiving methods. UQB presented the purchase order document to its *Shari'a* scholars and reviewed the transaction steps:

- The *mudaraba* would obtain commitments to fund from a group of Islamic institutions.

- Each time Global Telecoms would put out a request for tender, the *mudarib* would price the transaction.
- Whenever the *mudaraba*'s price and specifications were agreed, the members of the *mudaraba* would be called upon for funds.
- The *mudarib* would then source the goods or contract their manufacture.
- Completed goods would be delivered to a bonded warehouse designated by Global Telecoms.
  - There the goods would be inspected and accepted or rejected.
  - Upon acceptance, title would transfer to Global Telecoms and a promissory note would be issued to the *mudaraba* in the name of the minority supplier as agent for the *mudarib*.
- From the bonded warehouse, the goods were picked up by a bonded shipper under contract to Global Telecoms, and delivered to the required site.
- Global Telecoms typically paid for the goods within 180 days as stipulated in the purchase order and promissory note.

The Global Telecoms programme ran for two years and generated over US$1 billion in sales to Global Telecoms. Although approved by leading *Shari'a* scholars, the *mudaraba* subscriptions were taken up mostly by small European banks with unutilised credit limits for Global Telecoms. Their motivation was that, despite the terms of the sales (no delay or penalty payments for late payment), the mark-up on the sale delivered a higher coupon than an equivalent six-month exposure to the company in a corporate loan or commercial paper programme.

The more common syndicated *murabaha* transaction is similar in process and, like the Global Telecoms transaction, the *mudaraba* agreement is similar to conventional syndicated loan agreements. The distinction is that there is not usually a partnership with the seller of goods. Instead, there is usually an agency appointing the buyer, the beneficiary of the credit, to perform certain functions on behalf of the *mudaraba* or syndication such as inspection, acceptance and shipping.

Retail fund aggregation

Another very popular use of *mudaraba* is for retail funds aggregation. The plethora of private Islamic funds buying real estate or making private equity investments, and a large number of investment portfolios all apply the *mudaraba* concept as the core means of organising capital. And, most equity fund investment, whether the highly successful National Commercial Bank funds offered with Wellington Investment Management or the numerous funds and unit trusts offered around the world also adapt the *mudaraba* to their needs.

In Malaysia, unit trusts are a popular means to aggregate capital to buy listed investment securities. These unit trusts in the Islamic sector are structured as *mudarabas*. The contract between subscribers and trust is implied and is called an *amana* contract.[14] This variation of the concept means that the market has adopted a standard, unwritten contract between the *mudarib* and the investors.

Example: Meezan Bank, Pakistan

In Pakistan, Meezan Bank operates its deposit scheme so that the bank and its shareholders are deemed to be the *mudarib*. The depositing consumers take the position of *rabb al-maal*. Whether or not the underlying business takes an attractive rate of profit, the consumer may not earn a large share, and the basis of the lower profit for the consumer is defined in the *mudaraba* agreement. The shareholders' profit-sharing ratio cannot be less than their investment. The consumer's loss is solely in proportion to invested funds. The bank's *Shari'a* board permits daily calculation of the applicable net asset value. Consumers are free to add or decrease funds at any time.[15] '...the deposit side of the Islamic bank is a major departure from the original form of the [mudaraba] enterprise, while at the same time using the basic principle of profit and loss sharing.'[16]

Non-bank financial institutions

The case of Pakistan's *modaraba* companies

Established by The Modaraba Companies and Modaraba Floatation and Control Ordinance of 1980, *mudarabas* have been active in Pakistan as a means to expand both the Islamic financial sector and create more access to credit. The Ordinance defines a *modaraba* (the preferred local English spelling is with an 'o' and not a 'u') as 'a business which a person participates with his money and another with his efforts or skill or both his efforts and skill and shall include Unit Trusts and Mutual Funds by whatever name called.'[17] Certain restrictions apply to protect the integrity of *modarabas*, namely a 20 per cent reserve with State Bank of Pakistan; and a commitment of 15 per cent of liabilities to National Investment Trust Certificates or public company securities.

Pakistan's *modarabas* are structured as limited liability companies and may be quite small. The predominate business has been leasing (more than 70 per cent of *mudaraba* activities) and trade finance (up to 20 per cent). (The business focuses vary year to year according to the business decisions of companies, but leasing and trade finance are always the top two activities.) Most *modarabas* choose to be listed on local stock exchanges where they represent up to 10 per cent of market capitalisation.

In Pakistan, *modarabas* are often floated by businesses to expand their funding. The tool has some inflexibility as a *modaraba* must distribute all of its profits as dividends. But, the certificates are structured as redeemable instruments to promote the self-financing of domestic businesses.

Musharaka[18]

> 'A new form or procedure in *Musharaka* cannot be rejected merely because it has no precedent in the past. In fact, every new form can be acceptable to *Shariah* in so far as it does not violate any basic principle laid down by the Holy Qur'an, the *Sunnah* or the consensus of the Muslim jurists.'[19]

Musharaka literally means 'sharing'. The concept is a highly flexible tool for organising business interests between business partners. Classically, multiple partnerships were crafted with variable terms and conditions as a means of venture management that bears more in common with merchant banking, and synthesises lending but with greater risk–reward factors and greater investor say in project management.[20] There are examples of sub-partnerships formed within *musharaka* to allow for the expansion of trade to new parties under specific limitations.[21]

Shirkatul milk and *shirkatul 'aqd*

There are generally two forms of *musharaka* established in the *Shari'a*: *shirkatul milk* and *shirkatul 'aqd*. There are also credit-driven derivatives of the concept such as the declining-balance partnership. Although we will find that our modern applications of *musharaka* are typically limited liability entities, the traditional concept is of an unlimited liability business venture.

Shirkatul milk is a partnership of two or more owners of a property held in common. This form of partnership may be established without a specific contract as in the case of inherited property. There are optional forms and compulsory forms. However, the method's primary limitation is that the object of the partnership, the underlying property is not divided or unitised. This creates restrictions for use or specific division of the property, and further problems using this sub-form in the banking and financial sectors.

Shirkatul 'aqd is a mutual partnership by contract. This form of *musharaka* is the focus of this chapter. Although capital contributions may be in kind or by services provided, they are typically cash and valued at an agreed par value. There is no obligation to value the disparate components of capital equally. A further form of this sub-method is a partnership in goodwill (*wujuh*, literally 'face'), in which there may not be any form of cash investment, but a partner contributes his name, credit or track record with a particular value.

The basic rules applied to both methods of *musharaka* are that the capital is quantified and specific.

Basic rules of *musharaka*

Like *mudaraba*, a cardinal rule of *musharaka* is that profits and losses must be shared in the same proportion. This proportion is governed by the actual earnings or losses, and not the relative volume of contribution. Losses must be shared in the same proportion as profit. The profit cannot be structured to give a guaranteed rate or yield to one party. A general principle of partnership in *Shari'a* is that partners have the right of pre-emption, unless the property is tightly defined or there is mutual agreement.[22] Generally, this stipulation is removed by the mutual agreements of contract that make *musharaka* more feasible in the banking environment.

Within a *musharaka*, one partner may deputise another partner to perform specific functions of a business.[23] In theory, every partner may manage the enterprise, but the partners may elect one or more to manage the *musharaka*.[24] 'Every contract of partnership contains a contract of agency.'[25]

In classical examples of *musharaka* arrangements recorded in Egyptian and other courts, there is a strong precedent for infinite life relationships, helping to set a parallel to the modern corporation.[26] In addition, like modern company shares, classical partnership interests are heritable. A classical stipulation is that a partnership may not be dissolved without the knowledge of all partners.[27] Since *musharaka* is thus analogised to comprehend the modern corporation, the formal process of a bankruptcy notice fulfills this obligation.

Some banks practise *musharaka* in a manner similar to *mudaraba*, effectively reducing the bank's risk and operational liability profile.[28] When applied in the banking markets, the valuation for interim withdrawal or profit distribution/loss allocation is 'constructive liquidation'.[29] This is a form of net asset value determination which seeks to define the price a willing buyer would pay for the assets of the enterprise.

Musharaka deposits

University Bank in Ann Arbor, Michigan[30], offers a profit-sharing deposit which is a form of limited *musharaka*. The limitation is based on Federal Deposit Insurance Corp. (FDIC) restrictions on losses at a licensed bank. In western markets such as the United States, deposit insurance is a direct outcome of the banking system collapse that began in October 1929. 'Government Guarantees on deposits have maintained public confidence in the safety of the banking system' even if they have introduced a modest element of moral hazard.[31] Thus, in the posted *fatwa* supporting the product, the *Shari'a* scholars define this as a specific exception to the rules of *musharaka*.

For the regulator, allocation of the profit or loss ratio at the top line removes most mathematical probabilities that a low-risk transaction could actually suffer a capital loss. This is bolstered by the bank's guarantee of its underwriting and preparedness to substitute assets or *sukuk* in the event that underlying assets suffer any payment defaults.

In addition, the bank has established specific reserves and general reserves. These may be used either to offset displaced commercial risk, which is the risk that the yields on the underlying assets will be too low to retain market share and the bank may bolster the yields by drawing on a specific reserve. Or, they may be used by the bank in its election to consume losses in lieu of the depositors.

For the retail consumer, allocation of the profit and loss at the top line removes any concerns that the bank will over-allocate its expenses to this deposit class and insulates the consumer from any excessive costs or expenses elsewhere in the bank's business. Below is an example of the product in action.

Example: University Bank

University Bank offers several different *musharaka* products. In lieu of a set formula, the bank manages its yield to consumers in two ways. First, the bank agrees to a specific ratio, ostensibly 90:10 in favour of the bank. But, the bank also may elect to forgo some of its profits in order to ensure that the consumer earns a competitive yield compared with the market. Second, the bank recalculates the paid profit into a simple interest formula for regulatory purposes as required by the Federal Truth in Savings Disclosure rules.

At University Bank, the profit-sharing, limited *musharaka* deposit may only invest in *Shari'a*-admissible instruments within the bank's portfolio and business lines:

- *sukuk al ijarah* from mortgage alternative programme;
- *sukuk* from state programmes contemplated;
- other traded permissible instruments; and
- non-traded permissible instruments.

In the US market there are certain regulatory risks that depend upon the locus and charter of a bank. For instance, the United States has a long history of contingent interest deposits and these have been approved by the Federal Deposit Insurance Corporation as deposits and explicitly ruled not to be securities. But, periodically, the Securities and Exchange Commission will challenge their status as deposits and insist that these are securities. In the absence of specific Islamic regulations, such regulatory turf war will prevail in markets such as the United States.

In the cases of University Bank, HSBC Amanah in London and New York, and the new Islamic Bank of Britain, some consumers have questioned whether Muslims may deal with conventional banks or Islamic banks operating in a predominately conventional environment. These consumers, in this type of scenario, suspect the conventional bank of seeking an attractive source of funds. The predominate answer of *Shari'a* scholars has been that so long as the bank complies with the rules of *musharaka* or *mudaraba*, as applicable, and the underlying transactions are permissible, then such deposits are permissible.[32]

Deposit profit distribution methods[33]

The business of calculating profits and allocating them to consumers in an Islamic bank is fairly straightforward.

In this approach, the customer deposit accounts are segregated into different types and tenors. For the purpose of determining the current account share of profit, the balance should be adjusted by deducting net fixed assets, even though the profit allocable to current account will eventually accrue to shareholders. Shareholder funds are assumed to be the weighted average balance. The relevant sharing ratio is applied to determine the bank's share of the profits and the balance is set for distribution to the consumers. So long as the differential is disclosed, the bank may use different ratios for different products, risks and tenors.

Other forms of bank account

In this book we do not examine either the use of *wadia*, a form of safekeeping, or *qard hassan*, interest-free loans. The former are not meant by design to be profit-generating deposits. The latter are meant, in the *Qur'an*, to be for charitable purposes. As such, the *qard hassan* is not intended to be used for a commercial activity.

Declining-balance partnership

Sometimes called 'diminishing' in lieu of 'declining' joint ownership in property or equipment. This variation of *musharaka* is extremely flexible as a tool of credit extension whether for business working capital, asset acquisition, or property investment. So far, the method has been unitised most extensively for consumer home acquisition. The method may be used applying either *shirkatul 'aqd* or *shirkatul milk*.

In the case of property, the declining-balance partnership comprises a contract of property ownership. The majority partner is the financier and the manager or the property is the beneficiary of the finance or the consumer.

The consumer will promise to purchase units from the financier. The promise to buy units should not be contingent upon the acquisition of the property. In other words, one would make the purchase whether or not the promissor kept his promise.[34] The partnership may lease the property on to the consumer with the investor claiming into profit the rent according to his share in the property. The *Shari'a* does not allow the rental and acquisition agreements to be fixed as one conditional on the other.[35] The solution is a contract of partnership with unilateral promises of unit purchase and to enter into a lease, an independent contract of its own from the partnership to the consumer. Some scholars allow the joint purchase contract to incorporate the lease from the partnership to the consumer as the lease is a future commitment and such commitments are allowed for leasing.[36] Sh. Taqi also advises on the use of this method for small businesses and services such as taxi services using *shirkatul milk*. Likewise, Sh. Taqi recommends this method for inventory finance.

Although this method has been very popular for residential and commercial property acquisition, it is a useful method for pre-export finance. A method for managing risk is to define delivery conditions so tightly that if the producing partner fails to deliver, it is negligence and the bank is not liable to deliver the goods.[37]

Variations have been used for build-operate-transfer (BOT) projects including the Bosphorus Bridge in Istanbul, as well as toll roads in Malaysia and Iran. In such BOT transactions, *musharaka* project certificates are issued and indicate a pro rata share in a project's ownership. The Hanafi school allows such certificates to be sold and traded without consideration for liquid assets.[38]

Shares and certificates

Shares in an operating company are deemed by most Islamic scholars active in the field to be a form of *musharaka* ownership. These shares participate in the divisible ownership of the business and ought not be controversial. As we shall see in Chapter 9: Islamic asset management, this position allows for Muslim participation in global equity markets.

Preferred shares, however, have not been permitted due to their stipulated fixed rate return. Such a return, which is independent of the actual business performance, is *ribawi*.[39] Moreover, the non-voting status and establishment of a preferred position during business failure are generally viewed by *Shari'a* scholars as contrary to the nature of partnership or *shirkah*.

Yet, an unexplored space for the field of Islamic finance is the degree to which a functional equivalent of preferred shares may be established by using either *mudaraba* or a sub-business *musharaka*.

Pre-emption

All methods of joint ownership are subject to the concept of *shufa'a* or pre-emption. According to Jabir bin Abdullah, the Prophet said:

> 'There is pre-emption in everything which is shared, be it land, or a dwelling, or a garden. It is not proper to sell it until he informs his partner; he may go in for that or he may abandon it; and if he does not do that then he [his partner] has the greatest right to it until the partner permits him [to act].'[40]

As a practical matter, either the operating agreements applied in diminishing *musharaka*, or the other equity forms, define the terms under which the managing partner operates sales with the pre-agreed consent of the other partners. Likewise, forms such as *ijarah-wa-iqtina'a* – in which the lessee has equitable rights in the property – have stipulated procedures which preserve pre-emption. Ostensibly, pre-emption seems like a challenge to the efficacy of applying *musharaka* in modern Islamic banking. Realistically, the right of pre-emption and its prospective disruptiveness to a financial investment is managed by proper documentation and definition of procedures.

Conclusion

In this chapter, we have looked into the breadth and applicability of *mudaraba* and *musharaka*. In some cases, the bank will invest alongside the *mudaraba* investors as is the case with University Bank. But, in the classical case of *mudaraba*, the investor is solely at risk of capital loss, whereas in *musharaka* the method puts all investors at risk in the proportion that they have agreed. Both methods result in a useful tool for intermediation and risk management. Both allow for considerable flexibility in the structuring of investments and deposits; both are under-applied and their use will grow with the evolution of the field. Our emphasis has been their use as a means for Islamic banks and Islamic banking windows to gather deposits. We have also touched lightly on the various, as yet undeveloped, aspects of applying these methods for corporate and commercial finance. Perhaps most importantly, we have learned that the two forms adapt to the concept of limited liability companies and allow for the development of funds and investments in global markets. Since the Islamic banking model is to utilise *mudaraba* and *musharaka* to collect funds for onwards investing it requires that we examine those methods for onwards investing.

---

1 Hanna, Nelly, *Making Big Money in 1600: The Life and Times of Isma'il Abu Taqiyya, Egyptian Merchant*, (Syracuse: Syracuse University Press, 1998), p. 34.

2 Usmani, M.T., *An Introduction to Islamic Finance*, (Karachi: Idaratul Ma'arif , 1998), p. 55. Sh. Taqi points out a clear understanding of the fact that the classical scholars had not contemplated the modern large scale commercial enterprise with multiple layers of business complexity.

3 Hanna, *op. cit.*, p. 55.

4 Usmani, M.T., 'The Principle of Limited Liability' in Usmani, Muhammad Imran Ashraf, *Meezan Bank's Guide to Islamic Banking* (Karachi: Darul Ishaat, 2002), p. 224. The primary points of this sub-section are informed strongly by Sh. Taqi. Nonetheless, Sh. Taqi has not yet determined a final position as to the permissibility of this concept.

5 Hanna, *op. cit.*, p. 41.

6 Hasan, Zubair, 'Islamic Banking at the Crossroads: Theory versus Practice', paper presented at a seminar on Islamic wealth creation at Durham University, July 2003, p. 7.

7 Shirazi, Habib, *Islamic Banking* (London: Butterworths, 1990), p. 31.

8 Comair-Obeid, Nayla, *Les contrats en droit musulman des affaires*, (Paris: Economica, 1995), pp. 177–8.

9 Tyser, C.R. et al, tr. *The Mejelle* (Kuala Lumpur: The Other Press, 2001), p. 233.

10 Hasan, *op. cit.*, p. 35.

11 Shirazi, *op. cit.*, p. 41.

12 Usmani, M.I.A., *op. cit.*, pp. 190–192. Also see Usmani, M.T., *op. cit.*, p.66.

13 Usmani, M.I.A., *op. cit.*, p. 206.

14 Ali, Mohammed Imad, 'Unit Investment Trust in Malaysia', presented at a seminar on Islamic wealth creation at Durham University, July 2003.

15 Usmani, M.I.A., *op. cit.*, p. 175. Also see Usmani, M.T., *op. cit.*, pp. 68–74.

[16] Khan, Tariqullah, 'An Analysis of risk sharing in Islamic finance with special reference to Pakistan' (unpublished doctoral thesis, 1996), p. 202.

[17] *Ibid*, p. 115.

[18] Usmani, M.T., *op. cit.*, p. 32. *Musharaka* is not a classical term of *fiqh*, the classical term of *fiqh* being *shirkah*. However, *shirkah* has a broader meaning than *musharaka*, which is typically what is meant by *shirkat al amwal*, p. 33.

[19] *Ibid*, p. 30.

[20] Hanna, *op. cit.*, p. 57.

[21] *Ibid*, p. 58.

[22] Khan, Dr. Muhammad Muhsin, tr., Sahih Al-Bukhari, Vol. III (Beirut: Dar Al Arabia, undated)., p227.

[23] *Ibid*, p. 281.

[24] Usmani, M.T., *An Introduction to Islamic Finance, op. cit.*, p. 42.

[25] *Mejelle, op. cit.*, p. 218.

[26] Hanna, *op. cit.*, p. 55.

[27] *Mejelle, op. cit.*, p. 222.

[28] Comair-Obeid, *op. cit.*, p. 179.

[29] Usmani, M.I.A., *op. cit.*, p. 189.

[30] The bank is a client of the author's company SHAPE™ Financial Corp.

[31] Gross, David, B., *The Government's Role in Promoting Financial Sector Stability in Housing Matters: Issues in American Housing Policy* (Washington, D.C.: Fannie Mae, 2004), p. 79 and p. 84.

[32] Mufti Ahmed Suliman, *Advice on Using Banks for Mudaraba?* Posted to ibfnet@yahoogroups.com on 2 March 2005.

[33] Based on a one-day workshop by M. Ikram Thofeek.

[34] Usmani, M.T., *op. cit.*, p. 89.

[35] *Ibid*, p. 87.

[36] *Ibid*, p. 90.

[37] Usmani, M.I.A., *op. cit.*, p. 198.

[38] *Ibid*, p. 206.

[39] Ahmad, Abdel-Rahman Yousri, 'Islamic Banking Modes of Finance: Proposals for further Evaluation', presented at a seminar on Islamic wealth creation at Durham University, July 2003.

[40] Siddiqi, Abdul Hamid, tr. Sahih Muslim, Vol. III (Lahore: Sh. Muhammad Ashraf, 1992), p. 846-847.

4 The *murabaha* and simple sales transactions

Abdulkader Thomas and Bryan Kraty,[1] with Sudin Haron, Mustafa Hussain, and Stella Cox

Introduction

In Islamic banks, *murabaha* – sales, *ijarah* – leasing and *salam* – pre-paid sales, are the workhorses. According to one of the leading Islamic scholars active in the field, Sh. Muhammad Taqi Usmani, *murabaha* and *ijarah* are not originally meant to be tools of finance, but modern needs have allowed scholars to permit their reformulation when *salam, istisna'a, mudaraba* and *musharaka* are not readily applicable.[2] One might view these contracts as the building blocks of most Islamic banks and banking departments. Certainly, these represent the most commonly applied concepts[3] in the global Islamic finance environment, although that is subject to very gradual erosion over time as new concepts are developed and gain commercial viability. Simple case studies will be laid out and the stage will be set for more complicated concepts to be applied in the following chapters.

Murabaha

This term simply means a 'profitable action', in which the Arabic root *r b h* is the source word for the term 'profit'. Any sales activity is presumed to be geared to seeking a profit, hence works of Islamic scholarship, classical and modern, contain 'books of sales' (*bai'*) in which the term *murabaha* is a sub-set within the forms of *bai'*. *Murabaha* is not specifically a credit sale,[4] but it is a sale in which the cost of the good or goods to be sold is fully disclosed.[5] In Islamic finance, a *murabaha* is an unconditional contract of sale between buyer and seller where the goods, cost price, mark-up and payment date are all clearly defined and agreed. The simple elegance of the *murabaha* contract has allowed easy adaptation to a regulated banking context. This, in turn, has allowed *murabaha* to constitute the vast majority of Islamic banking transactions.[6]

When applied in a credit situation, *murabaha* is unlike a conventional loan in which cash is granted to the consumer who then buys the goods. In the *murabaha* transaction, the intermediary buys the goods and sells them to the consumer on installments at a mark-up. The sale is immediate, not prospective or conditional upon future events. A sales contract, however, may impose duties, conditions, upon the seller subject to mutual agreement. For instance, the place of delivery may be stipulated in the contract.[7] Qaradawi points out that:

> 'the majority of scholars permit it [*murabaha*] because the basic principle is the permissibility of things, and no clear text exists prohibiting such a transaction.

> Furthermore there is no resemblance to interest in such a transaction, since the seller is free to increase the price as he deems proper, as long as it is not to the extent of blatant exploitation or clear injustice, ...'[8]

This interposition of a financier in the purchase and sales process is what makes the *murabaha* transaction Islamically legitimate in the banking context. Unlike a traditional loan, this process causes the financier to assume certain risks between purchase and resale. Services rendered by the bank are therefore regarded as quite different from those of a conventional bank, which simply lends money to the client to buy the goods. As we shall see below, the bank may take security applying traditional encumbrances. *Murabaha*, due to its nature, enjoys widespread use for import – export finance.

Conditions of sale

Defined object

For a sale to be valid, there are several primary conditions. Foremost, the object of the sale must exist at the time of the sale (with the specific exceptions discussed in later chapters of *salam*, and its derivative *itisna'a*). Then, it must have a contract consisting of at least an offer and an acceptance. The contract may be verbal as when one goes to the market and states, 'I wish to buy 12 of your papayas'. The vendor shows the papayas, states a price, which one accepts for the papayas, and then one pays for them. Or, as is standard in the banking context, there is a written contract of which there may be many variants.

As in the fruit example, the sales contract must have a valid and permissible object, such as the fruit; a price that is mutually agreeable; and possession allowing for delivery into the buyer's possession. The fruit fulfills all the requirements of a valid object of sale: existence, valuable, consumable, capable of being owned, deliverable, specific and quantifiable. Within the fruit example, there is no contingency, such as 'I will sell you the 12 papayas after I find them in the market'; or conditionality, such as 'I will sell you the 12 papayas once they ripen'.

Clear term

A sale may have reasonable conditions, if the goods are specified and exist, that they may be delivered to a specific place within a specific time-frame. In this case, the sale is immediate, instant and absolute.[9] All Islamic sales transactions have a specific post acceptance condition which is the buyer's option to inspect the object of the contract. After that the buyer may accept or reject the object and the contract is completed or invalidated.

Contract validity

For a *murabaha* contract to be valid, the conditions of offer or acceptance must be complied with; the seller must have valid title or possession, the buyer must take title;[10] the object of the sale cannot be used lawfully; nor may the item itself be forbidden by Islam. In the event that these conditions are not met, the contract of sale is *bai' baatil* or an 'invalid sale'.[11] Likewise a sale is invalid if one or both parties are not mentally competent.

In one *athar*: 'Tawus said that if somebody bought a thing with mutual agreement and then sold it, then that was his property and the profit would be for him.'[12] When considering title, the question is typically of possession. The *Shari'a* has afforded considerable flexibility when defining possession and it allows for *physical* and *constructive* possession. The latter means that the owner may not have physical control of the object, but has control including all the rights, liabilities, and risks of ownership running through to total loss.[13]

Possession is distinguished from custody in *Shari'a*. According to Ibn Umar, 'if at the time of a transaction, the animal sold is living, but it dies while still in custody of the seller, then the buyer is the loser.'[14] On the one hand, *Shari'a* scholars would carve out negligence by the custodian. On the other hand, the concept extends to perishable and non-perishable goods. A custodian, in *Shari'a*, must follow either the agreed instructions of the buyer or demonstrate reasonable care for the goods, but has no more than a limited fiduciary obligation to the buyer until the buyer removes the goods from custody.

A sale may be voided if it is defective, *bai' fasid*. In this case, some conditions of the contract or inspection of the object indicate a failure of contractual conditions or defect. If these are cured, the sale may be completed, otherwise, the sale should be voided and the goods and price returned to the respective parties.[15]

Forms of sale

The forms of sales include *musawama*, which is discussed later in this chapter; *murabaha*, which is detailed in this chapter; *muqayada* or non-monetary barter; *sarf* or currency exchange; *salam*, which is detailed in this chapter; *istisna'a* which is discussed in Chapter 7; and *muajjal* or deferred payment. (The *muajjal* is covered as either a variant of *murabaha* or *musawama*, and rarely utilised as an independent term in this book.)

The *Shari'a* also instructs the ethics of buying and selling beyond informing the formality of transacting. Abdullah Ibn Umar said, 'Do not urge someone to return what he has already bought (ie, in an optional sale) from another seller so as to sell him your own goods.' This speaks of the *adab* or 'proper behaviour' of commerce and is akin to forbidding *twisting* in financial transactions whereby a securities or insurance sales person talks a consumer out of a satisfactory product that the consumer has already contracted to purchase in order to replace it with the sales person's own product, whether or not there is a benefit to the consumer.[16]

The five options of sale as formalised in classical *fiqh* are:

- buyer's option to rescind: time limited, seller has similar option, but ceases before execution of contract;
- option of inspection: the right to see and verify the object of the sale;
- option of defect: right to return if defective;
- option of quality: right to specified quality; and
- option of price: right to fair price within market range.

> '... in order to make the *murabaha* contract effective in the business of inventory or short-term trade financing, it was necessary to depart somewhat from the classical model by combining a promise to buy on the part of a client with the actual purchase by the bank of goods from third party suppliers. Then, in addition to the actual *murabaha* contract, a further transaction is appended; the promise to purchase that is made by the client or prospective buyer.[17] This arrangement, however innocent in appearance, actually brought up a host of issues for the early *Shariah* boards. Nonetheless, as the needs of modern trade were such that a *Shariah*-compliant alternative to trade financing by means of conventional, interest-based financing was required, the classical *murabaha* was transformed into the modern *Murabaha li'l-Amir bi'sh-Shira*, *murabaha* with an order to purchase that has now become commonplace to Islamic banking.
>
> 'Following the success of this experience, *Shariah* boards went on to engineer and approve a host of hybrid nominates, using a single nominate like *murabaha* in different configurations like parallel *murabaha*, reverse *murabaha*, back-to-back *murabaha* and reverse parallel *murabaha* contracts; ...'[18]

Although it is allowed for regulated western economies which require it, the general principal of *Shari'a* scholars has been that there is no obligatory or contractual rebate for early repayment in a *murabaha* transaction. A non-contractual reduction, offered by the seller is accepted by all Islamic scholars for *murabaha* transactions that are paid early.[19]

The *murabaha* contract is 'an unconditional contract of sale between buyer and seller where the goods, cost price, mark-up and payment date are all clearly defined and agreed'. The price is set by mutual consent (hence 'offer and acceptance'). Ibn Qayyim pointed out that 'parties may wish to postpone either the payment of the price, or the delivery of the object of sale, to a later occasion.'[20] In *murabaha*, the price is deferred. In *salam*, the object is deferred.

Murabaha and cash management

Exhibit 4.1 shows the application of *murabaha* as a cash management tool. In this case, the investor appoints an agent, perhaps a bank, to purchase and sell goods, typically non-monetary commodities such as coffee, aluminum and copper. The sales are made with payment deferred at a price higher than the spot market. For the sales offer to be acceptable, the goods must be Islamically acceptable, exist and be owned by the seller,[21] and be immediately identifiable (allocated), that is, known to the buyer. The object of sale must have an independently verifiable value. In a *murabaha* contract, there must be certainty of price without conditionality.

Exhibit 4.1 ***Murabaha* trade financing**

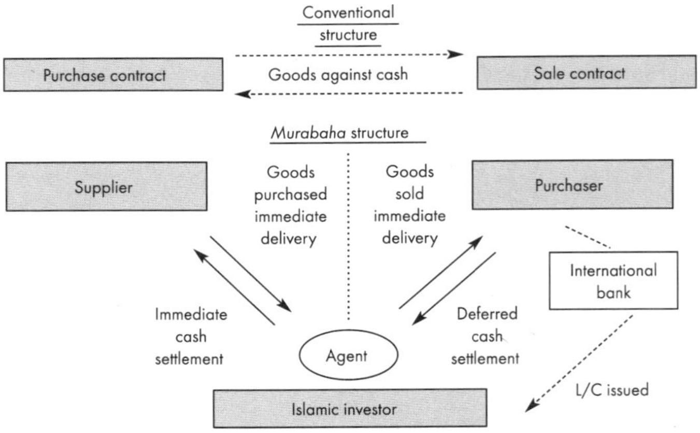

Source: Stella Cox and Lawrence Oliver.

When this model is applied with the bank stepping in as a merchant intermediary and not an agent of the buyer, then a number of Islamic banks permit the consumer to reject an item after promising to purchase it and after the bank has possession of the goods. This rejection is permitted to show that the purchase is a true merchant purchase and not conditional upon the consumer's promise. As a result, the bank must have the object, later to be the collateral, in hand prior to signing the formal sales contract. In this approach, no side letters which invalidate or contradict the core contract of sales are permitted.[22] This more restrictive view of the *murabaha* contract is frequently linked to a more restrictive position on possession. For instance, certain Islamic banks have specific space allocated to them in merchant warehouses where goods to be offered under *murabaha* are stored or moved to demonstrate physical possession, not merely constructive possession.

However a sale is conducted, if it results in a debt, the property sold may be mortgaged and the receivable evidenced by a promissory[23] or supported by a third-party guarantee. Ideally, there is no payment by the guaranteed party for the guarantee. With respect to trade, there is some difference of opinion among scholars.[24] The general view in favour of mortgaging and securing debts is supported by the behaviour of the Prophet Mohammed (PBOH) when he contracted a debt, purchasing grain on credit and mortgaged his armour to the seller.[25]

Murabaha sale versus loan of money

Up to now, many bankers and their regulators are comfortable taking the view that *murabaha* is a synthesised loan or form of debt. There are four distinctive features of a *murabaha* sale compared with a loan of money.

1. The banker in a *murabaha* must have some form of factual possession, registered or not, constructive or physical.

2. A *murabaha* transaction may be extended. However, the extension or rollover may not result in an increase. This is the basic rule of *riba*, which forbids the creditor to offer a further deferral in payment for more money.
3. If the payment is late, no form of penalty may be charged for the profit of the creditor (even if a third-party collection agent may charge the costs of collection).
4. Most Islamic scholars do not like net sales, sales discounts or early payment discounts when these are structured into the contract. But, Islamic scholars do not mind if the financier elects to give discounts.[26]

In export trade finance cases, the investor signs a separate agreement with the buyer to act as agent to sell the goods onwards in the market.[27] This has the benefit of pre-export working capital finance or of allowing the exporter to provide finance to the end-buyer who is not the bank's customer. In the case of collections, an exporter may appoint the bank as its agent to collect the receivable and pay the bank a fee, which the bank holds from the payment.[28]

Murabaha in a banking context

When we examine the primary elements of the *murabaha* in a banking context, we need 1) a willing buyer and seller to agree upon the object of the contract, its price, when the price will be paid and the specification of the object. Then, once the seller has 2) delivered the goods and the buyer accepts them, 3) the buyer is obliged to pay the seller the cost of the goods, which is known in *murabaha*, plus a profit margin. *Murabaha* is not necessarily a delayed payment or credit contract and the payment may be made at closing, delivery, or over time (see Exhibit 4.2).

Murabaha stimulates financing when a bank buys the goods, directly or indirectly, and offers them subject to a specific contract on deferred payment terms to the bank's customer. The manner in which most banks seek to mitigate delivery risk is to require the buyer to sign an agreement unilaterally promising[29] to purchase goods from a bank. The promise is a unilateral promise binding the prospective buyer and not the banker. In some schools, scholars view promises as binding. The OIC Fiqh Academy, for example, requires that promises are binding in commerce when they are one-sided; induce the promise to incur some liabilities; and subject to enforcement as well as actual damages if broken. In many jurisdictions, including the United Kingdom and the United States, the promise to buy is sufficient to pursue a collection judgement against the client if he or she refuses delivery when the goods meet the contractual specifications.

Exhibit 4.2 ***Murabaha* – basic contract**

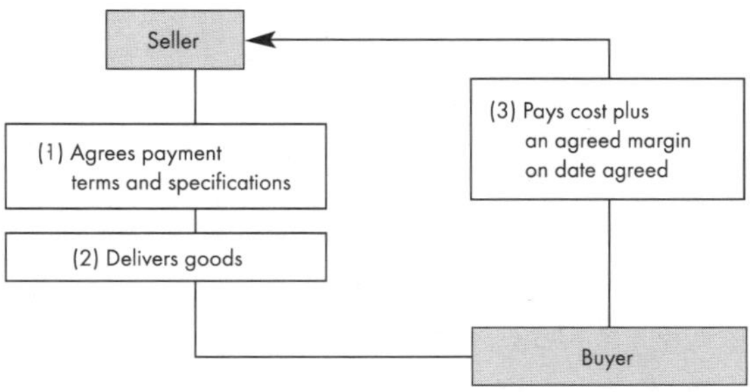

Source: Author's own.

Exhibit 4.3 ***Murabaha* financing agreements**

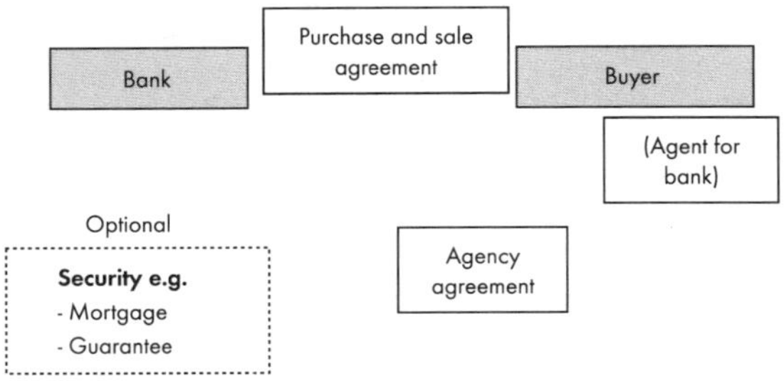

Source: Author's own.

The most frequent means protecting the bank from buyer rejection is to appoint the buyer as agent for the bank to order the desired goods. As agent, the buyer will be responsible for defining the specifications, executing the order and then inspecting the delivered goods. As a result, the buyer is not usually able to reject the goods and escape contractual payment obligations except in extraordinary circumstances.

In cases of a bank-executed *murabaha* with the buyer acting as the seller's agent, the primary agreements are the actual purchase and sales agreement, the *murabaha*, and the agency appointing the buyer to act on the bank's behalf in sourcing and ordering the goods (see Exhibit 4.3).[30] Since security is permitted, there are many cases in which the goods are hypothecated or the buyer provides a guarantee or letter of credit to comfort the bank that it will be paid the correct amount on time, in accordance with the contract.

Murabaha in trade financing

Although much of the modern *murabaha* trade supports the money market – such as cash management of Islamic banks through the purchasing and selling of metals on the global exchanges – there is a growing support of trade in favour of commercial parties using *murabaha*. The following case study[31] examines the mechanics of a raw material purchase for the manufacture of stainless steel.

Case study: raw material purchase

In this case, the investors engage an agent (supplier) to procure chromium for sale to an industrial user (buyer). The supplier is a reputable institution in the metals industry and the buyer is an independent manufacturer of steel and has no ownership or management relationships with the agent, investors or suppliers.

Deal structure

The investors and the agent require a fund management agreement, a *mudaraba*, in which the agent represents the investors. The agent will collect certain expenses and have some participation in the transaction. The agent executes a master purchase and sales agreement with the buyer. Independent schedules to the agreement define the terms of offer and acceptance each time goods are identified. Since the investors are represented by a bank and not a traditional commercial entity which knows the steel business, the investors' agent executes an agency agreement with the buyer, appointing the buyer to act as its agent to purchase the goods specified in the schedules.

When the buyer approaches the agent bank, the party representing the investors, the buyer is a non-Islamic entity seeking financing. The buyer will obtain a specific agency for the purchase and then as agent provide the purchase details and indicate its acceptance of the goods under the appropriate schedule of the master murabaha (see Exhibit 4.4).

When the purchase order is issued by the buyer to the supplier, the agent bank advises the investors of their disbursement obligations and issues a letter of credit to the supplier guaranteeing payment subject to the terms of the underlying documents (see Exhibit 4.5).

Once the supplier conveys the shipment notification with the bill of lading, the agent bank pays the supplier and the goods are shipped to the buyer's location (Exhibit 4.6).

The buyer, akin to the obligor in a financing, may pay the obligor in a single payment after a specific term, which is the most common approach in the Islamic banking market. However, if mutually agreed, the payments may be made in installments. These payments are conveyed to the investors and represent a return of their original capital and a mark-up on the sale, typically a Libor-defined factor (Exhibit 4.7).

Most trade transactions are for periods of between three and 12 months, with six months being the most common. But, there is no limitation on the term and murabaha installment sales may be used for long-term transactions such as home acquisition.

Exhibit 4.4 **Agency and offer mechanics**

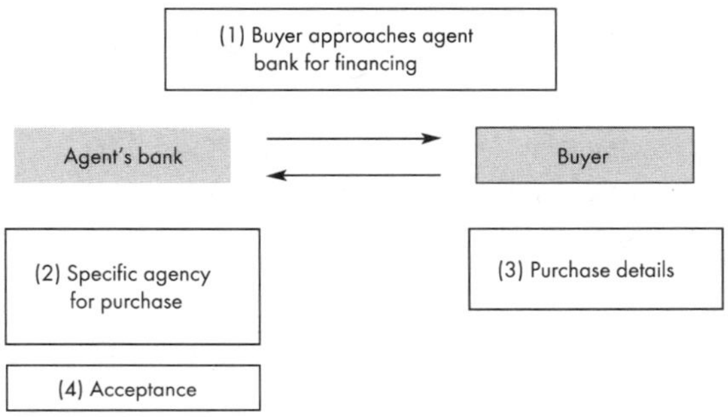

Source: Bryan Kraty.

Exhibit 4.5 **Ordering and funding**

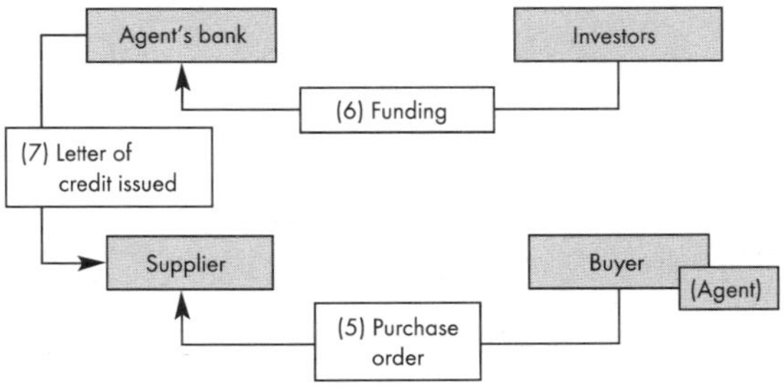

Source: Bryan Kraty.

Exhibit 4.6 **Shipping and payment 1**

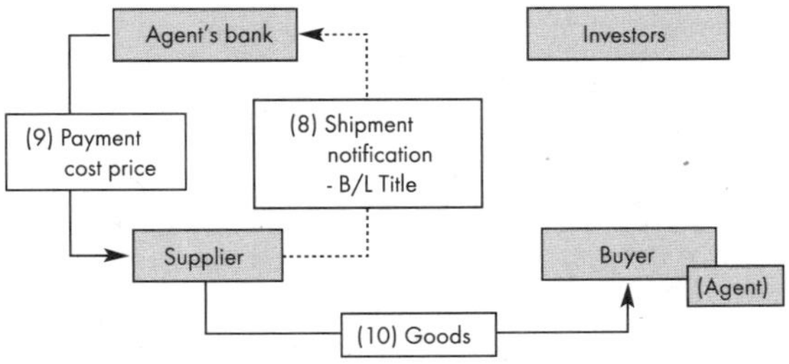

Source: Bryan Kraty.

Large trade transactions such as this are frequently syndicated either domestically or internationally.

Pricing and documentation

Generally, the pricing for *murabaha* transactions is in line with similar conventional trade finance facilities. Transactions are determined on a case-by-case basis in line with tenor, credit quality of buyer, strength of security, and so on. Most Islamic traded deals are priced in line with peer conventional deals.

Exhibit 4.7 **Shipping and payment 2**

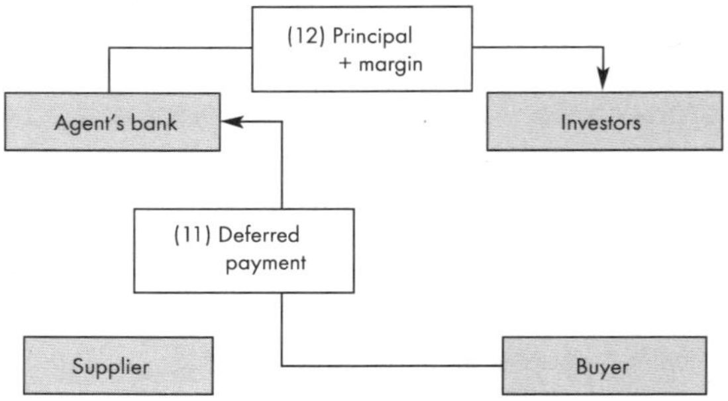

Source: Bryan Kraty.

When accounting for a *murabaha* transaction, the Islamic financier treats the deal as a short-term receivable funded by the *mudaraba* funds on hand, themselves a matching liability. Since the Islamic institution may not come into direct title or merely hold unregistered title for a negligible period, the object of the trade will not itself appear as an asset for the financier. The obligor shows a short-term liability on the balance sheet asset.

The documentation in many *murabaha* cross-border trades is similar to customary international trade documentation such as freight documents, invoice, certifications, insurance, and so on. These follow the sales agreement (the *murabaha*) which may be a master agreement for revolving facilities or multiple shipments.

Among Islamic bankers, renewable is preferred to revolving as the funds do not roll over like a loan; rather, they are returned to the investors and called anew for incremental draws under a master agreement. When the financier will not negotiate the acquisition of goods, there is an agency agreement between the financier and the buyer. There are various contract notes. If the deal is syndicated, there will be the *mudaraba* or investment management agreement. Finally, there are any relevant security documents such as letters of credit, guarantees, mortgages, receivables, cash, and so on, as specifically required in the documentation.

Murabaha versus *bai' bithaman al muajjal*

Newcomers to Islamic financing often enquire whether or not there is a difference between *murabaha* and *bai' bithaman al muajjal*. A sale in which the buyer and seller agree on deferred payment is *bai' muajjal* or *bai' bithaman al muajjal*, in which the word *bai'* means 'sale' and the word *muajjal* means 'delayed' or 'deferred'. In Malaysia, *murabaha* is used to refer to short-term credit sales and *bai' bithaman al muajjal* is used for long-term credit sales. According the Sh. Muhammad Taqi Usmani,[32] deferred credit sales are governed by the following primary conditions:

- the time of payment must be agreed in advance;
- if there is an increase compared with the cash price, it must be agreed at the time of the sale and the buyer must have the true option to pay the lower cash price or higher deferred sale price;[33] and
- the price may not be increased if there are delays in payment, but the remaining installments may be accelerated if there are any defaults in paying the installments on time.

The case of Malaysia

May one sell or securitise *murabaha* debts? The classical view is that once a good has been sold and there is a document representing monies owed, then the document is the same as money and is no longer connected to the goods. Its sale, therefore, is akin to the trading of monies and subject to the rules of *riba.*[34] The Malaysian view is: so long as a receivable is connected to a true trade transaction or the commercial transfer of a non-monetary asset, then the receivable may be traded freely at whatever price willing parties negotiate.

Bai' al-dayn – the sale of debts

In Malaysia, the sale of debts is formalised as *bai' al-dayn.* This refers to a transaction that involves the sale and purchase of securities or debt certificates that conform to *Shari'a* under current Malaysia regulation. Securities or debt certificates will be issued by a debtor to a creditor as evidence of indebtedness.

On 21 August 1996, the Shariah Advisory Council of Securities Commission of Malaysia passed a resolution that allows the usage of *bai' al-dayn* in the Malaysian capital market for the following reason:

> 'Some of the Islamic jurists allowed this concept subject to certain conditions. In the context of the capital market, these conditions can be met when there is a transparent regulatory system, which can safeguard the *maslaha* (public interest) of the market participants.'

This is an area of deep dispute between Malaysian authorities and their counterparts in the GCC and south Asia. The latter argue that the Malaysian approach is based on a weak *hadith* and a decision, later reversed, by Imam Shafi'i. The former point to Imam Shafi'i's distinctive decisions according to the circumstances of Iraq and Egypt – both places where he was an active judge.

Islamic sales contracts

Murabaha and bai' bithaman ajil

As a result of their position, the Malaysians have built an extensive financial and securities infrastructure applying the contract of sale. This includes a banking universe governed by the central bank, Bank Negara Malaysia, which offers the following formal definitions of Islamic sales contracts in the banking sphere:

> ***Murabaha:*** Refers to the sale of goods at a price, which includes a profit margin as agreed to by both parties. Such sales contract is valid on the condition that the price, other costs and the profit margin of the seller are stated at the time of the agreement of sale.
>
> ***Bai' bithaman ajil:*** Refers to the sale of goods on a deferred payment basis at a price, which includes a profit agreed to by both parties.

Likewise, the Securities Commission of Malaysia provides its own governance of sales contracts once these pass into the marketable and private debt securities universes:

> ***Murabaha:*** A contract that refers to the sale and purchase transaction for the financing of an asset whereby the cost and profit margin (mark-up) are made known and agreed by all parties involved. The settlement for the purchase can be settled either on a deferred lump sum basis or on an installment basis, and is specified in the agreement.
>
> ***Bai' bithaman ajil:*** A contract that refers to the sale and purchase transaction for the financing of assets on a deferred and an installment basis with a pre-agreed payment period. The sale price includes a profit margin.

There are specific practical applications that follow from the formal regulatory definitions in Malaysia:

> ***Murabaha* note issuance facility (Munif):** It is a short-term (not more than one year) financing arrangement between the customer and the financiers (investors), where the customer agreed to purchase back its own asset at a certain selling price. Potential financiers are invited to bid (to purchase the asset at a price lower than the selling price, that is, the price where the bidder will sell back the asset to the customer) and the highest bidder will be selected. Upon execution of a *murabaha* purchase agreement and a *murabaha* sale agreement, the successful bidder will make an up-front payment and the customer will issue *murabaha* notes to this successful bidder. The issuer will make payment upon maturity.
>
> ***Bai' bithaman ajil* bond:** This bond is used to provide a financing arrangement to a customer who requires a fixed asset. The financier will purchase an asset and resell it to the customer on a deferred payment basis. The customer will issue bonds to reflect indebtedness in line with the financing arrangement. The customer (issuer) will make payment upon maturity (secondary and primary notes).

Less widely applied sales concepts

Although the *fiqh* literature is rich with different sales approaches, some of these methods have not found widespread adoption due to the tendency of Islamic banks to introduce new concepts slowly and then to expand the new concepts to their maximum capacity for utilisation. Others have been inhibited either by regulatory issues or the slower development of specific sub-markets for such products. Periodically, product complexity is an inhibitor of product adoption.

Musawama

Ostensibly this is a sale like *murabaha*. Whereas the *murabaha* is a fixed price sale in which all components of the sale are known to the buyer and seller, a *musawama* transaction is a truly negotiated sale in which the buyer does not necessarily know the seller's costs.[35] So far, *musawama* is only permitted in the limited number of jurisdictions in which banks may properly play the merchant role.

The primary applications of *musawama* have been in both car-dealer bank-funded inventory programmes, in which a car dealer manages a sum of money for an Islamic bank and negotiates sales prices with consumers. In these cases, the ultimate sales price may be paid upon delivery of the car, or may be paid over time after the delivery of the car to the buyer. Some Islamic banks, notably Kuwait Finance House and Qatar Islamic Bank, operate their own auto dealerships and do not disclose car purchase prices to consumers, thereby concealing the margin. These transactions are true sales and represent *musawama*.

In *musawama*, the traditional risks of a bank – including credit and cost of funds invested – are augmented by risks relating to inventory management, marketing risks related to the underlying goods and consumer fashion, and inventory aging.

Istijrar[37]

This is similar to *musawama*, but is more like a standard purchase order agreement whereby there is a master purchase agreement governing all terms and conditions except price. The buyer draws goods under the agreement, subject to the conditions pre-negotiated. The price must be disclosed prior to the drawing, unless the buyer and seller agree to a 'market value price' in a market that has limited price fluctuation.

There are two forms of *istijrar*. In the first, the price is disclosed and the price is paid, making the sale final upon receipt of all of the ordered goods. In the second, the price is not disclosed until all transactions are completed, and the sale is complete upon possession. Prior to delivery, *istijrar* may be cancelled if there is a significant variance between market norms and the agreed price.

Istijrar or the use of a master agreement may be adapted within the contexts of *ijarah*, *murabaha* and *mudaraba*. It may not be applied to debtors of a bank, but may be used as a means to secure goods to be sold to a bank's clients. An agency concept may also be applied in *istijrar* whereby the client secures the goods on the bank's behalf as in an agency *murabaha*. In the agency *istijrar* case (called pseudo *istijrar* by some scholars), the bank should have a stronger form of possession than simply constructive possession.

Muzara'a

This method is applied to the finance of agricultural inputs for a specific period of time. The approach crosses into a form of partnership. *Muzara'a* is for the cultivation of general agricultural products and *muqasat* is for orchards. Until recently, these forms of transaction have not been widely applied. This, however, is expected to change with the expansion of Islamic finance into micro credit and agricultural finance.

Problematic sales types

The Prophet Mohammed (PBOH) instructed 'Do not sell the fruits before their benefit is evident.'[37] *Muzabana* – the sale of an unripened commodity for dried commodity – or *ariyyah* – fruit for dried dates – is governed by special conditions. In this case, the scholars worry that the sale of items, mentioned in the *hadith* governing *riba*, are not only at risk of being *ribawi*, but are susceptible to *gharar*. But the exception is for charitable purposes.[38] Likewise, sale by estimation is forbidden with respect to those things which may not ripen or are otherwise not measurable when suitable for sale.[39]

Bai' al-' inah

A concern of Islamic scholars is to prevent the combining of two sales of the same object between the same counterparties. The issue here is that the time and price differential is a means of synthesising a loan at interest. This is the concept of *bai' al-' inah*, and it is forbidden by the majority of Islamic scholars who believe that the profit differential constitutes the forbidden *riba*. A large number of scholars have gone on to ban the combining of two contracts in a single contract. In fact, this is less clearly an issue if the joining of the two contracts does not result in observable or disguised *riba*.

The case of Malaysia

This is not the case, however, in Malaysia where *bai' al-' inah* has been formalised as a permissible practice. In Malaysia, *bai' al-' inah* refers to trading whereby the seller sells his assets to the buyer at an agreed selling price to be paid by the buyer at a later date. After that, the buyer immediately sells back the assets to the seller at a cash price, lower than the agreed selling price.

On 29 January 1997, the Shariah Advisory Council of Securities Commission of Malaysia passed a resolution that allows the usage of '*inah* in the Malaysian capital market for the following reason:

> 'The Shafie' and Zahiri mashed viewed *inah* as permissible. A contract was valued by what is disclosed and one's *niyyah* (intention) was up to Allah to judge. They critised [sic] the *hadith* used by the majority of the Islamic jurists as the basis for their argument, saying that it (the *hadith*) was weak and therefore could not be used as the basis for the *hukm* (judgment).'

The requirements for *bai' al-' inah* objects and all forms of installment credit sales, *murabaha* and *bai' bithaman al ajil* as well, are as follows:[40]

- must exist in corporeal forms;
- must be owned by the sellers;
- must be permissible and used in a permissible manner;
- they must be lien free;
- they must be specific; and
- they must not be one of the specific *ribawi* items (currencies, gold, silver, wheat, barley, dates and salt).

Although there is considerable effort to achieve conversion between Malaysia and other Islamic markets, *bai' al-' inah* is one of two areas that does not appear susceptible to reconciliation between markets.

Letters of credit

A common thread in both *murabaha* and *salam* transactions is the use of letters of credit either as a tool of guarantee or a means of ensuring belief ('credit' is derived from the Latin verb 'to believe') in long-distance transactions that parties will fulfill their obligations under the documents defining them. Although the general view of Islamic jurists is that the payment for a guarantee by the beneficiary of a guarantee is forbidden under the rules of *riba*, that is, the guarantee is money, so one is paying money for money, a letter of credit is a customary instrument of international trade allowing two parties to conduct a sale with a trusted intermediary standing between them to ensure that the terms of documents are complied with in order to allow payment. On this basis, Muslim scholars permit letters of credit and other documentary assurances between distant or unfamiliar parties in a trading transaction.[41]

Historical means of conveying funds which are covered in the traditional sources of Islamic law include *suftaja* and *hawala*. The former is a Persian word that pre-dates the time of the Prophet Mohammed (PBOH) and means 'bill of exchange'. The concept has little variation in concept in comparison with western bills of exchange and is governed by the rules of *riba*.

Hawala is a method of transferring debts without discounting. Since the transport of cash money, in and of itself, is dangerous, the concept of *hawala* allowed one to exchange debts in a way that allowed an independent party, a traveller, to carry one's rights and settle them against one's obligations. *Hawala* is also governed by the rules of *riba*, even if the modern adaptation of this form of monetary transmission has become a beneficiary of modern telecommunications and the internet.

Conclusion

The first instinct of Islamic bankers was to turn to the sales contract as a means of financing business and managing excess funds. A properly constructed sales contract has a clear term, a defined object and the capacity to seize the object, as well as a clear yield. Often, sales contracts are deemed to be easily compared to loans with limited operational difference. So the first major step by Islamic banks has been to apply the *murabaha* concept expansively and liberally.

However, this is problematic. On the one hand, *murabaha* has limited flexibility from a *Shari'a* perspective. Late payments cannot be punished and the price cannot be changed in the event of a late payment. With the bold exception of Malaysia and specific south-east Asian markets, the resultant debt from a *murabaha* transaction may not be sold at a premium or discount, and is not securitisable. In some markets, a bank intervening in the sales chain finds itself the warrantor of quality and that the manufacturer's warranty goes away (as is currently a challenge facing the Islamic Bank of Britain). Therefore, *murabaha*'s dominant position as an Islamic banking tool is steadily eroding as bankers become more comfortable with the other nominative contracts and their derivatives.

Checklist: *murabaha* transaction steps[42]

1. The Buyer and the Agent Bank (acting on behalf of the Financier) execute a Master Financing Agreement.
2. The Buyer negotiates with the Seller the terms and conditions of the purchase of the Goods as it would in the ordinary course of business.
3. When such negotiations are finalised, the Buyer requests the Agent Bank's permission to proceed with the purchase of the Goods by sending a completed 'Transaction Notice' to the Agent.
4. The Agent Bank (if it agrees with the terms contained in the Transaction Notice) confirms acceptance to the Buyer by sending a 'Transaction Approval'. Buyer proceeds with the purchase of the Goods as the undisclosed Purchasing Agent of the Financier.
5. Upon the receipt of Approval, the Buyer purchases the Goods described in the Transaction Notice on the terms and conditions as specified in this notice and confirmed by the Transaction Approval notice as an undisclosed agent for and on behalf of the Financier.
6. The Buyer delivers to the Agent Bank: (i) Invoice for Goods (or other forms of Memorandum of Title) **BEFORE** the Financier pay the Purchase Price to the Buyer.
7. The Financier on the Value Date pays the Purchase Price to the bank account of the Buyer acting on their behalf. The Agent Bank assumes title to the goods.
8. The Buyer (acting on its own behalf) enters into a deferred sales purchase agreement by making an Offer to the Agent for the purchase of the Goods at an agreed marked-up price and date. [This is a

procedural step to comply with the Islamic finance requirements and the terms are set out in the Master Financing Agreement].

9. Upon receipt of this offer, the Agent Bank accepts by countersigning and returning the Offer to the Buyer. [Again this is a procedural step to comply with the Islamic finance requirements].
10. The Buyer pays to the Agent Bank the Deferred Price on the Deferred Payment Date.

---

1 Kraty, Bryan and Abdelhaq Kafsi, *Islamic Finance & Mechanics* (Bahrain: unpublished manuscript, November 2004). Portions of this chapter owe a debt to this document as well as diagrams produced by Bryan Kraty.

2 Usmani, M.T., *An Introduction to Islamic Finance*, (Karachi: Idaratul Ma'arif , 1998), p. 19.

3 In certain Islamic banking experiments, the *qard hassan*, a 'goodly loan' has been used as a business method in lieu of the methods described in this chapter or as a current account depository tool. In this book, we do not treat this tool as a banking instrument because the *Qur'anic* implication is that the *qard hassan* is solely for charitable purposes.

4 Kamali, Mohammad Hashimj, *Islamic Commercial Laws: An Analysis of Futures and Options* (Selangor, Malaysia: Ilmiah Publishers, 2002), p. 132. He provides a useful analysis of the juristic differences leading to the historical consensus that a sale may be completed, paid for, after the goods are delivered allowing for a credit transaction.

5 Usmani, M.T., *op. cit.*, p. 95.

6 Bahrain Monetary Agency, *Islamic Banking & Finance in the Kingdom of Bahrain* (Bahrain: Bahrain Monetary Agency, 2002), p. 25. As of 2002, the BMA felt that the volume was approximately 75 per cent of the total Islamic transactional market.

7 Tyser, C.R. et al, tr. *The Mejelle* (Kuala Lumpur: The Other Press, 2001), p. 23.

8 El-Helbawy, Kamal et al, tr., Al-Qaradawi, Yusuf, *The Lawful and the Prohibited in Islam* (Indianapolis: American Trust Publications, undated), pp. 269–70.

9 Usmani, M.I.A., *Meezan Bank's Guide to Islamic Banking* (Karachi: Darul Ishaat, 2002), p. 76.

10 Title may be *registered* as is the common case with real property, a house, and large personal property, a car, or *bare legal* as in rightful possession.

11 Usmani, M.I.A., *op. cit.*, p. 73.

12 Khan, Dr. Muhammad Muhsin, tr., Sahih Al-Bukhari, Vol. III (Beirut: Dar Al Arabia, undated), p. 185.

13 Usmani, M.T., *op. cit.*, p. 98.

14 Sahih Bukhari, *op. cit.*, p. 196.

15 Usmani, M.I.A., *op. cit.*, p. 74.

16 Sahih Bukhari, *op. cit.*, p. 197.

17 In fact there are two promises inherent in this transaction; the promise of the client to buy from the bank, and the promise of the bank to sell to the client. The entire matter became the subject of much discussion by the scholars at the First Conference of Islamic Banks at Dubai in 1979. Their collective *fatwa* approving this arrangement was a significant milestone in the jurisprudence of modern Islamic finance.

18 DeLorenzo, Yusuf, 'Shariah Boards and Modern Islamic Finance: From the Jurisprudence of Revival and Recovery to the Jurisprudence of Transformation and Adaptation' presented to International Islamic

Financial Standards Board, May 2004, London. This book will only cover the basic iteration for simplicity's sake.

[19] Usmani, M.T., *op. cit.*, pp. 141 - 143.

[20] Kamali, *op. cit.*, p. 107.

[21] Usmani, M.I.A., *op. cit.*, p. 126.

[22] Aqeel, Abdul-Rahman, 'Shari'ah Precautionary Procedures in Murabaha and Istisna' ' in *Proceedings of the Second Harvard University Forum on Islamic Finance* (Cambridge, MA: Harvard Islamic Finance Information Program, 1998), p. 128.

[23] Usmani, M.T., *op. cit.*, p. 103.

[24] *Ibid*, pp. 129 - 131.

[25] Sahih Bukhari, *op. cit.*, p.161. Also, Sahih Muslim, *op. cit.*, p. 844.

[26] Usmani, M.I.A., *Meezan Bank's Guide to Islamic Finance*, *op. cit.* 130. Also see Kamali, *op. cit.*, p. 135, for a more liberal view.

[27] *Ibid*, p. 198. Also, see Usmani, M.T., *An Introduction to Islamic Finance*, *op. cit.*, p. 107.

[28] *Ibid.* p. 198.

[29] Usmani, M.T., *An Introduction to Islamic Finance*, *op. cit.*, p. 121.

[30] Bukhari, *op. cit.*, p. 283. Umar and Ibn Umar deputised or appointed as their agent another person to exchange money and weigh goods. One may also appoint an agent who is not present, p. 284.

[31] Kraty, Byran, Euromoney Islamic Finance Summit Workshops 2003 - 5.

[32] Usmani, M.T., *op. cit.*, pp. 102, 103.

[33] *Ibid*, p. 117.

[34] Usmani, M.I.A., *op. cit.*, p. 206.

[35] Usmani, M.I.A., *op. cit.*, p. 126.

[36] *Ibid*, p. 144. Also visit: www.meezanbank.com.

[37] Bukhari, *op. cit.*, p. 219.

[38] Siddiqi, Abdul Hamid, tr. Sahih Muslim, Vol. III (Lahore: Sh. Muhammad Ashraf, 1992), pp. 806 - 8.

[39] Bukhari, *op. cit.*, p. 216.

[40] Mansor, Ustaz Mohd Bakir Haji, 'Islamic Money Market: Shariah Perspective', presented at Euromoney Asian Islamic Banking & Finance Summit Workshop with Bank Negara on 'Implementing Islamic Money Market: Issues and Challenges' on 23 September 2004.

[41] Usmani, M.I.A., *op. cit.*, p. 195.

[42] Kraty and Kafsi, *op. cit.* (Unpublished manuscript).

Lease finance and *ijarah*

5

Abdulkader Thomas and Bryan Kraty,[1] with Mustafa Hussain, and Stella Cox

Introduction

Unlike *murabaha* with its very rigid limitations, *ijarah* is a truly flexible tool for Islamic banks. The nature of the underlying asset allows for its sale during the life of the lease; flexibility in pricing the lease; and adaptability to changes in lessee or property circumstances. Still a reformulation of a commercial method for financial institutions, Islamic leases are a closer fit to modern banking practices.[2] Nonetheless, the details that define a lease or its derivative as Islamic are significant. As much as the *ijarah* transactions are commonly applied concepts in the global Islamic finance environment, simple errors in application may render an Islamic lease invalid from a *Shari'a* perspective.

Lease finance and *ijarah*

The concept of *ijarah* is based on a wage paid for delivery of a service (such as hiring a doctor, a laborer, and so on), the use of equipment, the use of real property, or usable capacity (the usufruct is such that the 'use' concept is much broader than one traditionally thinks[3] so long as leased property is fully, clearly identified by the parties). *Ijarah*, like *murabaha*, is initiated by offer and acceptance.[4]

This is not specifically a method of finance, rather a business process that fits conveniently within the banking spectrum. Thus, as Sh. Muhammad Taqi Usmani points out, the result is that *ijarah* transactions must comply with *Shari'a* rules which are similar to, but not the same as, western banking approaches to leasing.[5] A number of Islamic experts argue that the Islamic form of leasing applied in Islamic banking today is a hybrid instrument, not truly an operating lease and not truly a financial lease, but incorporating elements of both.[6] Due to the easy compatibility of the *ijarah* concept in a leasing environment, it enjoys a growing utilisation in Islamic finance.[7]

In conventional leasing, there is the granting of the use of an asset in exchange for rent. The asset must have some use, which may be broadly defined, and is usually not consumable. Ownership remains with the lessor, but the lessee pays running costs. Conventional leases may be either structured as operating or financial leases. The rentals can be fixed or variable. '... there are similarities between Islamic leases and conventional leases which make the instrument attractive to non-Muslim investors, thereby expanding the investor base and strengthening the integration of capital markets.'[8]

Similarly, in an Islamic lease or *ijarah*, like a conventional lease, the asset or service must have a valuable use. Certain consumables such as money, food, or fuel may not be leased.[9] Nonetheless, some forms of lease that are permissible include capacity. There is some disagreement about leasing land without improvements; but ground rents do not appear to be absolutely forbidden.[10] Nonetheless, ground rents for unutilised and unusable property or agricultural property have *hadith*-based restrictions. It turns out that these restrictions relate solely to the case of *muzara'a* and the issue is not prohibition, rather disapproval so as to protect the low-income cultivators and prevent exploitation of the weaker from the stronger.[11] The focus of Muslim jurists has not been on the economics of a lease, but on the consumption of the asset, or the benefits' capacity.[12]

Contract conditions

To be valid for *Shari'a* purposes, a leasing contract must be transparent, detailed, and agreed in advance of signing. In contrast to a conventional lease, the lessor assumes all costs of purchase and transport. The lessor must maintain legal and beneficial ownership and risk and this usually means that the lessor contracts the casualty insurance, and bears the primary responsibility for taxes. Nonetheless, there has been a development in the United States whereby some *fatawa* permit the lessee to be charged for certain taxes based upon the unique and defined benefit to the consumer.

But, the lessee is responsible for every harm to the asset caused by how the lessee operates the asset, due to misuse or negligence. This latter point has entered contemporary *Shari'a* debates because it frames an argument for the lessee to buy some form of casualty insurance. The lessee bears costs of using the asset, that is the cost of ordinary operation under the lessee's control. In an Islamic lease environment, the rent may commence only after delivery of the asset, but a lease may be set for a future date subject to this condition, a concept called *ijarah mawsufah*.[13]

Lease characteristics

The characteristics of a lease that complies with Islamic principles is similar to an operating lease, but may be structured to have the economics of a financial lease through a put option[14] mechanism or a promise to purchase. The investors have beneficial ownership of the financial assets and related risks. This means that the asset owner has responsibility for paying these costs, but they may be built into and recovered in the rental.[15] A lessee, nonetheless is an *Amin*, which means that he has certain obligations to the care of the leased asset, so long as such obligations do not extend to failures beyond the lessee's control.

Lease rentals

Lease rentals may be either fixed or floating. Adjustable rentals for international corporate transactions are often redetermined every three, six or 12 months. In consumer transactions, the rentals may be fixed for three or five years, and then redetermined. When the rentals are floating or adjustable, the basis for determination and adjustment must be pre-disclosed prior to signing the lease contract.[16] The typical, and so far indispensable, benchmark for adjustable rentals, although disliked, is either the US dollar Libor or Treasuries.[17] Rentals are normally computed against the investment basis of one party in the property, which is permissible so long as both parties agree.[18]

Rent should be charged only when the property has been delivered or made available to the lessee at a specific time and place agreed by the lessee. The lessee may act as the investor's agent to purchase assets.[19] As a practical matter, the lessee is made responsible for insuring and maintaining the property, generally through a side agreement that specifies duties, values and performance. Such agreements have become common as lessees are often more expert in the leased assets and have physical control, therefore making it easier for them to perform these tasks. A further practical consideration is that the insurance umbrella of a lessee using large amounts of similar equipment is normally less expensive than what an investor will obtain if the investor's exposure to the asset class in a specific jurisdiction is limited. In the event of a total loss, the lease is automatically terminated and the lessor has no rental claim from the lessee; the lessor's only recourse is to claim any insurance proceeds for which it is eligible.

Event of default

In the case of an event of default, a *Shari'a*-compliant lease contains customary clauses that may result in termination. In specific cases, termination is triggered when either the lessor exercises the put option, or calls on the defaulting lessee to fulfill its promise to purchase. In some structured lease transactions, the lessee is obliged to pay a 'termination amount' to purchase leased assets.

A default often flows from one or more late payments. There are several approaches to what may be recovered by the lessor following a late payment. Structured leases often claim compensation as liquidated damages with Islamic investors donating the balance to charity after deduction of administrative costs.[20] Another approach is for the lessor or its servicing agent to charge the actual costs of collection. In cases where the rental is floating, there may not be an administrative charge, but the lease may allow for an increase in the rental at the next increment thereby allowing the lessor to recover the expenses associated with late payment.

A frequent means of curtailment is a sale of the leased assets to the lessee. In this case, the lessee may, at the end of the lease term, purchase the leased assets either by exercising the call option and paying the exercise price or the embedded call documented within any promise to purchase.

Islamic lease structure

In a typical true lease circumstance, the bank and lessee will agree to the terms and conditions of the lease, specifying the object, when it will be available to rent, and the rental rate. The bank will pay for the asset from the dealer or manufacturer and take possession, and then the bank will lease the asset on to the lessee, usually through a special purpose vehicle (SPV) (see Exhibit 5.1). It is also permissible under *Shari'a* for the lessee to own the asset, sell it to the bank, and then lease it back.

In the case of a sale and leaseback, the sale of the asset should be at fair market value and the title must pass prior to the asset being leased back.

Exhibit 5.1 **Islamic lease mechanics**

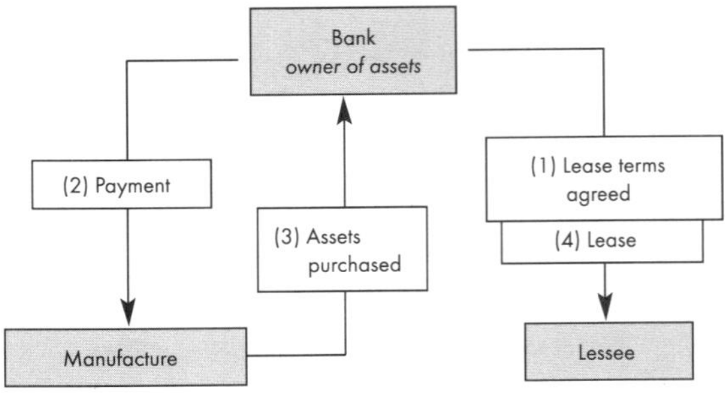

Source: Author's own.

There is no *Shari'a* objection to sub-leases[21] so long as the lessee benefits from any excess coming from the sub-lease. These must be agreed in advance with the consent of the lessor.

The *Shari'a* permits the assignment of a lease provided that due consideration is paid for passing title, or elements of ownership move, and all rights and obligations of the lease must be assumed by the new lessor. However, the assignment or sale of rent only is not permitted.[22] This latter point has important implications for securitising a leased asset. The certificate representing the securitised asset must attach to asset ownership and include proportionate rights and obligations: the certificate represents an undivided part of asset.[23]

Ijarah-wa-iqtina'a

A lease with acquisition (*ijarah-wa–iqtina'a*) or a lease ending in ownership (*ijarah muntahia bittamleek*) is the Islamic structured synthesisation of a financing lease. In this lease contract there is not a stipulated transfer, rather a unilateral promise of transfer may be made by the lessor relating to the lease term, or a unilateral promise with a purchase schedule may be offered.[24] In lieu of a lessor's unilateral promise, there may be a unilateral promise from the lessee to buy the asset at a pre-negotiated price. The purchase price for the asset transfer may be either a market value purchase or bargain purchase price. Ideally, the lease itself is not contingent on any promise to sell or buy, but such promises may be executed at the closing. In the event of lease termination, the decision must be mutual. The lessor may not force the lessee to buy the asset, and the lessee may not oblige the lessor to sell at a bargain price.[25]

The characteristic uses of this lease method are medium-term trade finance of equipment, financing new capital equipment or plant, medium and long-term finance of real estate, and re-financing under sale and leaseback. Periodically, the obligor, the lessee, may provide supplemental security. In corporate and commercial real estate, the tenors are usually three to five years, sometimes longer. With residential real estate, the tenors may extend to 30 years. In the US market the leases may incorporate an amortising feature over 25 or 30 years. The feature is much shorter with a higher residual for non-US transactions. Leases ending in acquisition may be syndicated bilaterally, internationally or domestically.

The rental pricing may be fixed or variable in line with similar conventional finance facilities. The rental may be determined on a case-by-case basis in line with tenor, credit quality of supplier, quality of the asset, strength of security, and so on.

Accounting for the asset as off-balance sheet depends on specific structures, particularly residual value at term, and the tax rules applied in the jurisdiction of the asset, lessee or lessor.

Documentation

Islamic leases ending in ownership arrangements are similar to conventional finance leases and enjoy well-established international precedents. The documentation necessarily includes the lease or *ijarah* contract which may be a head or master lease between the financial institution and its corporate customer, and then on-lease or sub-lease agreement between the master lessee and its customer, as pre-approved by the master lessor. There is not universal support for master and head leases among Islamic scholars: some scholars are concerned that one is simply transferring cash flows with no asset connectivity; others do not object when the underlying sub-lease is a true sub-leasing.[26]

When the lessee takes on the insurance and maintenance tasks, then there is normally an agency agreement governing the duties, payments and any impact on the rental. There may be a separate agency letter allowing the lessee to act on behalf of the lessor in acquiring the property to be leased.

The lease which ends in a transfer of property from the lessor to the lessee either has a letter of promise from the lessee to buy the property or a letter of promise from the lessor to sell the property. These letters are effectively pre-negotiated sales contracts. In structured cross-border transactions, instead of the promise letters, there are formal put and call letters. The view of many *Shari'a* scholars is that such letters must be unilateral and may not be combined. In other words, if there is a promise to purchase, there should not be a promise to sell; if there is a put, there should not be a call. The reasoning for this view is that the combination of the two unilateral, but opposite, promises transforms the lease into a sale and creates the risk of either *bai' al-'inah* or infects the contract with *riba*.

There is no *Shari'a* objection to structuring a lease agreement with additional security such as guarantees, mortgages, liens on receivables, or hypothecation of cash accounts, and so on. The more complex cross-border leasing transactions often require the supplemental security because of uncertainties relating to the recovery of the leased asset by the lessor in the event of an uncured or incurable default.

Finally, in the event of syndication, there is an investment management agreement.

When it comes to Islamic investors, they often use *ijarah* as an important tool for equipment import; project finance; corporate balance-sheet management; and working capital management for their clients. Profits may be from the rental, the margin of the rental over an index; facility fees; syndication fees; and other fees relating to the management of the property.

Project finance applications

Leasing has proven very popular in the project finance arena. In these cases, the application of leasing is usually a combination of construction finance (*istisna'a*) during the construction phase followed by a redeemable lease (*ijarah-wa–iqtina'a*) that buys out the completed project either in tranches or whole on completion.

In parallel with the *istisna'a*, the Islamic financial institution agrees on-sale to either the manufacturer or another end-buyer at a profit, reflecting the use of its capital, as above. This can be outright purchase, deferred sale or re-financing, for example, by way of lease finance. This type of arrangement is ideal for use in connection with the pre-construction finance needed, for example, in connection with the construction of a petrochemical plant.

Ijarah mawsufah bil thimma

Shari'a scholars permit leases to be executed for a future date.[27] Termed as a future, pre-paid lease, this is another structure to provide working capital provided for construction against an undertaking to lease such plant or equipment. In this case, pre-rentals are payable by the lessee on the understanding that the equipment will be leased. If plant is not manufactured or acquired according to the specifications laid down in the agreement to lease by a certain date, such pre-rentals will be repayable by the financiers.

In the project finance environment, the characteristic approach is to structure sequential contracts of *istisna'a* and *ijarah*. These are combined to allow for the financing construction of new capital equipment or plant, when the need is for tenors that stretch beyond three years. Frequently, one is dealing with tenors between five and 10 years.

The profit calculation is fixed in tranches for the construction period and may be either fixed or variable when the lease comes into force.

The most recent development in leasehold estate investment is the leasing of *intifa'a*. Applied to the construction of Zam Zam Towers in the Holy City of Mecca, this tool allowed the investors to separate property and right of occupancy,[28] somewhat along the lines of a time-share in the West. The advance payments of the future *intifa'a* or occupancy benefit were applied to the construction costs.

Case study: equipment leasing funds

Starting in the mid-1990s, Islamic banks and their advisers discovered that periodic gaps in the US credit markets did not correlate to the business cycle. As a result, corporates in the process of retooling plants to meet expanding demand or updating basic equipment such as forklifts or robots to maintain production or service standards. Service standards were able to access funds from Islamic investors when the US credit markets tightened. Subsequently, the universe of leasing funds has become global, with the largest concentrations of assets in the United States, Europe, and south-east Asia.

The typical fund followed the classical method of syndicating investors, usually Islamic banks, western banks, high net worth investors, agencies and others, applying the *mudaraba* technique. Funds are aggregated in suitable offshore jurisdictions to facilitate tax minimisation. For instance, some US-bound funds preferred to domicile themselves in Ireland as elements of the Irish-American tax treaty would allow a master lease representing a large-scale equipment purchase to be treated as debt with the master rental payments treated as interest for tax purposes.

The master lease to a specialist US leasing company is structured as an Islamic lease. The US company then sub-leases the equipment to other US companies. In some cases, the sub-leases are unmodified from standard local market leases. This practice is frowned upon by *Shari'a* scholars and there has been a growing process of adaptation of local market operating leases to meet Islamic rules.

Such leasing funds often provide the basis for medium-term fixed or adjustable rate investing. In addition, such funds are increasingly applied to liquidity management with the adaptation of *sukuk* methodology.

Case study: auto leasing

The prospective market for Islamic auto finance (IAF) is estimated to be robust given both the strong demand for new car imports in all of the main Islamic consumer markets, and the rising share of institutions providing IAF products in all of those markets.[29] This market has three branches: consumer auto acquisition; fleet acquisition for businesses; and import – export finance.

In one of the most innovative Islamic securitisations of 2004, Bemo Securitization worked with Hanco, a major Saudi Arabian fleet lessor to acquire an existing universe of autos from Hanco, thereby releasing cash to Hanco, which then serviced the onwards leases to local-market users of the cars. Hanco's goal was a repositioned balance sheet and transition towards providing a fleet management service instead of buying autos and leasing them.

The company was able to offer a pool of cars under lease to a diverse universe of credit risks, domestic Saudi and international companies. The cars were diversified by age, type, and usage. All obligors engage in time-delimited true operating leases of cars. As a result, Hanco has maintenance and replacement obligations to ensure that lessees are able to have uninterrupted use of their vehicles.

Because the *Shari'a* allows each car to be unitised, the fleets may be securitised with the leases running with the unitised ownership of the autos. Thus, a *sakk* or certificate holder owns a pro rata share of the fleet of cars and the risks of ownership and benefits of lease that run with that ownership. The repositioned Hanco continued to earn servicing and maintenance fees for managing the customer relationships and maintaining the cars. More critically, the company was now in a stronger financial position to enhance its market share. The slimmed down company now stood to enjoy a superior yield on its equity whereas investors could enjoy a stable return from short and medium-term leasing of their assets.

Case study: Zam Zam Towers and *sukuk al intifa'a*[30]

As part of the master plan for the ongoing improvements of the Holy Cities of Mecca and Medina, the various governates and charitable trusts or *awqaf* owning significant properties have entered into ambitious plans to modernise and expand facilities for pilgrims and visitors. In Mecca, the King Abdul Aziz Waqf is developing a multiplex of high-rise towers. Zam Zam Towers was a sub-project secured by an affiliate of the Kuwait-based International Lease Investment Company (ILIC, an Islamic Development Bank-sponsored entity) called Munshaat.

Munshaat entered into a 24-year reversionary ground lease with the *waqf* and had an obligation to build a high-quality service facility for pilgrims that met specific goals of the *waqf*. The company then engaged in a detailed study of demand for short-term accommodation in Mecca as well as the prices for such accommodation according to the Islamic calendar. Then, the company engaged in a forward-thinking radical re-conceptualisation of the project, applying awareness of time-share vacation facilities and fractional ownership within the framework of the governing reversionary ground lease.

Ownership issues

Since the long-term ownership of the building necessarily would go to the *waqf* and there were limitations on non-Saudi Arabian ownership of real property, Munshaat recharacterised the property into multiple estates: the ground belonged to the *waqf*; the building could belong to Munshaat as a Gulf Cooperation Council company ultimately controlled by the Jeddah-based Islamic Development Bank; and the *munfa'a*, or benefit of the space, could be sold for up to 24 years.

Munshaat, then entered into a BOT contract with the *waqf* governed by the reversionary lease, and sub-contracted construction of a 31-storey, 1,240-unit building to a prominent Saudi Arabian builder. The US$390 million contract was funded by an extraordinary issuance of Islamic securities. These securities represented a fractional ownership of the right to use a specific part of the building during a specific period. The shares were priced according to season, unit location and view. The shares were made fully exchangeable and represent a 24-year guaranteed right to utilise, for a specific time each year, a pre-specified space.

The securities were sold prior to construction, thereby funding the construction. The *sukuk* or securities represent a forward lease for the property, meaning that Munshaat bears a refund risk if the project is not completed. Among the novel features of this project is that the holder of a *sakk* may elect a number of options from which to benefit from: he or she may simply show up at the reserved time; exchange times through a specialised affiliate of Munshaat; contract for Munshaat to sub-lease the contracted time to a willing tenant who wishes to visit Mecca at that time; or sell the *sakk* to a willing buyer for a profit or loss, with that buyer then acquiring all of the attendant rights and benefits of the *sakk*. The underlying property rights represented in the *sukuk*, however, are limited in time and nature.

Since the *sukuk* represent a specific form of property, the certificates may be sold on an installment basis. This facilitates one of the goals of the sponsor Munshaat: to make it easy for a large number of people to acquire the certificates and the access and use of property that they represent.

Munshaat's innovative *sukuk al intifa'a* issuance has established a model that is easily replicable in global markets. Based on an adaptation of a classical series of concepts, all of which centre on the flexible approach to the sale and utilisation of property facilities, this is the first modern lease derivative in Islamic finance.

Case study: Telekom Malaysia's US$60 million syndicated lease

Telekom Malaysia presents the classic case of a syndicated Islamic lease transaction. Since the 1980s, Islamic banks and their conventional counterparts have become very active in syndicating large-ticket equipment, ship and aircraft leasing deals. Although such syndications are migrating to the *sukuk* market, this remains an area of significant club activity and plays an important role in the expansion of the Islamic banking market.

Key terms and structure

The key terms to the Telekom Malaysia deal were the creation of a US$60 million facility based on the existing installed microwave and switchgear belonging to Telekom Malaysia. The cash released from this plant would be utilised by Telekom to finance its investment abroad. The transaction was structured to comply with *Shari'a* as a sale of the equipment to a special purpose vehicle (SPV) established by Telekom's bankers and its subsequent lease back to the company under the rules of *ijarah-wa-iqtina'a*. The salient terms of the lease were as follows:

Rentals	:	Based on six-monthly Libor + 2%
Lease term	:	Five years
Purchase price	:	Single payment at lease maturity (fully amortising feature built into the rent)
Re-purchase	:	Option at nominal value

Because the obligor was located in a country with foreign exchange restrictions and the funds would be applied outside of that country, a structure was defined that would allow the company to make payments in foreign currency from foreign currency revenues outside of the country (see Exhibit 5.2).

This meant first that Telekom would sell its assets into a trust formed under domestic Malaysian law. The Islamic syndicate funded the trust to complete the purchase. Then the trust leased the assets to an offshore SPV formed by Telekom which, in turn, leased the assets back to Telekom (see Exhibit 5.3). If the proceeds were solely required for domestic market purposes and payments were freely convertible, then the second SPV would not have been necessary and the lease could have been executed directly by the trust and Telekom.

Exhibit 5.2 **Malaysia Telekom syndicated lease structure**

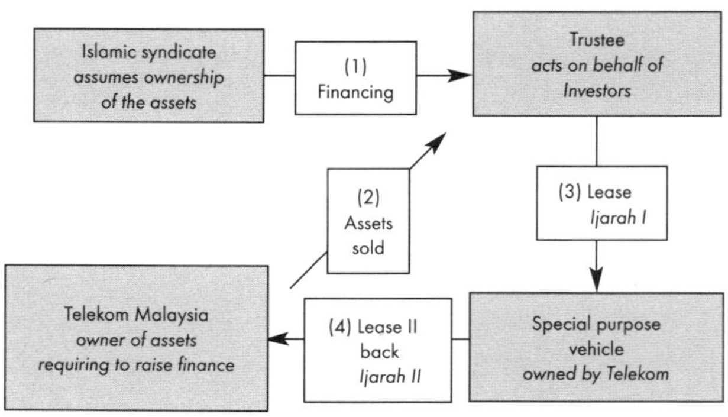

Source: Author's own.

Exhibit 5.3 **Rentals and purchase at maturity**

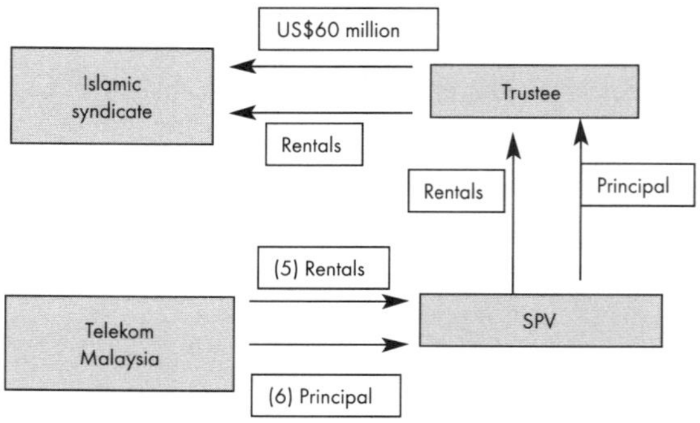

Source: Author's own.

The business flow of the transaction was similar to, but not the same as, a secured-term loan. The lease was structured so that the rent recovered 100 per cent of the invested amount, allowing a bargain purchase price at

Exhibit 5.4 **Telekom – call options**

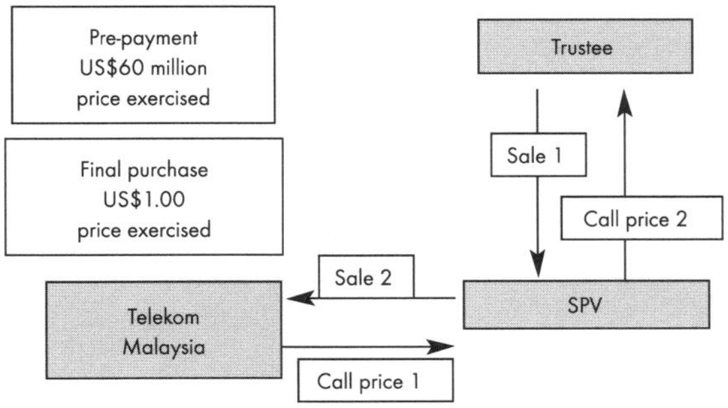

Source: Author's own.

Exhibit 5.5 **Lessor – put options**

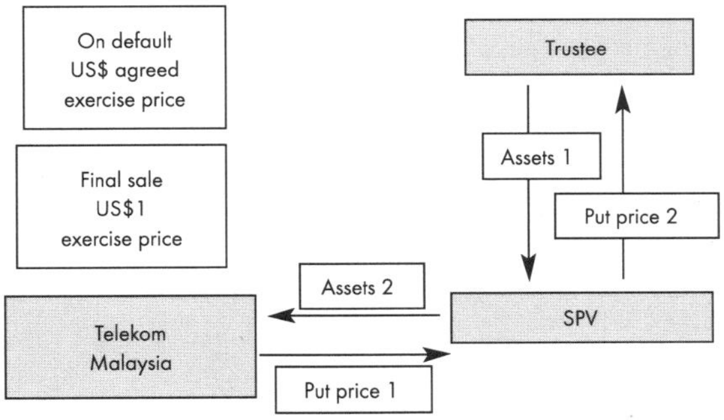

Source: Author's own.

term. Thus, each month, the flow of payments represented 100 per cent rental including 1/60th of the initial capital value of the equipment. Were Telekom to retire the transaction early, then the buyout price for the equipment was the full initial capital value of the equipment or US$60 million.

In an event of default or at such time that Telekom wished to buy the assets, an embedded call and put option mechanism was built into the lease (see Exhibit 5.4). This option could be put to Telekom in an event of default under either *Ijarah* I or II allowing the lessor to recover its funds through the put option, in turn allowing the SPV to sell the assets back to Telekom either at term for the bargain purchase price of US$1.00 or the full initial capital value in the event of default. Likewise, the SPV has granted a corresponding put option to the Investors, allowing it to put the equipment back to them in exchange for the agreed value.

Whereas the call is driven by the investors, the put is driven by Telekom (see Exhibit 5.5).

Successful execution of this transaction required the following universe of agreements, some of which integrated terms and conditions similar to conventional secured-term loans, yet retained the integrity of an operating lease.

Documentation

The main agreements in the Telekom lease were as follows:

- Islamic syndicate – *mudaraba* agreement
- Trustee – trust agreement
- Telekom and trust – purchase and sales agreement

- Trust and SPV – *Ijarah* I
- SPV and Telekom – *Ijarah* II
- SPV – assignment of title to equipment
- Syndicate and Telekom – service agency agreement

The syndicate was obliged to operate under the principles of *mudaraba*. A trust was settled on the syndicate's behalf, requiring a trust indenture or trust agreement. Then, the transaction required a purchase and sales agreement between the company and the trust, moving the assets from Telekom's balance sheet via a true sale onto the balance sheet of the trust. Now the trust could lease the assets to the SPV under *Ijarah* I, and leased onwards to Telekom under a second lease (*Ijarah* II). Title to the equipment may be assigned for security or tax purposes to the SPV. Since the syndicate has no knowledge or capacity to provide insurance and maintenance for the equipment on a cost-effective basis, the syndicate executed a service agency with Telekom to provide these services for a minimal fee.

Although this was viewed by all participants as a very successful deal, the strengthening Malaysian economy and improved credit position of Telekom meant that the deal was renegotiated within two years of closing under terms more favourable to Telekom.

Main differences between Islamic and conventional leases

The first distinctions relate to ownership and status of the lessor. There is nothing in Islamic theology that prohibits the standard structure of using a bankruptcy-remote offshore SPV lessor. However, the relationship between the SPV lessor and the financiers is slightly different since in Islamic transactions beneficial ownership of the equipment is very important. As there are often several investors or financiers, an agent (*mudarib*) will be appointed to coordinate and represent their combined interests. The *mudarib* acts very much like the standard agent bank and security trustee in a lending transaction, collecting and distributing funds on behalf of the investors and protecting their various interests.

Event of default or loss

In the event of termination and total loss, it is not uncommon, notwithstanding the Islamic sensitivities in respect of total loss proceeds, for the lessor to impose an absolute payment obligation on the lessee to pay the relevant termination sum or agreed value following an event of default or an event of loss. In this case, in order to comply with *Shari'a* principles, the Islamic investors may have to waive separately such claims on the lessee, that non-Islamic financiers would not.

Similarly, in the case of an event of total loss, only Islamic investors would rely purely on the receipt of sufficient insurance proceeds to recoup their investment. Where the loss is a result of negligence of the lessee, however, all parties may make a full claim on the lessee.

Put and call arrangements

Traditional leases often incorporate put and call arrangements that take effect following a lease termination or expiry. In order to make these compatible with Islamic principles, there are some changes in the procedures for claiming the full termination sum due upon lease expiration.

Under an Islamic lease, any put option or similar vehicle must be unilateral and documented separately from the lease itself. In a *Shari'a*-compliant case, following an event of default, or at lease expiry, the lessor will offer the equipment for sale to the lessee for an amount equal to the relevant termination sum or put option price. If the lessee fails to pay this amount, within an agreed period, then the lessor is entitled to 'put' the equipment to the lessee for this amount, thereby crystallising the claim against the lessee. For this to be compliant with *Shari'a* principles, the drafting must be very precise and the lease and the put vehicle may not be too closely bound. A call option may also be granted by the lessor to the lessee, under which the lessor will agree to sell the equipment to the lessee upon expiry of the lease or upon an agreed early termination. The preponderance of scholars prefer that only one put or call, however it is structured or termed, is executed when the lease is put into effect.

Broken funding

Often, a payment will take place on a date later than scheduled causing funding issues for investors, especially western institutions participating in a *Shari'a* structure. The question of 'broken funding' is a sensitive issue as it suggests that the underlying basis of the transaction is the provision of money, not equipment. From a *Shari'a* point of view, the former is intolerable, the latter is encouraged. Nonetheless, *Shari'a* scholars are worried that the leniency that is a hallmark of *Shari'a* will be abused and are not averse to the structuring of methods that will ensure that unnecessary, habitual tardiness does not mar either a transaction or the industry. In a number of structured deals, broken funding has been addressed through one of the following means.

1. In the event of a payment on a non-payment date, the amount then payable would be the full rental comprising the lessor's principal and profit thereon due on the following due date. This would effectively more than cover the investors' broken funding costs. At the same time the lessee may object given that it would pay more.
2. A formula is used to calculate the amount of rental payable when there is a payment on a non-payment date. This, however, is sometimes not acceptable by the *Shari'a* board, which will need to approve the documentation. Hence the aim would be to achieve broken funding coverage under (1) first, failing which (2) will have to be incorporated.

Late payment

Just as broken funding is a sensitive area in *Shari'a* analysis, so too is the imposition of a penalty for late payment of rentals. Such a penalty is correctly viewed as *riba* unless structured correctly. Liquidated damages, unlike default interest, may have limited acceptance among some *Shari'a* scholars; however liquidated damages may be claimed instead using the same concept. The main issue here though lies in the fact that any amount received by the security agent (*mudarib*) as liquidated damages would need to be shared pro rata between the commercial financiers. As a rule, however, the preference of Islamic jurists is that such damages must relate to the cost of collection in order to be taken into the accounts of the lessor; otherwise the excess over the cost of collection must be given to charity.

Servicing

With respect to insurance and maintenance, in a conventional lease the lessee would be responsible for procuring and paying for the insurance and maintenance of the equipment. Technically, in an Islamic lease the lessor is responsible for each of these, but it can appoint the lessee as its agent either under a separate service agreement or (depending upon the approach of the *Shari'a* committee) under the lease itself.

Conclusion

Leasing in Islamic finance is the nearest concept to conventional financing. *Ijarah* presents a long-term method of investing in property, plant, equipment and capacity using, effectively, an operating lease contract. *Ijarah-wa–iqtina'a*, a redeemable lease contract, is similar to a finance lease. When brought into the Islamic banking arena, the client selects the assets to be acquired by the Islamic financial institution, which then purchases these assets from the manufacturer or the client and leases the assets over a fixed period. This type of financing can be used to refinance assets owned by the client in a sale and leaseback arrangement.

In conformity with the *Shari'a*, the owner of the equipment, in our case the entity acting for the Islamic financial institutions, must be paid rent, which can be fixed or variable and must exercise all the rights and obligations attributed to ownership such as maintaining, insuring and repairing the asset. The lessee gains use of the asset for the period of the lease, subject to paying the rental. In the event that a lessee fails to pay an installment of rent at a due date, a penalty is not chargeable since this is similar to charging interest. In practice penalties are usually payable on default.

The terms of *ijarah* contracts are very similar to those of a conventional finance lease. In most cases where an Islamic financial institution is financing equipment or property, it will not wish to be left with the residual ownership of property that is not in its line of business or the task of disposing of it at the end of the lease period. So the leases are often structured with the means for the investor to dispose of the asset to the lessee in the event of default or at term.

[1] Kraty, Bryan and Abdelhaq Kafsi, *Islamic Finance & Mechanics* (Bahrain: unpublished manuscript, November 2004). Portions of this chapter owe a debt to this document as well as diagrams produced by Bryan Kraty.

[2] Usmani, Muhammad Taqi, *An Introduction to Islamic Finance*, (Karachi: Idaratul Ma'arif, 1998), p. 19.

[3] Tyser, C.R. et al, tr. *The Mejelle* (Kuala Lumpur: The Other Press, 2001), p. 66. This citation raises the renting of capacity from a wet nurse. Also see Khan, Dr. Muhammad Muhsin, tr., Sahih Al-Bukhari, vol. III (Beirut: Dar Al Arabia, undated), p. 225. The general concept of lease is noted in the *hadith* without restrictive or expansive comment.

[4] *Mejelle*, *op. cit.*, p. 63.

[5] Usmani, M.T., *op. cit.* p. 159.

[6] Johnson, Johnnie, 'Islamic Leasing', presented at International Conference on Islamic Leasing, 24, 25 April 2005, Kuwait.

[7] BMA, *op. cit.*, p. 28. *Ijarah* constituted about 15 per cent of all Islamic transactions as of 2002.

[8] Iqbal, Zamir, 'Financial Engineering in Islamic Finance', *Thunderbird International Business Review*, Vol. 41 (4/5) 541-560 (July-October 1999), p. 549.

[9] Usmani, M.T., *op. cit.*, p. 160.

[10] Bukhari, *op. cit.*, p. 300 and p. 311. Also see *Mejelle*, *op. cit.*, p. 66; as well as Qaradawi, *op. cit.*, p. 282.

[11] Siddiqi, Abdul Hamid, tr. Sahih Muslim, Vol. III (Lahore: Sh. Muhammad Ashraf, 1992), p. 812-7.

[12] Kahf, Munther, *Sanadat al Ijara wa al Ayyan Al Muajara* (Jeddah: Islamic Development Bank: Research No. 28, undated circa 1994), p. 25.

[13] Usmani, M.T., *op. cit.*, p. 160. Also see Habil, Dr. Abdurrahman, 'Mawsufa, the Jewel in the Ijara Crown', *Islamic Banker*, (February 2004) pp. 6, 7.

[14] Kahf, Monzer 'Analysing the conversion of existing instruments into Shari'ah compliant issues', presented at Securitisation.World Middle East, 2005, 12-14 April 2005. Options represent financial rights and are not salable, but the option concept is not *ip so facto* forbidden.

[15] Usmani, M.T., *op. cit.*, p. 167.

[16] Kahf, *op. cit.*, p. 51.

[17] Usmani, Muhammad Imran Ashraf, *Meezan Bank's Guide to Islamic Banking* (Karachi: Darul Ishaat, 2002), pp. 153-156; Usmani, M.T., *op. cit.*, pp. 118-120, p. 161 and 168-171; Khan, Tariqullah, *An Analysis of Risk Sharing in Islamic Finance with Special Reference to Pakistan* (unpublished doctoral thesis, 1996), p. 65; and, Hussain, Mustafa, 'Remedies in Islamic Leasing: A Comparative Analysis', presented at the International Islamic Leasing Conference, 24, 25 April 2005, Kuwait.

[18] Usmani, M.T., *op. cit.*, p. 163.

[19] Kahf, *op. cit.*, p. 28.

[20] Usmani, M.T., *op. cit.*, p. 139. For an opposing view, see Kamali, Hashim M., 'Shariah Issues of Islamic Leasing', presented at International Conference on Islamic Leasing, 24, 25 April 2005, Kuwait. Also see, Mustafa Hussain, 'Remedies in Islamic Leasing', presented at International Conference on Islamic Leasing, 24, 25 April 2005, Kuwait.

[21] Usmani, M.I.A., *op. cit.*, p. 161. Also see Usmani, M.T., *An Introduction to Islamic Finance, op. cit.*, p. 177.

[22] Usmani, M.I.A., *op. cit.*, pp. 162, 163.

[23] Usmani, M.T., *op. cit.*, p. 179.

[24] Usmani, M.I.A., *op. cit.*, p. 159.

[25] Usmani, M.T., *op. cit.*, p. 175.

[26] *Ibid*, p. 180. Kahf, *op. cit.*, p. 42. Kahf demonstrates the conceptual permissibility.

[27] Usmani, M.I.A., *op. cit.*, p. 150. Also see, Kahf, *op. cit.*, p. 47.

[28] Kahf, *op. cit.*, p. 47. Also see Kahf, Monzer 'Analysing the conversion of existing instruments into Shari'ah compliant issues', *op. cit.* Dr. Kahf points out that an asset, its ownership, its capacity to benefit, and its ownership may all be separated. Moreover, he supports the contention that the sale of the capacity (usufruct) may be used to finance construction.

[29] Mardam-Bey, Ibrahim, 'Recent developments in Islamic auto finance products' in Jaffer, Sohail, ed., *Islamic Retail Banking and Finance: Global Challenges & Opportunities* (London: Euromoney, 2005), pp. 107, 108.

[30] Homoud, Fuad, 'Workshop on Sukuk al Intifa'a: Their Basis and Characteristics', presented at the International Islamic Leasing Conference, Kuwait, 24, 25 April 2005.

Salam

6

Abdulkader Thomas and Bryan Kraty,[1] with Mustafa Hussain, and Stella Cox

Introduction

The three core nominative contracts involve either the sale of a good or the sale of the use of a good. In *murabaha* and *ijarah* as we have seen, the predominant practice is to deliver the good or its use now, whether payment is now or later. *Salam* – pre-paid sales – stands as an exception to the rule of sales, with the goods paid for in advance, but delivered later.

Salam has a specific derivative – *istisna'a* – which is the topic of Chapter 7. As we shall hold as a cardinal warning, *salam* is instituted in the banking and financial fields as the adaptation of a commercial contract.[2] Unlike *murabaha*, and more like *ijarah*, the adaptation of *salam* to the financial markets is straightforward. It is not difficult for professionals in the commodities exchanges of London, Chicago, Tokyo and Singapore to exclaim that *salam* is simply a futures contract. In this chapter, we will look at this concept more in its current adaptation as a short-term finance tool; later, in Chapter 12, we will revisit the application in the slowly evolving Islamic derivatives and hedging practices.

Salam

> 'Whoever wishes to enter into a contract of *salam*, he must effect the *salam* according to the specified measure and the specified weight and the specified date of delivery.' Prophet Mohammed (PBOH).[3]

Salam might be called future delivery financing and has been applied, notably, in the agricultural sector since before the life of the Prophet, when it was a documented business method.[4] Over the generations, *salam* has been expanded in commerce to meet the needs of trade financiers, and *salam* has spawned a derivative: *istisna'a*.[5] In certain cases, *salam* transactions may grant a merchant either priority on a specific producer's output or perhaps allow a buyer to secure a future price that is lower than the prevailing current market price.[6] Like western capital market derivatives, *salam* allows an enterprise to limit its risks, define future profit opportunities with reasonable accuracy, and to manage production timing to demand cycles.[7] In fact, many western financial analysts find close parallels between *salam* and futures contracts;[8] some even find strong similarities to options. The parallel may be taken viewed in the context of this definition by Warren Edwardes: 'Basis: The difference between the spot cash market price and the price of a futures or forward contract on the underlying financial instrument.'[9]

Features and definition

Like *istisna'a*, *salam* is one of the commercial contracts which is excepted from two of the most important conditions of a valid *Shari'a*-compliant commercial contract: at the time of contracting, the object need not exist, and the seller need not have valid possession of the object.[10] A condition governing *salam* contracts, perhaps to restrict these concessions and drive it towards processing (agriculture, construction or manufacture) is that the minimum period, in the view of many scholars, is ideally no less than 30 days, although this is not the uniform requirement of scholars as it has been noted that the Prophet Mohammed (PBOH) did not require a minimum period for a valid *salam* contract.[11] Some scholars are of the view that there must be a minimum interval between the contract payment and delivery of goods.[12]

Salam may be defined simply as a cash sales contract executed for the purchase of goods promised for future delivery. In contrast to a credit sale *murabaha*, under which goods are delivered and payment is deferred at a price higher than the spot price, the payment under *salam* is in full, while order and delivery of goods are deferred and the price may be lower than either the spot price or a credit *murabaha* price. In *salam*, the full price is paid in advance. In *salam*, and not its derivative *istisna'a* (see Chapter 7: Complex transactions: *istisna'a*, pre-export or manufacturing finance working capital and project finance), if the payment is partial, then there is a comparison to sale of a debt and many scholars deem this to be a violation of the rules of *riba*.[13]

In a *salam* transaction, the goods are commodities,[14] freely available in the market. The goods which are the object of a *salam* sale must be of specified quality and quantity without ambiguity. Although one might envisage that the goods will be a specific commodity from a specific farm or producer, the *salam* contract may not envisage such specification.[15] Only the date and place of delivery must be specified. The *salam* contract may not be applied for either spot delivery or cross sales.

Checklist: *Salam/istisna'a* financing transaction steps[16]

Part I Off-take mechanism (for goods being purchased)

Before entering into a *salam/istisna'a* the Financier, who will be acquiring title to the goods/equipment, on deferred delivery, has to have in place a creditworthy pre-agreed on-sale (or other exit strategy) mechanism with the end-Buyer.

1. The Supplier (*trader/manufacturer/construction company*), as Agent for the Bank, negotiates price/specifications/quality/quantity/delivery and other terms and conditions for sale of the goods/equipment with the Buyer.

2. The Buyer and Agent Bank (acting on behalf of the Financier) execute an Agreement for sale of goods/equipment being acquired by the Financier. This agreement has to accurately specify the quantity/quality/specification/delivery etc. This off-take could be via a number of mechanisms such as:

   - forward purchase agreement (a parallel *salam* or *istisna'a*);
   - redeemable lease agreement (*ijarah-wa-iqtina'a*);
   - letter of credit; and
   - purchase order.

Part II *Salam/istisna'a*

1. Once Part I is executed Agent Bank signs a *salam/istisna'a* agreement and any associated security agreement(s) with the Supplier in line with the above.
2. Supplier draws up a Transaction Notice with terms reflecting the purchase agreement above.
3. The Agent Bank (if it agrees with the terms contained in the Transaction Notice) confirms acceptance to the Supplier by sending a Purchase Order.
4. Agent Bank pre-pays Supplier (*can be stage payments in the case of an* istisna'a) for the goods/equipment for delivery.
5. *Under an* istisna'a, *the Supplier manufactures or constructs equipment and may receive total funds in advance or receive stage payments upon meeting pre-agreed completion criteria.*
6. Agent Bank assumes title to goods/equipment which are delivered by the Supplier to the end-Buyer who signs off on acceptance.
7. Buyer pays Agent Bank as per mechanics agreed under Part I.

Transaction structure

When utilised in the financial markets, the *salam* sales contract effectively provides a means of finance. Banks and investors can make a return by paying funds in full to a trader under *salam* for future delivery of commodities knowing there is a third-party buyer and a ready supply in the market. The buyer may secure the seller's delivery commitment with a mortgage, guarantee or letter of credit.

The trader will enter into a parallel sale secured by a promissory note, letter of credit or another *salam* agreement. This transaction, sometimes viewed as a form of *tawarruq*,[17] cannot be used to buy back the object of the original *salam* contract. This structuring of a parallel deal organises an unwinding of the original deal in a manner that turns the *salam* into a financing tool.

The financier in a *salam* transaction often appoints the trader as their agent to sell the goods to a third party at higher price on a cash or deferred basis (see Exhibit 6.1).

The basic mechanics are that the bank (as buyer) and trader (as seller) agree the object – the goods, payment and delivery. The buyer then orders the goods from the seller in the knowledge that the goods have been pre-sold and makes full settlement of the cash due at the time of placing the order. Then, at the agreed date, the seller, acting as agent for the bank, delivers the type, quantity and quality of goods as specified in the contract to the buyer on behalf of the bank. Profits from this sale are then shared with the bank.

Exhibit 6.1 **Process of *salam* transaction**

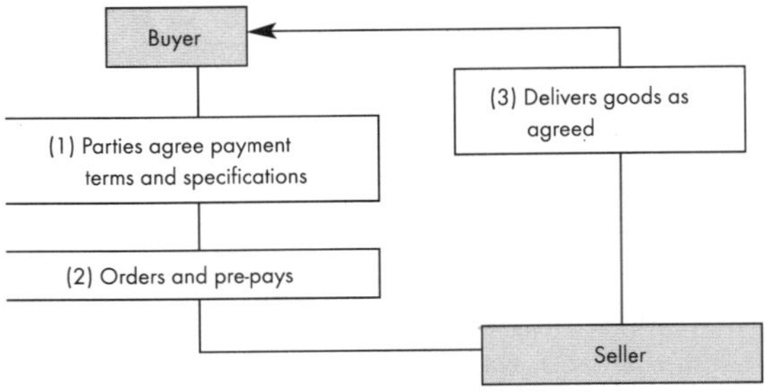

Source: Bryan Kraty.

Exhibit 6.2 ***Salam* as financing**

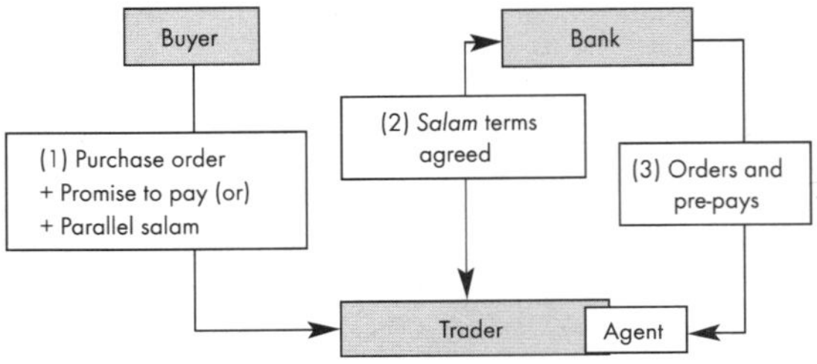

Source: Bryan Kraty.

Documentation

The main agreements can be outlined as follows.

- Deferred delivery agreement – between the bank and the trader.
- Agency agreement – between bank and trader, if trader acts as bank's agent.
- Optional security (eg, guarantee or mortgage) – between bank and trader.
- Letter of credit, promise to pay – between trader and end-buyer.

Salam is not necessarily a contract; in fact, like other Islamic commercial methods, it might be better characterised as a process. The bank will require a deferred delivery agreement with the trader. When the trader acts as the bank's agent, then they will execute a specific agency agreement identifying how the trader represents the bank. Between the bank and the trader there may be a collateral or supplemental security agreement comprising a mortgage or guarantee. These arrangements then move on between the trader and the end-buyer, where yet again additional collateral may be added to the transaction.

It is not hard to make these arrangements synthesise a financing for a business or a trader (see Exhibit 6.2). In this case, our buyer will issue the purchase order to the trader, who acts on behalf of the bank. The buyer's order will be supported by a promise to pay or a parallel *salam* arrangement. The trader and the bank execute their *salam* arrangement, with the bank pre-paying for the goods, and the funding passing through the trader to the buyer.

The trader then delivers the goods to the buyer on behalf of the bank. When the buyer settles with the trader, the proceeds pass through the trader to the bank.

Parallel *salam* and liquidity management

Salam has become a liquidity management tool for Islamic banks as well as a means of supplying manufacturers. When a bank steps in to the deal, the trader will act as the bank's agent to execute the purchase and sale of goods. In Exhibit 6.3, the trader as the bank's agent executes a purchase order with a buyer and supports it with either a promise to pay or an unwinding parallel *salam*. In the meantime, the trader has closed a *salam* agreement with the bank which pre-pays the trader for the goods to be delivered. In this transaction, there are two deals: the purchase and sale between the bank and the trader; and the purchase and sale between the trader and the market.

Exhibit 6.3 ***Salam* process**

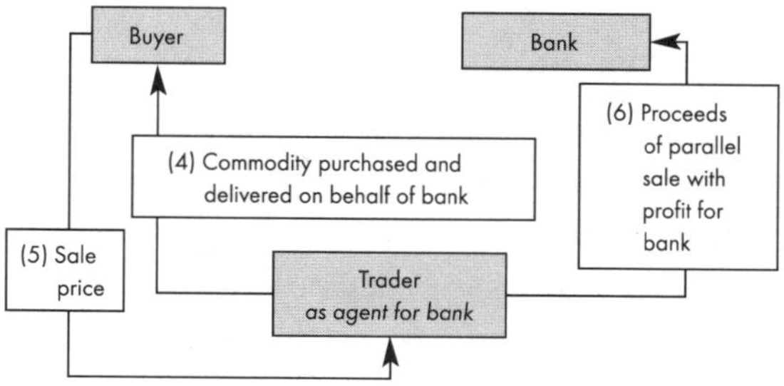

Source: Bryan Kraty.

There are some significant *Shari'a* issues when engaging in a parallel *salam* arrangement. Foremost, the two independent contracts may not be reliant one on the other[18] or linked in any direct manner.[19] As a result, if a counterparty under the first contract fails to deliver, the goods still have to be delivered under the parallel contract. Moreover, the parallel contract may not be used to buy back the goods delivered under the first, which is deemed to be a form of *bai' al-'inah* and forbidden by *Shari'a* scholars outside of Malaysia. The primary protection against the incidental contracting of *bai' al-'inah* is to ensure that the buyer under the parallel contract is an independent third party.

Commodity financing

Salam is a natural fit in the commodities processing finance arena. As shown in Exhibit 6.4, a manufacturer gives notice to its banker of its requirements and makes its advance payment. The bank makes a pre-payment to a broker as its agent and the broker makes the purchase, authorising the selling broker to deliver the sold goods to the manufacturer.

Salam offers a number of advantages to traders and brokers. Foremost, there is no impact on a company's leverage as this is an advance payment not a debt. The execution of multiple *salam* agreements will allow for a company's turnover to be increased indefinitely. When it comes to receivables, the company's counterparty is a bank. And, best of all, the company is able to take its profits

Exhibit 6.4 ***Salam* as commodity process financing**

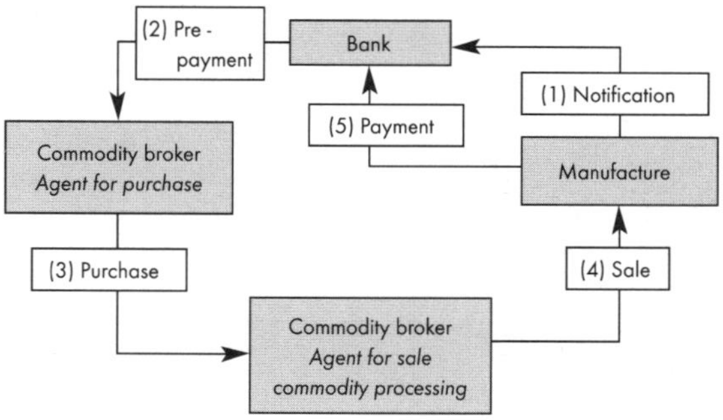

Source: Bryan Kraty.

in advance. When applied robustly, *salam* minimises a company's capital requirements whilst enhancing its turnover.

Example: Arabian Bottling

For many years, Arabian Bottling, the leading carbonated drinks distributor in the GCC, allowed its finance team to experiment with both novel forms of finance as a means to broaden the company's access to financial resources. The team was led by two European intellectuals with a deep curiosity in the regional culture. As a result, the team frequently experimented with Islamic banking with the knowledge that they were assisting the banks to develop products. In return, the banks often offered better pricing to the client. Arabian Bottling, however, was not always in need of credit, as it was in a cash business. In the early phase of Islamic banking, Arabian Bottling frequently placed funds with Islamic banks in the London Metals Market via *murabaha* placements through GCC-based Islamic banks.

Among Arabian Bottling's successes was the decision to adopt *salam* as a routine means to lock up aluminum supplies at favourable prices in order to reduce the risk of supply or price volatility. When the first transaction was pursued, Arabian Bottling was approached by Original Islamic Bank (OIB) in Bahrain. OIB had been criticised privately about its London *murabaha* trades as a means to manage excess liquidity. OIB had originally launched its *murabaha* business by making placements on behalf of OIB.

Now, answering the criticism of its adviser, OIB proposed to the finance team at Arabian Bottling that, in lieu of the seemingly artificial metals trades, so criticised because the end-buyer was often not an industrial user, the company should integrate its placements into the forward purchase of metals to supply its business and effectively hedge supply and price. Arabian Bottling understood that this was not a means to deposit funds, but a means to hedge supplies. But, more critically, the company adopted *salam*, first with OIB to manage its inbound supply of aluminum for manufacturing cans. But, over time, Arabian Bottling developed its *salam* process into a bidding programme involving Bahrain-based Islamic banks, London banks and global metals brokers. In exchange for a fixed price, set amount of aluminum and certain delivery date, Arabian Bottling was prepared to make an advance payment.

Working capital applications

A *salam* contract may meet the purposes of a working capital loan, when constructed as a contract of acquisition of goods with pre-agreed specification (see Exhibit 6.5).

Payment is made as a lump sum in advance. The delivery schedule and purchase price are agreed at the outset and take into account aspects such as material, labour, profit margin and costs. Settlement under the *salam* is delivery of the commodities or goods.

Exhibit 6.5 ***Salam* for working capital**

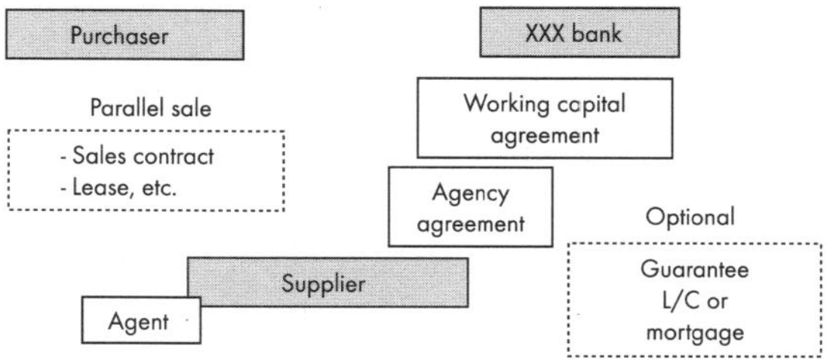

Source: Bryan Kraty.

Under a *salam* arrangement, a bank ends up owning the goods; so most regulatory regimes require that there must be a parallel sales agreement in place prior to completion. This is usually outright purchase by a customer of the supplier, but could be another mechanism delivering cash to the bank in exchange for the goods at the scheduled maturity. The supplier usually acts as agent for the bank to arrange an onward sale to its customers, with payment effected in favour of the bank via, for example, a letter of credit.

In the discussion of *salam*, we have seen that it may be applied as a useful tool for pre-export and working capital finance. In this case, the beneficiary is the supplier as opposed to the buyer, although it is conceivable that in a bank-managed deal, the bank as buyer is providing purchase finance to the end-buyer on the other side of a deal. Like *murabaha* debts, *salam* deliveries may be secured. Most *salam* transactions fall between three and 12 months. The investor in a *salam* transaction seeks to profit from the end sale of the purchased commodity, often securing a Libor mark-up over the investor's funds. 'Repayment' at maturity is through the delivery (and on-sale) of commodities. *Salam* transactions may be syndicated in bilateral, international or domestic syndications.

Documentation

The pricing of the investor's profit in a *salam* transaction is comparable to similar conventional trade finance facilities. The pricing may only be determined on a case-by-case basis in line with tenor, credit quality of supplier, strength of security, and so on. *Salam* transactions are accounted for as pre-payments.

Salam documentation is similar to traditional trade purchase and sales documents, and includes a sales agreement for deferred delivery of goods (the *salam*). There may be a master agreement for renewing facilities or multiple shipments. When the buyer is not a direct consumer of the goods, the *salam* is exited through a parallel sales contract. Otherwise, a traditional letter of credit, purchase order or open account documentation suffices to establish delivery of goods as paid for and ordered under the documents.

When the bank relies upon a third party to execute the purchase, and on-sale of goods, there is an agency agreement. There may be various contract notes supporting the different obligations. When the purchases are syndicated, there is an investment management agreement. Security documents including guarantees, mortgages, receivables, cash, and so on, are all feasible depending upon the terms of the *salam*.

Islamic investors have three primary points of engagement in a *salam* transaction. They may finance exporters either bilaterally or through clubs and syndications led by the Islamic investors or other financial institutions. They may provide corporate and/or cross-border guarantees to support other financial institutions. And, they may profit from a margin on the transaction, facility and agency fees for arranging facilities; and guarantee fees (an area of disagreement for many Islamic scholars).

Example: *Salam* as an open market operation tool

For a number of years, the Bahrain Monetary Authority (BMA) has issued *salam sukuk* to banks under its jurisdiction. The official position of the BMA is that these instruments are meant to offer additional short-term investments to the local banking market. Certainly this is true. But, the opinion of most Islamic scholars is that *salam sukuk* are not tradable. Thus, once the BMA issues the *sukuk*, securing the cash, the banks are obliged to hold the *sukuk* until maturity, thereby allowing the BMA to tighten the monetary supply. Conversely, at maturity, the BMA may reverse the transaction delivering cash back to the banks and expanding the monetary supply.

Conclusion

The Islamic capital market has undergone incremental evolution with each instrument adopted with some pain, and then exploited heavily to its logical conclusions. *Salam*, periodically practised, has become a diversified tool for liquidity management, monetary policy management and trade. Curiously, the agricultural roots of *salam* have not been fully exploited except in a few cases or a few markets such as Sudan. Cross-border risks and uncertain, or as yet unmodernised, agricultural practices have prevented the logical application of *salam* in predominately agrarian societies or in the agricultural sectors of larger countries such as Saudi Arabia, Egypt and Pakistan. Yet, we anticipate that the re-invigorated approach to Islamic banking in Pakistan and the rapidly expanding competition in the Saudi Arabian market will almost certainly lead to significant application of *salam* for agricultural production. Likewise, the strong parallels that *salam* bears to either futures or forward sales contract is already proving meaningful in the nascent Islamic hedge fund business and more broadly for securities in the Islamic markets. The securities applications of *salam* is examined more closely in Chapter 12: Risk management and derivatives.

---

[1] Kraty, Bryan and Abdelhaq Kafsi, *Islamic Finance & Mechanics* (Bahrain: unpublished manuscript, November 2004). Portions of this chapter owe a debt to this document as well as diagrams produced by Bryan Kraty.

[2] Usmani, M.T., *An Introduction to Islamic Finance*, (Karachi: Idaratul Ma'arif, 1998), p. 19.

[3] Siddiqi, Abdul Hamid, tr. Sahih Muslim, Vol. III (Lahore: Sh. Muhammad Ashraf, 1992), pp. 844–5.

[4] Usmani, Muhammad Imran Ashraf, *Meezan Bank's Guide to Islamic Banking* (Karachi: Darul Ishaat, 2002), op.cit., p. 133. Also see Usmani, M.T., *op. cit.*, p. 186.

[5] Hanna, Nelly, *Making Big Money in 1600: The Life and Times of Isma'il Abu Taqiyya, Egyptian Merchant* (Syracuse, NY: Syracuse University Press, 1998), p. 83. Hanna describes how 17th Century Cairo merchants funded the production of sugar, often taking delivery of the refined product, not simply the harvested cane.

[6] *Ibid*, p. 83. Also see Usmani, M.T., op.cit., p. 187.

[7] *Ibid*, p. 87.

[8] Bahrain Monetary Agency, *Islamic Banking & Finance in the Kingdom of Bahrain* (Bahrain: Bahrain Monetary Agency, 2002)., p. 74. The BMA feels that the better parallel is with a forward purchase contract.

[9] Edwardes, Warren, Key Financial Instruments: Understanding & Innovating in the World of Derivatives (London: Pearson Education, 2000) p. 237.

[10] Usmani, M.T., op.cit., p. 185.

[11] *Ibid*, p. 190.

[12] Usmani, M.I.A., *op. cit.*, p. 135.

[13] Usmani, M.T., op.cit., p. 187. The commodity must not be one of those enumerated in the *hadith* governing *riba*, and may not be either precious stones or a specific item.

[14] Usmani, M.I.A., *Meezan Bank's Guide to Islamic Banking, op. cit.* p. 134. Also see Kamali, Mohammad Hashimj, *Islamic Commercial Laws: An Analysis of Futures and Options* (Selangor, Malaysia: Ilmiah Publishers, 2002), p. 113.

[15] Usmani, M.T., op.cit., p. 188.

[16] Kraty and Kafsi, *op. cit.*

[17] Al-Suwailem, Sami bin Ibrahim, *Mawqif Al-salaf min al-Tawarruq al Munathim* accessed at www.islamicfinance.net, September 2004 and Khoja, Ezzidine, *al-Tawarruq* accessed at www.isalmicfi.com on 15 April 2005. The concept of *tawarruq* is described further in Chapter 11: Liquidity management. This method is not without controversy and has been challenged by some Islamic scholars such as Dr Suwailem, but supported by others such as Sh. Nizam Yaquby. See remarks at Sixth Harvard Forum on Islamic Finance, May 2004.

[18] Usmani, M.T., op.cit., p. 194. Moreover, if one delivery in a parallel *salam* is defective, then the second *salam* cannot be cancelled.

[19] Usmani, M.I.A., *op. cit.*, p. 135. To ensure the absence of linkage, the contracts should have distinct tenors.

7 Complex transactions: *istisna'a*, pre-export or manufacturing finance working capital and project finance

Abdulkader Thomas with Bryan Kraty

Introduction

This chapter begins by focusing on *istisna'a*, which is a concept derived from *salam*. *Istisna'a* allows for considerable flexibility in the funding of construction, project development or manufacturing. However, *istisna'a* does not complete the cycle and faces certain limitations in its syndication or securitisation according to some *Shari'a* scholars. Therefore, we will emphasise the complete transaction cycle in the case studies that finish the chapter.

We examine four cases of complex transactions: the SKS Power transaction in Malaysia, a hypothetical manufacturing case – Asian Telecoms, the Tabreed transaction in the United Arab Emirates, and a hypothetical refinery project in Saudi Arabia. Each of these cases must solve one or more structuring and legal issues in order to apply one or more Islamic methods for completion.

Istisna'a

According to Sh. Imran Usmani: '*Istisna'a* is a sales transaction where a commodity is transacted before it comes into existence.'[1] An *istisna'a* contract is used in a similar way to a working capital or construction or manufacturing loan. The transaction is constructed as a contract of acquisition, prospectively followed by the use of plant or equipment with pre-agreed specification.

Payment can be as a lump sum in advance or progressively in accordance with the progress. The delivery schedule and purchase price are agreed at the outset and take into account aspects such as material, labour, profit margin and other project costs. Settlement under the *istisna'a* is delivery of the completed goods – equipment, plant or project[2]. The late jurist Sanhoury, following the views of the Maliki, Shafi'i and Hanbali schools, viewed *istisna'a* as a variant of *salam*.[3]

We consider *istisna'a* to be a complex transaction instead of a simple variant of *salam* because its applications relate to construction, manufacturing and hedging at a level beyond basic commodities,

Complex transactions: *istisna'a*, pre-export or manufacturing finance working capital and project finance

which in *salam* are transacted in their natural state. Each *istisna'a* activity entails a higher level of detail and complexity with respect to mutual consent to price before initiation of the transaction as well as specification of the product to be manufactured, built or delivered.

Definition

Istisna'a is a cash sales contract made against promised future delivery of goods. *Istisna'a* may be derived from *salam*,[4] but it is unique:

- under *salam*, deliverables are commodity like;
- under *istisna'a*, deliverables are manufactured goods or constructed property; and
- under *istisna'a*, unlike *salam*, interim or progress payments may be made.

In *istisna'a*, progress payments may be deferred, and may attract penalties, agreed in advance,[5] for the late delivery of the contracted goods. To be valid, all specifications, delivery options, payment conditions and pricing must be agreed in the *istisna'a* contract. Even if the financier subcontracts the manufacture or construction of the object, the majority of *Shari'a* scholars take the view that the financier is responsible for the product warranties, even if the financier is able to assign or otherwise cover this risk. Orders may be cancelled prior to start of production, and delivery need not be specific, but should fit within a maximum time-frame and not a minimum. The object of manufacture should not be a commodity or the transaction is *salam*.[6] In *istisna'a*, there is no debt in the form of a traditional loan receivable as the obligation is for the delivery of manufactured goods.

Transaction structure

The core concept of *istisna'a* is straightforward. The purchaser agrees to terms of delivery and specifications; issues an order and makes periodic progress payments (see Exhibit 7.1). Within the time-frame agreed, the goods or construction of property or equipment is completed and delivered. The manufacturer has the requisite materials under its own control.

Exhibit 7.1 ***Istisna'a* structure**

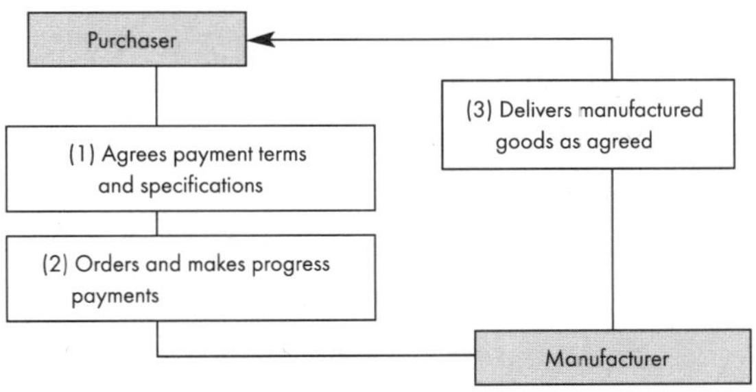

Source: Bryan Kraty.

When this model is transmitted to the banking environment, a financial institution will not enter into an *istisna'a* agreement unless the goods being manufactured on their behalf have identified a purchaser(s). The financier may engage in parallel with a qualified contractor, hire a contractor or an agent to engage in the construction or manufacture as specified in the contract. Sometimes this arrangement – whereby the financier appoints a third party to perform the manufacturing – is termed a 'parallel' *istisna'a*. In this case, the price for the goods sold under the parallel sale is higher than the cost of manufacture reflecting the trading profit of the bank.

Documentation

The main agreements can be outlined as follows.

- Working capital agreement – between bank and manufacturer.
- Agency agreement – between bank and manufacturer, because manufacturer acts as agent.
- Optional security (eg, guarantee, mortgage, pledges on receivables) – between bank and manufacturer.
- Exit documentation (parallel sales contract, forward lease agreement etc) – between manufacturer and purchaser.

Istisna'a documentation includes a sales agreement for deferred delivery of equipment or property (the *istisna'a* contract), which may be designed as a master agreement in order to allow for revolving facilities or multiple shipments. Most financial institutions require some clear exit documentation including a parallel sales contract, a forward lease, or some other terminal document. Since the bank will not perform the manufacturing or construction, it will engage in an agency agreement with the end-manufacturer.

The transaction will entail security documents which may include guarantees, mortgages, and pledges on receivables, cash, or accounts. Typically, each progress payment is accompanied by a note.

Like *murabaha* and *ijarah*, *istisna'a* may be syndicated, which would require an investment management agreement or *mudaraba*.

Key features

The characteristics of *istisna'a* to finance manufacture, construction or pre-export allow for flexibility for the bank to provide a facility to either the supplier or buyer depending on structure (see Exhibit 7.2). The tenors range from three to 24 months and may be longer. The profit is typically calculated as a margin over the cost of goods to be acquired. The financier's initial investment, the principal, is recovered at maturity with the profit when the ordered items are delivered (see Exhibit 7.3).

Exhibit 7.2 ***Istisna'a* for financing (a)**

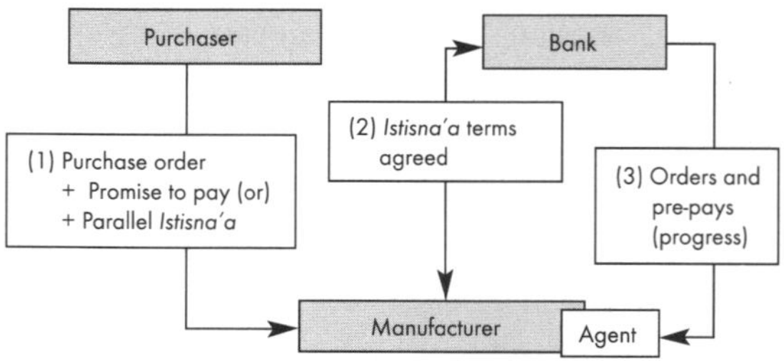

Source: Bryan Kraty.

Pricing for most *istisna'a* are in line with similar conventional finance facilities. But, *istisna'a* pricing may only be determined on a case-by-case basis in line with tenor, credit quality of supplier, strength of security, and so on. The accounting shows the *istisna'a* advances as pre-payment.

Exhibit 7.3 ***Istisna'a* for financing (b)**

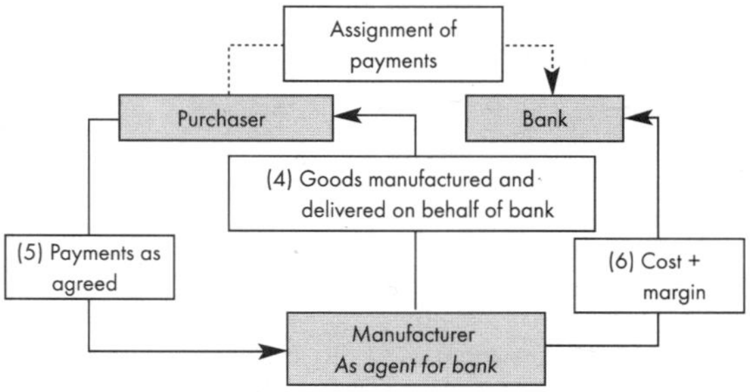

Source: Bryan Kraty.

An important issue with respect to *istisna'a* is that under an *istisna'a* agreement the financiers end up owning the output or constructed property. Therefore, a purchase mechanism needs to take effect upon completion. This is often a lease, but could be an outright sale or a mechanism with the effect of refinancing.

Although some scholars feel that *istisna'a* may be rejected if the orderer has not seen the item, the prevailing trend is that the manufactured or constructed item must be accepted if it meets the buyer's specifications. The provision of *istisna'a* ostensibly has risks greater than a traditional construction financing. These risks may be mitigated through various agreements with agents and contractors on behalf of the bank.

Istisna'a has proven a valuable tool for property construction: residences, commercial property; ship or aircraft construction; as well as large-scale project finance including oil installations, manufacturing equipment and plants, and infrastructure such as bridges and highways. In many *istisna'a* transactions, the exit has been structured via build-operate-transfer (BOT) mechanisms. Manufacturers have found *istisna'a* to be beneficial since it does not directly affect a company's leverage and is treated as an advance payment. Better still, the manufacturer has no risk on receivables since it contracts to be paid by a bank and earns profit in advance. In some environments, the process potentially avoids withholding tax, further improving the contracting party's profit margins.

Ju'ala as a sub-set of *istisna'a*

Ju'ala[7] is a pre-specified reward based on a contractor meeting defined targets using its own efforts. If the *ju'ala* is set low enough, then it embeds a liquidated damages penalty for the contractor for poor timing or delivery. The payment and reward are for service as opposed to goods. Again, the concept applies to future delivery. In Iran, for example, *ju'ala* has been creatively applied to build roads and other infrastructure projects.

Securitised and syndicated project finance transactions

In this part of the chapter we look at the practical application of *istisna'a* and the critical issues relating to project management in the following cases: SKS Power, Asian Telecoms, Tabreed and Saudi

Refinery projects. These cases demonstrate how *istisna'a* contracts may be exited with an *ijarah* contract; how *ijarah* can be used under specific circumstances to release asset capacity for the securitisation of *istisna'a* in a more restrictive setting. And we examine the particularly complex problems that require attention as one seeks to engage in sophisticated projects, whilst adhering to Islamic principles.

Case Study: SKS Power[8]

Although Malaysia has become a significant innovator in the field of Islamic bonds, much of that innovation has been concentrated in those transactions that are linked to the *murabaha* concept as applied in that country. SKS Power (now Tanjung Bin Power Sdn Bhd and referred to herein as SKS) was formed in 1998 in order to develop, finance, construct, commission, operate and maintain a 2,100 MW coal-fired power plant and ancillary facilities in Tanjung Bin, Johor. SKS and Tenaga Nasional Berhad signed a Power Purchase Agreement (PPA) in July 2002 for the sale and purchase of generating capacity and energy for an initial term of 25 years with a possible extension of 15 years. SKS was the first independent power producer in Malaysia to bear an element of demand risk under its PPA. The Economic Planning Unit of the Ministry of Finance granted approval to the project in August 2003.

In order to meet this commitment, SKS needed to build a facility. This meant that SKS had to raise RM5.6 billion to finance all costs associated with the site acquisition, development, design, construction, start-up and initial operations of the project. Fortunately for SKS, the Malaysian domestic market was very liquid at the time and a number of experienced managers were available. From these, SKS appointed Commercial International Merchant Bankers (CIMB) and five others as joint lead managers to manage the fund-raising exercise in the domestic debt capital market.

The task

CIMB accepted the mandate, which meant that they were obliged to coordinate the funding exercise; develop the funding structure and liaise with qualified *Shari'a* advisers for approvals of the as yet unproposed structure. Once these front line tasks were complete, CIMB would carry out the due-diligence process, including the review of a suitable Information Memorandum, review the legal documentation, and execute the bond or *sukuk*[9] allocation and distribution process.

The CIMB proposition

For the long-term financing, CIMB initially recommended a ground-breaking *istisna'a-ijarah sukuk* structure. This approach would be totally novel. The Malaysian capital market had been growing steadily, but the Islamic sub-segment was heavily dominated by debt-like issuances of *murabaha* or *bai' bithamin ajil* instruments. On the one hand, such instruments were highly analogous to traditional debt instruments, fitted easily with the Anglo-Australian securities laws, and could be securitised much like notes. On the other hand, only in Malaysia and in a few other areas had Islamic scholars permitted the securitisation of debts.[10] Thus, the CIMB proposition would break new ground on two fronts: it would securitise the construction financing and organise the take-out funding with a permanent lease of the facilities. The *sukuk* holders would have a seamless transition from the *istisna'a* period to the *ijarah* period.

Under the new structure, the *istisna'a*, construction financing, would be switched to an *ijarah*, leasing, once the plant was completed and ready to commence operations. The combination of *istisna'a-ijarah* would allow SKS to benefit from the tax deductibility benefits given to *ijarah* structures. However, as the structure was new and untested, CIMB had difficulties convincing SKS of its benefits. At the same time, legal and tax advisers were not prepared to give their opinions on the structure, citing other issues such as balancing charges, capital allowance, and so on. Related parties suggested to SKS that it would be better to issue *bai' bithamin ajil* (BBA) bonds as an allegedly more tried and tested structure.

In this specific environment, CIMB was obliged to postpone the finalisation of the long-term funding structure until the bridge financing was resolved. SKS decided to secure a local market revolving BBA bridging facility. With this in place, SKS was comfortable that it had time to negotiate and finalise the long-term funding structure proposed by CIMB, and agreed for CIMB to proceed with the *istisna'a-ijarah* structure.

Despite the pressure to simply issue a BBA bond, CIMB recommended an *istisna'a sukuk* structure as an alternative instead. The *ijara*h leg was dropped, thus making it more straightforward, but leaving a bullet payment at the term. CIMB persevered and managed to convince SKS to continue with the *istisna'a sukuk* proposal. In a timely manner, CIMB managed to secure unqualified opinions from the tax advisers. Indeed, the Ministry of Finance eventually approved CIMB's initial *istisna'a-ijarah sukuk* structure resolving all issues raised. It came just before submission of the structures to the Securities Commission. At the same time, the Ministry agreed to include *istisna'a* as one of the Islamic financing options eligible for tax benefits as proposed by CIMB. Nonetheless, after comparing the *istisna'a-ijarah sukuk* and the *istisna'a sukuk* structures, SKS instructed CIMB to proceed with the latter for submission to the Securities Commission.

The SKS challenge and practical problems

The fundamental structuring issue is to take what bankers had thought of as the rights and obligations under a traditional loan agreement, in this case a construction and permanent loan, modulise them, slot them into the *istisna'a* agreement and then carry forward the appropriate modules into a lease or *murabaha* take-out agreement.[11]

Solutions

The transaction isolates the SKS project into a special purpose vehicle independent trust (SPVIT and herein SPV). SKS executed its agreements in a two-step process (see Exhibit 7.4), each step isolating two unique transactional aspects:

Exhibit 7.4 **SKS transaction**

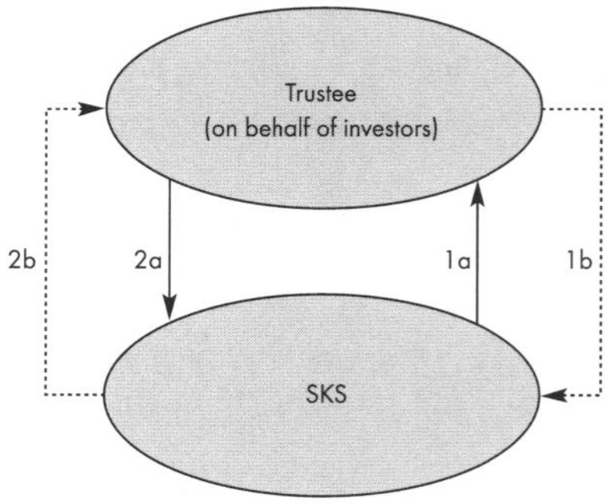

Source: Author's own.

Step 1a

SKS and the trustee execute an *istisna'a* purchase agreement, under which SKS agrees to construct and deliver to the trustee a specific asset. In this case, the asset is the work in progress funded by the interim BBA facility. The delivery of the asset will take place upon completion of its construction. The risk associated with the ownership of the asset passes to the SPV upon execution of the agreement.

Step 1b

The *istisna'a* purchase price was set at RM1 billion which is to be disbursed in one lump sum. This was the first series of the issuance.

Step 2a

The trustee and SKS execute an *istisna'a* sale agreement, under which the trustee agrees to construct and deliver the asset to SKS. The trustee sub-contracts the actual work to the contractor, which is agented to SKS. Delivery to SKS will take place upon the trustee taking delivery of the completed units under the *istisna'a* purchase agreement. The risk associated with the ownership of the asset passes to SKS upon execution of the agreement.

Step 2b

The *istisna'a* sale price will be equivalent to the aggregate of the *istisna'a* purchase price and profit related thereto as calculated according to a prescribed formula. The sales price will be payable according to an agreed payment schedule.

In certain perspectives, this approach may appear to be the same as *bai' al-'inah* on two accounts. Foremost, the work is begun by SKS and then sold to the SPV which agrees to sell it back. Most scholars, however, view that the work in progress delivered to the SPV is different from the final object and that the two transactions are not invalid. Within specific *Shari'a* views there should not be conditionality of the one contract on the other. Finally, almost all *Shari'a* scholars allow the financier to contract, in this case via the trustee, to construct the object, and to complete an agency agreement with the obligor to perform or sub-contract the actual work.[12]

Salient transaction features

Project costs	:	RM7.774 billion
Issuer	:	SKS Power Sdn Bhd (now known as Tanjung Bin Power Snd Bhd)
Proceeds	:	Paydown of bridge facility; finance site acquisition; construction; transaction; and initial working capital needs
Rating	:	AA3 (RAM)
Maturity	:	5–12.5 years
Principal amount	:	RM 5.6 billion in five tranches comprising one spot tranche and four forward tranches
Periodic coupon	:	Between 6.30 per cent and 8.90 per cent p.a. Payable semi-annually in arrears with the first profit payment commencing six months from the date of a specific issuance
Redemption	:	Unless redeemed, purchased or cancelled by the issuer, the *istisna'a* notes are due on their redemption dates
Term	:	Maximum term is 12.5 years from the final issuance

A landmark transaction: adding depth to the market

The SKS issuance was a landmark transaction bringing many rewards to the Malaysian markets. The transaction generated unique benefits to investors, the issuer, and the entire investment banking and securities community.

Malaysian investors added a new, alternative fixed income instrument that is *Shari'a* compliant and at the same time helps to diversify their investment portfolio. This opportunity further provided investors with the chance to invest in a highly rated *sukuk* issuance by an independent power producer with potential upside in their investment once the plant is fully completed and ready to commence operations.

As for the issuer, SKS was able to tap a wider investor base than its traditional investor universe by offering Islamic *sukuk*. In this case, the issuer was able to offer *sukuk al istisna'a* despite the absence of any tangible asset at the time of issuance. This was possible because *istisna'a* is the best Islamic structure for financing construction projects and manufacturing.

Moreover, SKS enjoyed a lower cost of funding since Islamic papers tend, in Malaysia, to be priced between five and 10 basis points less than conventional debt. Thanks to incentives designed to support the Islamic market, SKS's costs of issuance were are also lower than with traditional bonds

Complex transactions: *istisna'a*, pre-export or manufacturing finance working capital and project finance

since SKS was able to deduct expenses such as the arrangement fee, rating fee, and other issuance costs from the company's taxable income.

Exhibit 7.5 **Breakdown of Malaysian *sukuk***

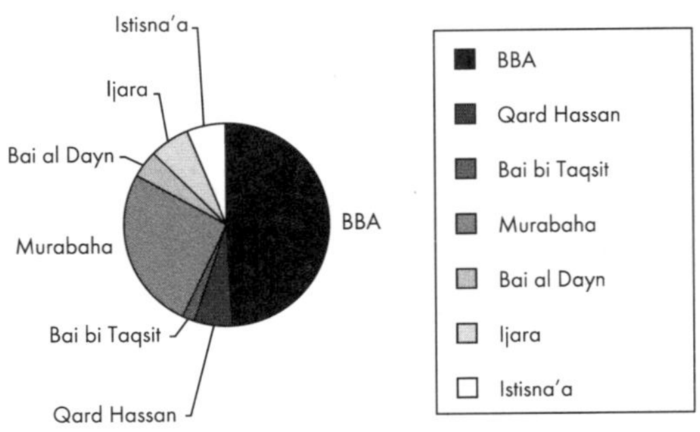

Source: Baljeet Grewal.

The Malaysian capital market has been dominated by debt issuances, most of which are unpalatable to Islamic investors in the Arabian Peninsula and South Asia (see Exhibit 7.5). For example, BBA, *bai' al-dayn, murabaha, qard hassan* and *bai bi taqsit sukuk* are all forms of debt that contravene the view of such investors that the trading of debt securities is susceptible to *riba*, if not *ribawi*. Although Malaysia's Islamic banks have grown to a 10 per cent market share or US$23.4 billion in assets, domestic *sukuk* outstanding are RM115.9 billion, or approximately US$30 billion, far outstripping the International Islamic Financial Market's assessment of global *sukuk* issuances, totalling only US$6 billion in 2004.[14] Beyond changes in Malaysia's capital controls, the introduction of more and varied instruments acceptable to Islamic investors elsewhere will bring greater depth and liquidity to the Malaysian market.

Prior to the SKS issuance, only about 7 per cent of Malaysia's *sukuk* issuances were *ijarah*-based, which is a more widely acceptable structure. The SKS issuance is the sole *istisna'a* issuance, doubling the universe of more acceptable issuances. Thus, the SKS transaction is a milestone, broadening the Malaysian capital market, and helping it to offer global investors more instruments to their liking.

In the course of structuring the offering, SKS and CIMB worked to secure new tax legislation in Malaysia relating to the issuance of *sukuk*. With the success of this transaction, CIMB and others anticipate that more *istisna'a* offerings will be forthcoming for project finance.

Syndicated and securitised pre-export and export finance transactions

Case study: Asian Telecoms

In June of 2004, Asian Peninsula's prime minister complained to the Ministry of Communications that the country was not successfully bridging the digital divide. He instructed the minister to accelerate installation of broadband infrastructure. At the regional level, each one of Asian Peninsula's states had its own Ministry of Communications which coordinated with the Federal

Exhibit 7.6 **Process timeline**

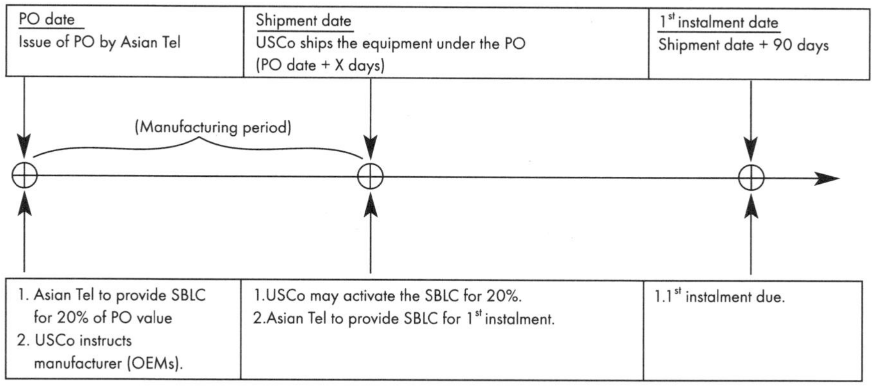

Source: Author's own.

Ministry. Southern State would take the lead and implement first. Asian Peninsula was committed to a dual-track Islamic–western banking system. Southern State was hoping to apply Islamic methods to fund its infrastructure expansion.

The order

Southern State's telecoms and internet company, state-controlled operator Asian Tel, had already agreed on its supplier USCo, a noted Silicon Valley-based internet backbone manufacturer and agreed upon the terms of a memorandum of understanding. The process for ordering is shown in Exhibit 7.6.

The process

When considering the classical nominative concepts, Asian Tel and its bankers had to choose from the following listed below.

- *Murabaha*: To Asian Tel, this, or its regional variation, *bai' bithamin ajil* (BBA), seemed a logical option for structuring the purchase contract. However, their *Shari'a* advisers pointed out that the materials did not exist in final form and would have to be assembled. So, post manufacturing, *murabaha* was a suitable application.
- *Istisna'a*: Asian Tel knew that USCo required pre-transaction finance. Asian Tel was not prepared to provide advance funds, and USCo was not competent to structure an Islamic transaction. Yet, this was the preferred option of Asian Tel's Islamic advisers.
- *Salam*: The primary condition of *salam* is that the item sold in advance must be readily available in the market. It would not apply in this context since the materials that were the object of the contract were not commodities and required transformation.

Exhibit 7.7 **Transaction structure**

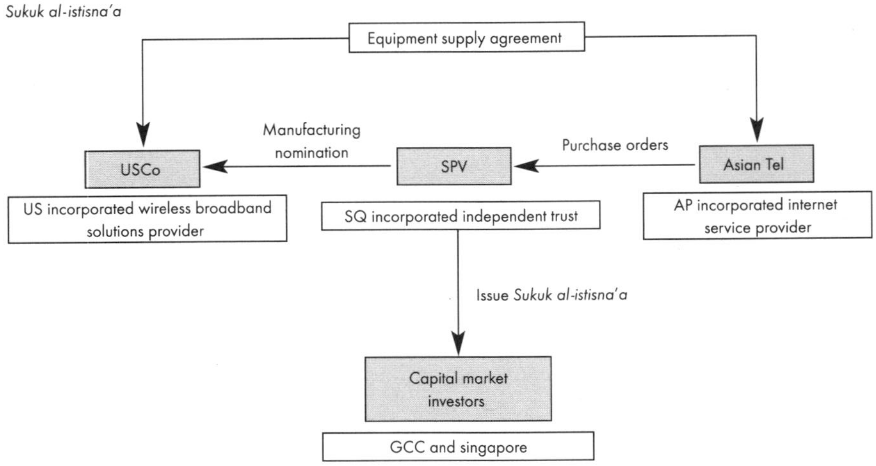

Source: Author's own.

- *Ijarah*: Although Asian Tel was amenable to *ijarah*, leasing the equipment, USCo would not provide lease finance due to its shortage of funds, and Asian Tel's bankers were reluctant to become the owners of equipment with a high obsolescence risk.
- *Mudaraba*: This flexible method would be applied by Asian Tel's bankers to structure the pool for the ultimate *istisna'a* and *murabaha* deals.
- *Musharaka*: As a government-controlled entity, Asian Tel's bankers were unable to become partners in its internet expansion. As for USCo, the company had no desire to bring direct partners into its operating business and warned the investment bankers of punishing international tax risks.

Exhibit 7.8 **Transaction documentation**

	USCo	Asian Tel	SPV
Incorporation and Trust Indenture			√
Equipment Supply Agreement	√	√	
Supply & Deferred Sales Contract			
• Purchase Order		√	
• Assignments of Broadband Cash Flow & Subscriptions	√	√	√
– Asian Tel acknowledgement of assignments			
Supply & Deferred Sales Contract Assignment	√		√
Letter of Credit (initial and installment)		√	
Purchase Orders		√	√
Nomination Agreement, as schedules:	√		√
Manufacturing			
Installation and Servicing			
Underwriting Bank commitment			
Assignment and acknowledgement of DPC	√	√	√
[Letter of Comfort]		√	
Sukuk al istisna Indenture			
Underwriter's commitment			√
Sakk al-istisna'a (Trust Participation Certificate)			
Subscription Agreements			√
Fatwa			√

Source: Bryan Kraty

The solutions

Asian Tel and USCo settled on a *sukuk al istisna'a* offering (see Exhibit 7.7). In this transaction, the confirmation of a firm order was supported by a letter of credit for 20 per cent of the delivered value. The investors were invited to invest in the underlying materials whilst USCo assembled them. Once the goods were ready for shipping, the *sukuk* holders relied upon the investment bankers as trustees of the SPV to execute the final installment credit sale to Asian Tel.

Steps to implement

In order to proceed with the transaction, the following documentation was required (see Exhibit 7.8).

Outcome

Asian Telecoms provided a unique opportunity for the buyer and the manufacturer simultaneously to secure off-balance sheet financing during the manufacturing period. The innovative method applied generated an attractive short-term income instrument for the capital markets that was secured in an innovative manner.

Syndicated and securitised corporate finance transactions

Case study: Tabreed *sukuk* issuance[15]

Introduction

The National Central Cooling Company (Tabreed) was established, with the assistance of the UAE Offset Group (UOG) in 1998, as an offset project for the provision of district cooling services. Tabreed has grown to become the world's largest district cooling company servicing the UAE and neighbouring GCC states.

Although Tabreed is the UAE's leading district cooling service provider, it is not without competition. Therefore, any funding decision must deliver efficient costs so as to maintain a competitive cost structure and facilitate future growth. Tabreed's management also wanted to tap new sources of capital, to support its conservative successful growth strategy and meet initial required capital outlays. The company wanted this debut, and for future capital market capital-raising efforts, to familiarise investors in the region and offshore with the Tabreed name and also create an accessible investor base.

The company targeted for its district cooling business high credit quality and stable users in a hierarchy of high volume cooling users (see Exhibit 7.9).

Exhibit 7.9 **Target business users**

Institutions	Commercial	Tourism/leisure	Residential
Military complexes	Office towers	Hotels	High-rise towers
Government buildings	Shopping malls	Stadiums	House compounds
Universities & schools	Industrial parks	Amusements parks	
Hospitals	Airports	Cinemas & theatres	
Mosques	Ports		

Source: Tabreed Financing Corp., Offering Circular, 1 March 2004, p. 41.

All of Tabreed's target clients benefit most from the economies of scale offered from district cooling compared with unit services. In the Arabian Gulf region, a desert with high humidity in the densely populated coastal areas with major concentrations of property in government ownership and large entities, district cooling appears to be an extremely attractive economic proposition for Tabreed and its customers.

The decision to select Islamic financing

Islamic financial institutions and capital markets have enjoyed rapid growth since the early 1990s. The market players are flush with capital and often willing to deploy their funds at attractive rates compared with conventional lenders. Within the Arabian Gulf region, the evolution of *sukuk*[16] and strong government support by the members of the Gulf Cooperation Council have generated significant enthusiasm for Islamic products, the formation of new Islamic banks, and the expansion of the Islamic palate. This latter point is emphasised given the overall lack of applied Islamic capital market products and corporate solutions.

Tabreed's management was aware that the company's board had a preference for Islamic-compliant financing over conventional methods. In fact, the company had previously arranged financing products through regional Islamic banks and the finance team was well-acquainted with the relevant concepts. Therefore, management wanted to have a structure that would satisfy Islamic investors. But, they added the condition that any structure would need to meet conventional investor criteria. Bringing in conventional investors would not only validate any Islamic structuring decision, it would, if done well, generate the greatest possible investor coverage for Tabreed.

Following the structured issuance of *sukuk* by the Bahrain Monetary Authority (BMA) and the global *sukuk* issuance by Qatar and Malaysia, management was comfortable that the Islamic capital markets were evolving quickly and deeply enough to support an Islamic issuance. The decision enjoyed broad consensus within the Tabreed team and was an easy sell to its eventual advisers, the National Investment Company and CSFB, who knew that local, regional and international market players were evolving and getting up to speed on Islamic offerings.

The opportunities for companies and international Islamic capital markets nonetheless posed challenges. For instance, Tabreed and its advisers would be among the first UAE issuers of a complex *sukuk* offering. The decision to create a precedent that would facilitate the progress of the future development of the market would also require bringing market participants (bankers, lawyers and *shari'a* advisers) and regulators up to speed about the structure and concepts to be applied.

Tabreed was a perfect candidate for this ground-breaking initiative. First, the company had the right credit risk profile for a cutting-edge *sukuk* project. The company's management structure and internal and external financial and operating systems satisfied international requirements for securities issuance. Second, the company was familiar with Islamic finance through prior Islamic bank financings. Therefore, when the company approached its primary financial adviser, The National Investor, there was strong, mutual enthusiasm for a *sukuk* offering.

Tabreed and The National Investor spent eight months of intensive work preparing the offering. The team worked with consultants, *Shari'a* scholars, lawyers, regulators in the UAE, Luxembourg, Cayman Islands, and market sounding with local and international institutions. One key to this initiative was to focus on preparation given that many of the players were unfamiliar with the *sukuk* concepts. Then a pre-syndication with local and regional banks was organised leading to a full roadshow based on price discovery.

Asset mix

The issuer in this transaction is a special purpose company (SPV) called Tabreed Financing Corp. (TFC or the Issuer). Maples Finance Ltd established the Issuer in the Cayman Islands, which then contracted to purchase a portfolio of existing assets (called the 'Initial Plant') and assets which were planned to be built, the rights to build assets, specific sites and miscellaneous assets ('Additional Plants'), and collectively the assets to be purchased were called 'Plant'. In contrast to the SKS *sukuk al istisna'a* issuance in which the assets were fully equivalent to Additional Plants, the *Shari'a* advisers required that 51 per cent of the Tabreed assets must be the Plant and the balance may be the Additional Plants. The Issuer is trustee for a declaration of trust over the universe of assets meaning that the assets are held in trust for the certificate holders. The Issuer then contracted either or to lease the assets to the company. The structure of the financing is shown in Exhibit 7.10.

Issue of title

There was a question of transferability of title under UAE law. There was uncertainty if transfer of Plant to the trust would result in the disturbance or cancellation of the UAE Armed Forces contracts, as the government does not normally give formal approvals to transfers. Land for the Plants, especially the Additional Plants, is leasehold not fee simple. However, UAE law integrates land and improvements (no separate title), therefore the company guarantee is key.

Exhibit 7.10 **Deal structure**

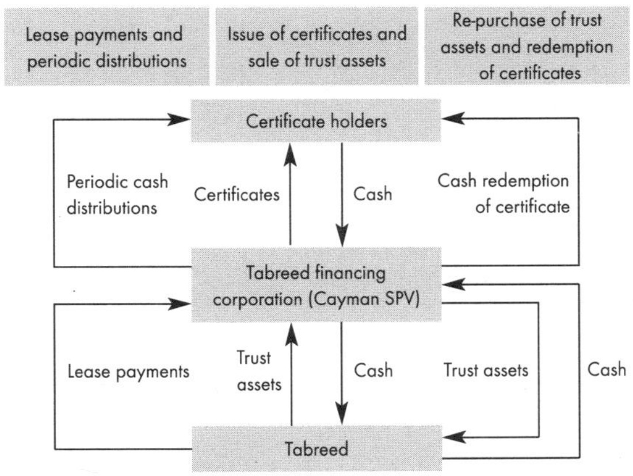

Source: Christian Mouchbahani.

Like many GCC states, the UAE applies a variation of the Sanhuri codes, themselves an adaptation of regional law and custom to Franco-Swiss-style codes. This means that there is an absence of a trust law in the UAE: meaning that any trusts would have to be established elsewhere. Therefore, the securities are governed by English Law and the Plant by UAE law and administrative practice.

Exhibit 7.11 **Tombstone of offering**

Summary Terms and Conditions

Issuer:	Tabreed Financing Corporation ("TFC")
Guarantor:	The National Central Cooling Company ("Tabreed")
Issue:	Certificates
Islamic Structure:	*Ijarah/Istisna'a*
Amount:	US$100 million
Maturity:	2009 (5 years)
Repayment:	Bullet
Periodic Distributions:	Fixed, payable semi-annually in arrears
Use of Proceeds (TFC):	(i) Purchase of certain existing central cooling plants (ii) Purchase of future central cooling plants to be manufactured (iii) Investments in other construction activities
Status:	Undivided beneficial ownership interest in the Trust Assets
Covenants:	(i) Negative Pledge (ii) Cross Default (iii) EBITDA/Total Debt Service not less than 1:1 (iv) Total Debt/Equity not greater than 2.76:1
Listing:	Luxembourg Stock Exchange
Shari'a Advisers:	Dr. Abdul Sattar Abu Ghuddah & Sheikh Nizam Yaqubi
Governing Law:	English, UAE

Source: Christian Mouchbahani.

The issuance

This was led by a local investment bank with close ties to the company's founding parents. The tombstone for the US$100 million offering is shown in Exhibit 7.11.

The offering memorandum identifies 16 primary agreements that were executed in order to launch this transaction (see Exhibit 7.12).

The Declaration of Trust establishes the trust governing the Issuer. The Purchase Agreement defines how the assets move into the Issuer's legal possession and the Purchase Undertaking how they may be taken back by the company. The various Islamic contracts are included as well. Undertakings have a different status in *Shari'a* than contracts/agreements. Hence, there are more unique documents in this transaction than one might find in a conventional securitisation of a sale leaseback deal.

Since the physical control remains with the company, various agreements are structured to ensure that the assets will be properly cared for and payments made on time. An additional feature of this transaction is an agreement to make sure that the excess cash is invested in accordance with *Shari'a*.

Exhibit 7.12 **Primary agreements identified in offering memorandum**

Declaration of Trust
Purchase Agreement
Lease Agreement
Servicing Agency Agreement
Insurance Agreement
Investment Agency Agreement
Deed of Covenant & Guarantee
Istisna'a Contract
Certificate Purchase Agreement
Undertaking to Lease
Purchase Undertaking
Sale Undertaking
Service Agency Agreement
Islamic Investment Agency Agreement
Administration Agreement
Form of Certificate

Exhibit 7.13 **Salient covenants**

Negative pledge: Issuer & Tabreed
Issuer acts solely as Trustee
Debt-to-equity cap of 2.76:1
Cross-default to individual leases
Lawfulness
Guarantee is deemed non-enforceable
Cross-default lessee obligations
Material Adverse Change
Bankruptcy
Good standing
Guarantor is funded to meet guarantee

The covenants (see Exhibit 7.13) trend towards ensuring that the guarantor can support the guarantee and does not default in its operations or in that of its affiliates when it is the obligor under the various lease and *istisna'a* agreements. Negative pledges were used to ensure that the company or its affiliates would not otherwise seek to encumber the Plant given some of the uncertainties of local law.

Outcome

The Tabreed case demonstrates that there is a clear demand for Islamic investment and corporate finance solutions. Like sovereigns, corporates of any domicile may increasingly apply Islamic corporate finance and capital market solutions under attractive issuance terms. In order for the transaction to succeed from a *Shari'a* perspective, Tabreed had to assure that 51 per cent of the pool supporting the *sukuk* were assets subject to *ijarah*. This ensured that the majority of the transaction was not 'cash' and accounted for the accreting asset nature of the assets under construction or *istisna'a*. Tabreed continued the process of expanding the cooperation between financial institutions, issuers and regulators to create greater precedence and more benchmarks in support of the growing global *sukuk* market.

Case Study: Saudi Refinery

A mid-1990s US$3.2 billion Saudi Refinery petrochemical plant expansion was set to be both the largest petrochemical financing in the world and the largest non-sovereign Middle East financing. This last point meant that the project's financial requirements would easily exceed the capacity of domestic and regional banks. But, foreign investors would face significant challenges in securing their invested funds based upon both local law and customs.

Financing issues

This complex financing fell to an experienced project finance lawyer[17] resident in Jeddah. The primary issues in front of counsel were the capacity to enforce security agreements and to operate in the absence of common law-style trust laws. For instance, in Saudi Arabia, the core concept that a valid contract is sufficient to transfer property between two parties is voided when one of the two parties is a foreign person or entity. Moreover, the Kingdom was known to have practical limitations on a lender's ability to seek indemnities from loss in connection with a defaulted loan.

The Saudi Refinery transaction was to involve multiple funding sources with distinct legal approaches across jurisdictional lines, as well as financiers with disparate credit and investment policies. Counsel had to assist these diverse lenders and investors to achieve comfort about the security of their financing in a country that lacked any specific statutes governing collateral or mortgages. Worse, Saudi Arabian notaries were infamous for impeding the registration of security interests relating to loans.[18]

The question of forum followed as a major challenge. As a *Shari'a* jurisdiction, Saudi Arabian courts would not enforce claims for interest. The Saudi Arabian Monetary Agency (SAMA), the central bank, had established the Banking Disputes Settlement Committee (BDSC) to govern disputes between banks and their clients. The Kingdom also had the Office of the Settlement of Negotiable Instruments Disputes (NIO) to govern action relating to promissory notes or other negotiable instruments and a Board of Grievances (BOG) to address commercial, non-bank related disputes, including foreign judgements. Usually, neither the BDSC nor the NIO inquire as to *Shari'a* compliance.

The challenges followed logically: how to register collateral and then direct the lenders to the forum of their choice and preference? The BDSC provided some advantages to conventional bankers. For instance, SAMA will provide legal and accounting reviews; prohibit a debtor from fleeing, and post a debtor's name on a list that restricts the debtor's ability to do business. But, if a creditor fails to secure satisfaction at the BDSC, then the financier must go to court, where one starts afresh with a new hearing, usually at the BOG.

In its own right, the BOG is rigorous and thorough and looks into all areas, allowing for a review of *Shari'a* compliance. Typically, Saudi courts only award out-of-pocket damages. Foreign judgements typically lead to an analysis of the underlying rules of contract as applied in Saudi Arabia. Moreover, a BOG procedure could take between two and 10 years. If a claim does not entail a *Shari'a* contravention, itself a question of public policy, then the process should only take one year. Of particular relevance to the prospective Saudi Refinery creditors, the BOG is the court for enforcing foreign judgements.

Layered on top of its existing procedures, the BOG often wishes to ascertain that the home countries of claimants will grant reciprocity for the BOG's judgements when enforcing foreign judgements. Saudi Arabia is member of New York Convention on the Recognition and Enforcement of Arbitral Awards of 1958. But, there are no specific rules issued or pending at BOG.

When it comes to project finance, lenders seek to be secured by cash flows, all project assets and all company assets applying a mortgage (known as a *rahn* in *Shari'a*). The Saudi Refinery security grantors are Saudi-based entities. With a diverse syndicate of regional lenders and global banks, the bankers had varying degrees of familiarity with local laws. The regional lenders would be satisfied with 'first perfected liens', and the global lenders sought maximisation of collateral.

Guarantee issues

On the analytical side, Saudi Refinery was complex, but clearly financable. The problem came with the collateral. The majority of the Saudi Refinery lenders wanted the collateral to be enforceable in New York and London. The locus of the project meant that collateral enforcement had to be consistent with *Shari'a*. Now, counsel's challenge began. He crafted a multi-step dialogue with Saudi scholars which made him realise that most Saudi jurists lacked familiarity with the interpretation of non-*Shari'a* collateral forms, even when these were consistent with *Shari'a* precepts. Therefore, counsel elected to start his collateral structuring in the first jurisdiction, and, arguably the most complex – the Saudi Arabian *Shari'a* environment – and solve as many perfection of collateral problems as possible. He would then move on to analyse the more flexible New York and English law rules that would comfort lenders the most.

Counsel's next step was to segregate the collateral into first line objects: offshore cash payments, and second line objects: onshore collateral. In this exercise, counsel took the view that lenders always have the right to action all collateral in the case of a default, but they rarely do so. This process would help counsel and the bankers determine the most favourable jurisdiction for the first line collateral. Ultimately, the lenders chose England as the jurisdiction for first line collateral.

Having isolated these elements, counsel moved to the next challenge and sought to overcome the popular opinion that security interests can be perfected in Saudi Arabia. To solve this project counsel enlisted a team of Saudi jurists, notably with Hanbali (the most dominant school in Saudi Arabia) *fiqh* training. In order to describe how collateral could be structured according to *Shari'a*, counsel developed more than 3,000 questions, which, when answered, would lead to a body of explanatory materials.

Counsel's universe of materials would result in a classical *fiqh* explanation of solutions in a form acceptable to Hanbali scholars. Counsel presented his questions discretely over an extended period to a member of the BOG who was also a respected scholar of Hanbali *fiqh*. The method of interaction was structured to develop fundamental principles of law that any Hanbali judge would understand and apply.[19]

To achieve these ends, counsel began with an analogy relating to a camel. Could a camel be pledged? If so, the camel was *marhoun*, an asset subject to perfection under a pledge or mortgage (*rahn*). Working with examples found in the classical texts of Islamic *fiqh* and its interpretation by Hanbali scholars, counsel built a body of argument to govern the perfection of security interests in the project's real estate (the site leases and easements); immovable property (the refinery itself); movable property (computers and equipment); cash, bank accounts, contracts, accounts receivable, intellectual property, technology licences and permits. Although some property crossed classification boundaries, counsel was able to define a status and appropriate action.

There are specific risks of mortgage and agency, if narrowly interpreted in Saudi courts: is the agency or *wakala* supreme – it is cancellable? Or is the *rahn* written widely enough to grant the sought-after security powers in the event of default? In Saudi Arabia, there is some precedence in court for agencies and powers of attorney, either with a specific term, not being revocable.

A specific and significant challenge in the Saudi Refinery deal was the site lease. In this project, the Royal Commission for Jubail and Yanbu owns land and leases it to the project company. In this financing, a leasehold mortgage was crafted to secure the obligations of the company under the various financing agreements, the specific facilities agreement and the notes.

As the deal progressed, the Saudi Industrial Development Fund (SIDF) entered the deal with concessionary terms for its segment of the financing. Their late entry led them to take a mortgage on the leasehold interests. SIDF, however, did not take a security interest in the project's non-real property interests and revenues. This was beneficial to all of the lenders, allowing for a strong local lender to control the leasehold estate. In Saudi Arabian mortgages, there must be a specific amount that is secured and subject to collection. Under local law, a mortgagee has a reasonable expectation to secure a judicially directed sale of property for the specific amount. But local custom does not necessarily contemplate immediate sale. This is, in part, because a *rahn* needs to specify how it is to be exercised and the specific remedies relating to action in the event of default. This is less clear for personal property than real property.

The mortgagee has responsibility for all expenses to preserve the mortgage. In Saudi Arabia, these expenses are real and include erecting and maintaining fences around the property; engaging security agents and paying the guards who patrol the site; and erecting clear signage. This is because in the Hanbali view, a *rahn* is by definition possessory. In court, if the mortgagee's behaviour is not possessory, then the mortgagee's position is *pari passu* with an obligor's general creditors.

In Saudi Arabia, possession may prove a problem to determine. Recordation is generally accepted in Saudi Arabia as a form of 'constructive possession'. But, since 1981, Saudi notaries have tended to refuse to record mortgages in the name of banks on the grounds that these are likely to be for interest-related debt. Banks have often tried to use nominees to achieve recordation, but the notaries have frequently seen through that strategy. If one cannot record a mortgage in a country that does not permit interest and where notaries do not wish to record mortgages, how can one perfect a lien? An accepted alternative to recordation with notaries in Saudi Arabia is to publish a notice of an encumbrance in the Kingdom's Official Gazette (the *Umm Al Qura*) as a tombstone announcement. In addition, bills of possession, signage, fencing or presence of a mortgagee's employees also suffice as a means to achieve constructive perfection of a mortgage or *rahn*.

But, now there was a new problem. Common law jurisdictions typically appoint a trustee to supervise or otherwise monitor collateral. In some cases, a bankruptcy-remote trust might be established to hold collateral. Civil law and *Shari'a* law jurisdictions, however, lack trust and trustee laws. Like much of the Arabian Middle East, Saudi Arabia, despite being primarily a *Shari'a* jurisdiction, had a civil code strongly informed by the civil codes defined by the Egyptian jurist Abdul Razak Sanhouri. Thus, local law appeared to lack any trust rules.

In the process of investigating Hanbali *fiqh*, counsel discovered the concept of an *adl* or 'a trusted and honourable person with fiduciary responsibilities' to specific parties, a person whose capacity was the combination of a trustee-arbitrator in common law. As he learned more about the *adl* concept, counsel determined that this was the *Shari'a* concept that best matched the concept of trust law in English law. For instance, the *adl* could be endowed with a power of sale require, even if it would require the mutual consent of all parties with an economic interest in the deal.

In structuring the management of the project security, counsel and his legal peers established two unique persons in the position of *adl*, an Onshore Security Agent and an Offshore Security Agent. This solution required two sets of security documents, harmonious with each other, UK law and Saudi Arabian law. The interdependent documents allowed the two security agents to coordinate and act correctly, ensuring that pledged assets, such as cash, moved correctly and within the permitted spheres so as to allow the exercise of remedies under the appropriate law. For instance, the Offshore Agent was responsible for security interests in cash proceeds from benzene and cyclohexane sales deposited in a UK account and subject to pledge under English law. The *adl* in Saudi Arabia was entrusted with all elements of the transaction that were not interest oriented. All of the interest elements were segregated and driven to offshore trust.[20]

Next, management of the security required that the project company grant powers of attorney to the lenders. These grants were accompanied by agency agreements where the banks are agents of the company with respect to specific collateral. But, many Saudi judges view both these grants and agencies as revocable at will by either side. None of the security grants or *assignments* are *hawala*[21] or transferred arrangements or rights. But, the *rahn-adl* structure defined by counsel confers more irrevocability than previously seen in complex Saudi transactions.

The Onshore Master Agreement and Onshore Common Agreement were designed to unify all collateral and rights, and remedies allow security agents to act against the entire package in a timely manner in both jurisdictions. The transaction documentation included a Material Adverse Effect

Clause as a final catch-all for prospective enforcement in the UK environment.

Outcome

Due to the deal's complexity, counsel and the lending counsels structured multiple resolution routes to provide multiple options in the case of disputes. The innovative approach taken to understand *Shari'a* law as applied in Saudi Arabia was an important part of the process and allowed for the lawyers to structure the *rahn-adl* concept, which now constitutes the primary project finance solution in Saudi Arabia and other *Shari'a* law jurisdictions. Although this was a conventional financing with interest-bearing loans, the structure relied upon a resolution of defined conflicts between Islamic law as applied locally and cross-border transaction funding. The latest developments in project finance in the MENA region all include significant *Shari'a* elements. Within Saudi Arabia itself, all domestic banks now have substantial *Shari'a* operations and a new fully Islamic bank is being launched.

Exhibit 7.14 **Collateral and governing agreements**

General	Onshore Master Security Agreement
General	Onshore Common Agreement
General	Deed of Possession
General	Security Trust Deed
General	Offshore Security Deed
General	Announcement & Notification
General	Proper Signage at the Site
Immovables, real property interests and related contracts	Onshore Mortgage (*rahn*) Agreement
Financial accounts	Onshore Pledge (*rahn*) and Assignment of Accounts
Financial accounts	Offshore Accounts Assignment
Financial accounts	Offshore Accounts Trust Deed
Contracts	Consents
Contracts	Onshore Pledge (*rahn*) and Assignment of Contracts
Proceeds, available receipts, and accounts receivable	Onshore Pledge (*rahn*) and Assignment of Available Receipts and Accounts Receivable
Intellectual property	Onshore Pledge (*rahn*) and Assignment of Intellectual Property
Approvals and permits	Onshore Pledge (*rahn*) and Assignment of Approvals
General personal property	Onshore Pledge (*rahn*) and Assignment of Personal Property
Equipment	Onshore Pledge (*rahn*) and Assignment of Equipment
General intangibles, chattel paper, documents and instruments	Onshore Pledge (*rahn*) and Assignment of General Intangibles, Chattel Paper, Documents and Instruments
Technology licences	Onshore Pledge (*rahn*) and Assignment of Technology Licenses
Technology licences	Offshore Assignment of Technology Rights
Letters of credit and performance bonds	Onshore Pledge (*rahn*) and Assignment of Letters of Credit & Performance Bonds
Letters of credit and performance bonds	Offshore Assignment of Letters of Credit and Performance Bonds

Source: McMillen, Michael, 'A *Rahn-Adl* Collateral Security Structure for Project and Secured Financings', in *Third Harvard University Forum on Islamic Finance: Local Challenges, Global Opportunities* (Cambridge, MA: Harvard University, 1999), pp. 121–2.

Future large-scale projects will likely exceed the capacity of regional and global Islamic banks. Should global banks be reluctant to participate in the Islamic tranches, then not only will they continue to apply the *rahn-adl* concept, but they will migrate towards the adoption of the emerging Facilities Coordination Agreement. This new complex inter-creditor management document is similar to the UK form Common Terms Agreement. Both forms address the relevant representations and warranties as well as covenants and events of defaults in conventional and Islamic transactions as applied in the Islamic sector. Both coordinate the pro rata utilisation of distinct facilities, repayments, and sharing provisions. But, the Facilities Coordination Agreement is structured to prevent contagion of Islamic facilities by conventional facilities.[22]

[1] Usmani, Muhammad Imran Ashraf, *Meezan Bank's Guide to Islamic Banking* (Karachi: Darul Ishaat, 2002), p. 139.

[2] Kraty, Bryan and Abdelhaq Kafsi, *Islamic Finance & Mechanics* (Bahrain: unpublished manuscript, November 2004).

[3] Comair-Obeid, Nayla, *Les contrats en droit musulman des affaires*, (Paris: Economica, 1995), p. 32. Also see Aqeel, Abdul-Rahman, 'Shari'ah Precautionary Procedures in Murabaha and Istisna'a' in *Proceedings of the Second Harvard University Forum on Islamic Finance* (Cambridge, MA: Harvard Islamic Finance Information Program, 1998), p. 128. The Hanafi distinguish between the two concepts.

[4] Al Qassar, Abdul Aziz, *Aqd al-Istisna'a, Al Mustathmiroon,* May 2003, no. 19, p. 60. Some scholars differ as to whether *istisna'a* is a derivative of 'sales' by way of *salam*, or *ijarah*, or a promise and not a contract. This will cause variation in how the *istisna'a* process is documented depending upon the *Shari'a* board.

[5] Usmani, M.T., *An Introduction to Islamic Finance*, (Karachi: Idaratul Ma'arif , 1998), p. 198. Unlike monetary debts, the price of an *istisna'a* and *ijarah* may be linked to actual delivery.

[6] Al Qassar, *op. cit.*, p. 60.

[7] Some analysts view *ju'ala* as a unique contract form, others as a form of *istisna'a*. Few scholars include *ju'ala* as one of the primary classical nominative contracts.

[8] Based on the presentation by Badlisyah Abdul Ghani, 'Successful Sukuk Issues: Case Study SKS Power', presented at Asian Islamic Banking & Finance Summit, Kuala Lumpur, 21,22 September 2004.

[9] For more information about *sukuk*, see Adam, Nathif, J. and Abdulkader Thomas, *Islamic Bonds: Your Guide to Issuing, Structuring and Investing in Sukuk* (London: Euromoney Books, 2004).

[10] For a comparative discussion of Malaysia vs other Islamic markets, see Adam and Thomas, *op. cit.*, pp. 48-50.

[11] Michael McMillen, comments at 'Introducing a New Alternative', presented at Virginia Commonwealth University, 3 December 2004.

[12] Usmani, M.T., *An Introduction to Islamic Finance, op. cit.*, pp. 199-200.

[13] Grewal, Baljeet, 'Islamic Private Debt Securities as a financing option for infrastructure projects', presented at Asian Islamic Finance Summit, Kuala Lumpur, 22 September 2004.

[14] Thofeek, Mohammad Ikram, 'Corporate Governance - Trends and Developments: Focus on Boosting the Global Sukuk Market', presented at Islamic Funds World, London, October 5-6, 2004.

[15] The case is based upon the presentation of Mouchbahani, Christian, 'Initiating the First Corporate Sukuk & First Gulf Listing in Luxembourg: Tabreed US$100 Million ISO Case Analysis', presented at The 2nd Annual Islamic Funds World, October 2004, as well as the Tabreed Financing Corporation Offering Circular dated 1 March 2004.

[16] For more information about *sukuk*, see Adam, Nathif, J. and Abdulkader Thomas, *Islamic Bonds: Your Guide to Issuing, Structuring and Investing in Sukuk* (London: Euromoney Books, 2004).

[17] This case draws heavily from Michael McMillen's (formerly of King & Spalding, now a partner of Dechert) written accounts, public addresses as well as private conversation with the author relating to various project financings in *Shari'a* environments.

[18] McMillen, Michael, J.T., *Islamic Sharia'ah Compliant Project Financing: Collateral Security and Financing Structure Case Studies*, accessed at www.djindexes.com on 24 January 2005. In this working paper, McMillen goes into security structures relating to US real estate investment as well as the Saudi Refinery and other cases.

[19] Michael McMillen, comments at 'Introducing an Alternative', Virginia Commonwealth University, 3 December 2004.

[20] McMillen, *op. cit.*, VCU.

[21] *Hawala* is a *Shari'a* term relating to the transfer of an obligation. If applied here, it would interfere with both the concept of the *adl* and the management of security interests under Saudi and *Shari'a* law.

[22] Ali, Rahail and Rustam Shah, 'Streamlining Co-Islamic Financings', *Islamic Banker* November/December 2003, pp. 6, 7.

Real estate

8

Abdulkader Thomas with appreciation to Mohammed Asaria and Tamara Box

Introduction

The preferred asset class for many Islamic investors has been real estate. On the one hand, property clearly meets the asset focus of most methods. On the other hand, many Islamic investors have a personal or corporate bias towards property, which may centre directly on its tangibility. In this chapter, we isolate specific cases that highlight how the means described in previous chapters including *istisna'a*, *intifa'a*, *murabaha*, *musharaka*, *ijarah*, and *ijarah* in tandem with a conventional mortgage, as well as *salam* are applied for the finance or acquisition of property or property development materials. All cases are live cases, when the underlying transaction is not in the public domain, so the names of the counterparties are not disclosed. The chapter ends with a close look at the Saudi Arabian market which is one of the more complicated property markets.

Mudaraba and *musharaka*

As examined in Chapter 9: Islamic asset management, *mudaraba* is a key method for organising property investment. It has been widely used for commercial property acquisition by Islamic investors in all environments. The typical approach is to organise the core investment into property, and then to cross borders according to the appropriate tax and property rules.

The classic structure applied in European property organises the investors into an offshore fund that may include specific sub-steps to enter different jurisdictions for tax purposes. The fund forms a partnership with an entity representing a seasoned fund and property manager. Frequently, such managers are local or regional market professionals are often sub-contracted to the actual *mudarib* who is the fund manager. The fund then acquires properties, most commonly through either *ijarah* or *murabaha* vehicles, and then on-lease these to market tenants (see Exhibit 8.1).

REITs

The next phase in many key markets shall be the adaptation of the real estate investment trust concept (REIT) to property acquisition wherever this delivers a benefit to the investors for tax, exit strategy or liquidity purposes.

Exhibit 8.1 **Classic *mudaraba* structure**

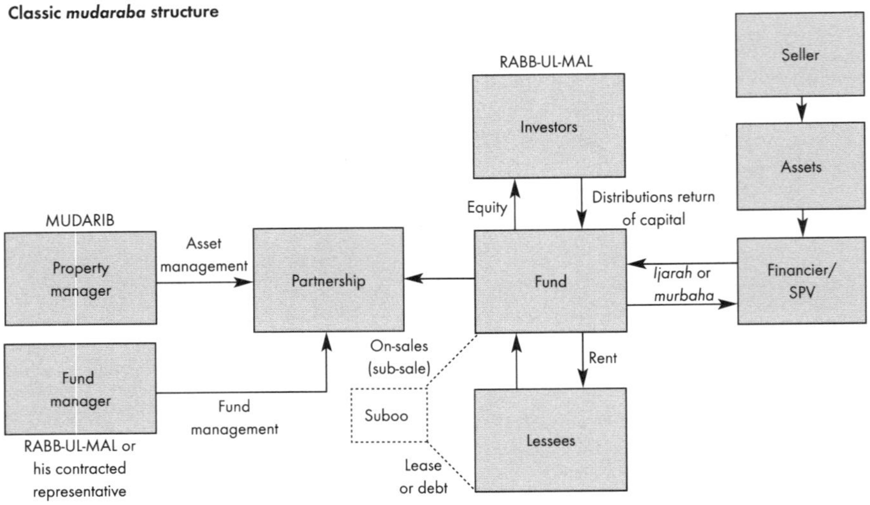

Source: Property IV conference, DTZ Corporate Finance Sep 2003, Oct 2003.

Exhibit 8.2 **Property acquisition using REIT concept**

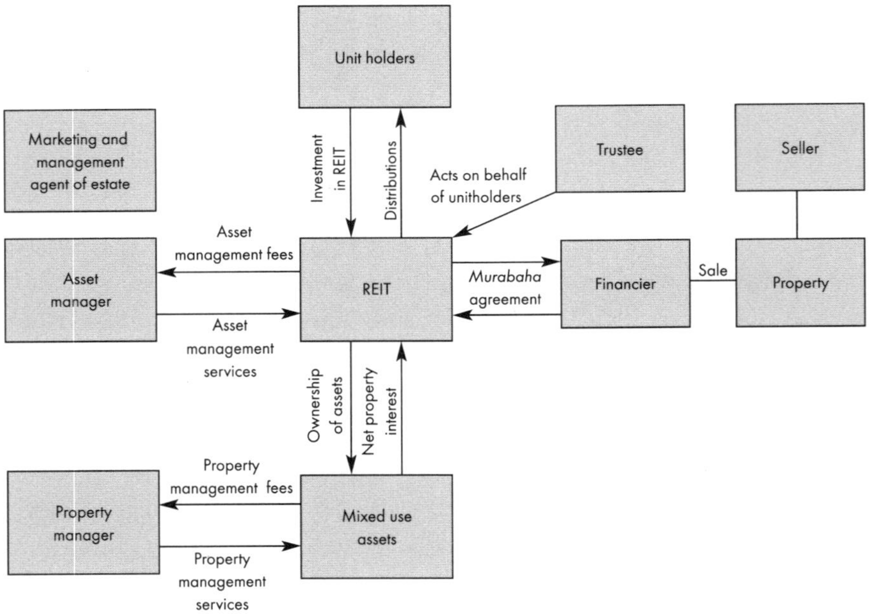

Source: Author's own.

In the case of a REIT, the investors take a view about preferring tax and, prospectively, monetisability. The REIT then engages in traditional asset management and property management contracts, purchases by *murabaha* or *ijarah*, and then on-leases (see Exhibit 8.2). Prospectively, the REIT may also take a view, if sufficiently capitalised, to offer the *murabaha* or *ijarah* acquisition and permanent funding for in-bound investors.

Istisna'a and *intifa'a*

Istisna'a has been embraced by international Islamic real estate investors as a way to enhance yields by building new properties. The FairMarket Apartment Company (FMA) of Denver, Colorado, formed a partnership with a major GCC Islamic investment house to build US apartment blocks. From FMA's perspective, it was very straightforward to develop a suitable product given the flexibility of their traditional lender.

Exhibit 8.3 **Reorganising traditional documents and obligations**

Construction (Istisna'a)
- Commitment for construction
- Disbursment mechanisms
- Conditions precedent
- Representations and warranties
- Covenants

Lease (Ijarah)
- Rent rate calculations
- Periodic rent
- Representations and warranties
- Events of default
- Remedies
- Indemnities

Project Transfer Agreement
- Mandatory prepayments
- Voluntary prepayments

Source: Michael J.T. McMillen, 'Islamic Financing Products in the United States: Structures and Current Developments', International Islamic Finance Conference – The Islamic Free Market Institute Foundation, Capital Hilton, Washington, D.C., 26 September 2002.

First, FMA and their lender partitioned the traditional real estate construction agreement into three universes of activity: construction; post-construction and project transfer (see Exhibit 8.3). The construction management documents entail the traditional terms of a construction loan, except that it effectively prices the contract in accreting terms. The investors make scheduled progress payments under the *istisna'a* or construction agreement, allowing FMA to secure supplies, pay staff and complete the work on schedule. In some contracts, the contract allows for pricing adjustments to reflect changes in incremental costs, or to award the contractor for early completion.

Upon completion, FMA delivers the completed property to the acquiring partnership at a fixed price that aggregates the financial yield sought by the investors. This is governed by the Project Transfer Agreement.

Should the partnership not be able to purchase the completed project outright upon issuance of a certificate of occupancy then there are several options. A typical option is to structure a forward lease. Under the terms of certain transfer agreements, the ownership entity may enter into a leasehold estate allowing for the financed party to redeem the lease and market the property.

ZamZam Towers, discussed in Chapter 5: Lease finance and *ijarah*, provides a new model which may be extremely advantageous on multiple fronts in many markets. First, the *sukuk al intifa'a* fit rather neatly into many definitions of debt for tax purposes. Certainly this is the case in the United States. Second, the concept can be applied to synthesise 100 per cent of construction funding, a mezzanine position or a full equity stake in a project. Since it is like a pre-paid lease, the proceeds may be paid prior to construction, held in trust and delivered to the project manager on a draw basis.

Murabaha

In Europe, a number of property investors have become comfortable with *murabaha* as a banking tool to finance investor acquisition of property (see Exhibit 8.4). UK and Irish banks, in particular, have offered *murabaha*, taking notional possession of title at closing and then selling the property at a higher price. On

Exhibit 8.4 **Property acquisition using *murabaha***

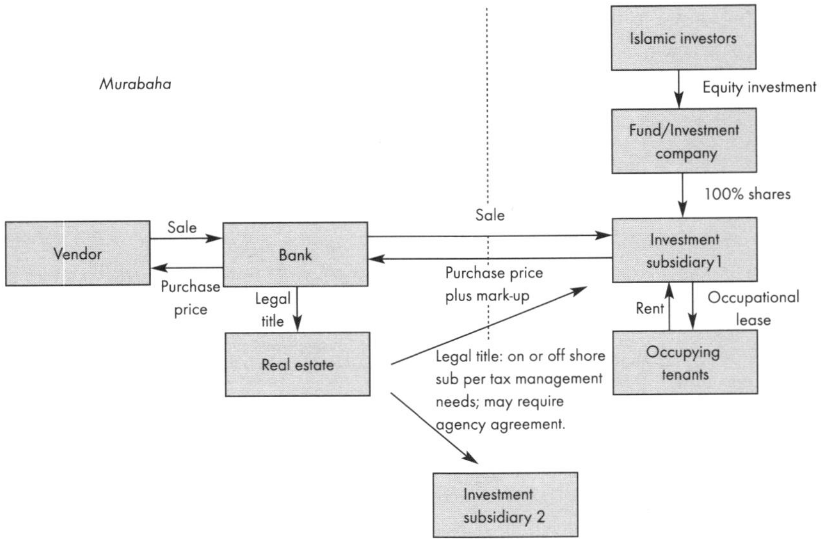

Source: Simon Berrill, DTZ Corporate Finance, 2005.

the one hand, they like such transactions because of the similarity to traditional mortgages. Indeed, they are able to secure their interests with a modified note and mortgage. This is because the structure is similar to traditional secured real estate lending, even if the process is different.

On the other hand, the negative issue with the process is a lack of flexibility. The bank financier is only able to go out so far, to a maximum of nine years. Thus, if the buyer cannot pay off in that time, Islamic rules do not allow an extension with a price change. Moreover, outside of Malaysia, such transactions are not easily securitised, since most other Islamic jurisdictions view the *murabaha* receivable as cash, which cannot be sold at variable prices.

Periodically, the financier or investor needs to avoid stepping into the direct chain of title for tax or regulatory reasons. In such case, the financier or investor appoints one of the transacting parties to act as its agent to acquire the subject property. The agent then steps into the chain of title on behalf of the financier and executes the sale on terms to the end-buyer. This method is most likely to be applied in jurisdictions where banks face the most serious limitations on their ability to own real estate. In the case of the investor, such a manoeuvre keeps the property title in an onshore SPV, which is often better for tax management purposes.

Musharaka and declining-balance partnership

The general principle of equity investment flows with the core organising principle of most Islamic investments. But, the use of true *musharaka* as a primary financing tool by major conduits or onshore financiers in support of offshore investors has been limited. Typically, the onshore party takes a minority position, no more than 5 per cent, sometimes 10 per cent, often contributed in kind – goods or services – and not cash.

But, declining-balance partnerships have been used for residential real estate in both the United States and the United Kingdom. In late 2004, a substantial private transaction was executed between a London conduit and a GCC investor for the acquisition of German property (see Exhibit 8.5).

Exhibit 8.5 **Example debt structure–declining-balace *musharaka***

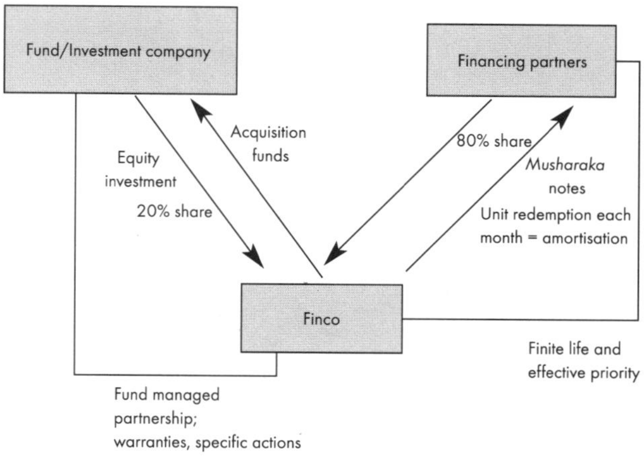

Source: Author's own.

In this transaction, the 'debt' capital is raised through *musharaka* participation notes. The investors in these notes represent 80 per cent of the capital and allow for a monthly unit or partial unit redemption that is tantamount to amortisation. The *musharaka* notes have a finite life. The *musharaka* investors and the fund would share in the profits according to agreed proportions, which may cap the prospective yield to the finance partners to a traditional real estate debt yield.

Ijarah and leveraged *ijarah*

Although many *Shari'a* scholars strongly encourage the *musharaka* forms, the most popular and most flexible property leveraging method is *ijarah*. In UK and other European transactions, the SPV must be ultimately owned or be a charity in order to manage tax issues. Beyond that, the process is straightforward and a large number of banks are now willing to participate in lease finance: providing funds to acquire the asset, and then on-leasing it to the investors' SPV with the investors taking responsibility for managing the property and dealing with tenants (see Exhibit 8.6).

In the United States, the government-sponsored mortgage giants, Freddie Mac and Fannie Mae both lend traditionally to SPVs which then master lease apartment projects to offshore investors.

Frequently, tax and corporate risk management issues mean that the structures are particularly complex in countries such as the United States. This is shown in Exhibits 8.6 and 8.7.

For instance, many offshore investors are obliged to structure multiple offshore companies to make varying percentage loans to an onshore SPV which then masterleases a project from the US financier. Sometimes multiple agreements are required to govern tax management, insurance and maintenance.

Exhibit 8.6 **Property acquisition using *ijarah* and leveraged *ijarah***

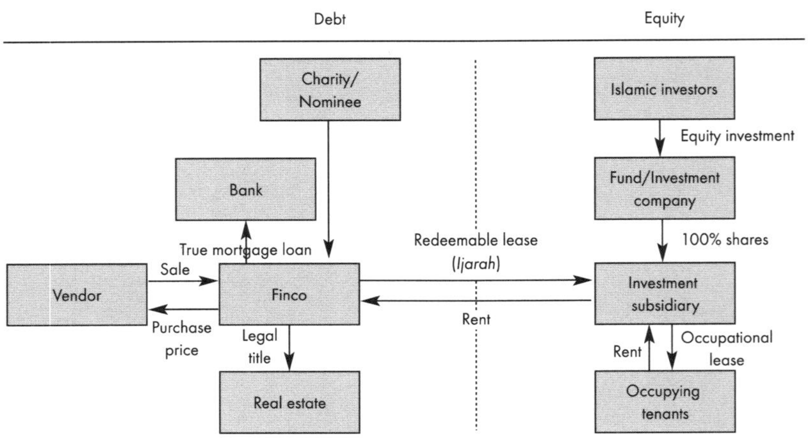

Source: Simon Berrill, DTZ Corporate Finance, 2005.

Exhibit 8.7 **Post-acquisition financing structure, overall transaction (without security documentation)**

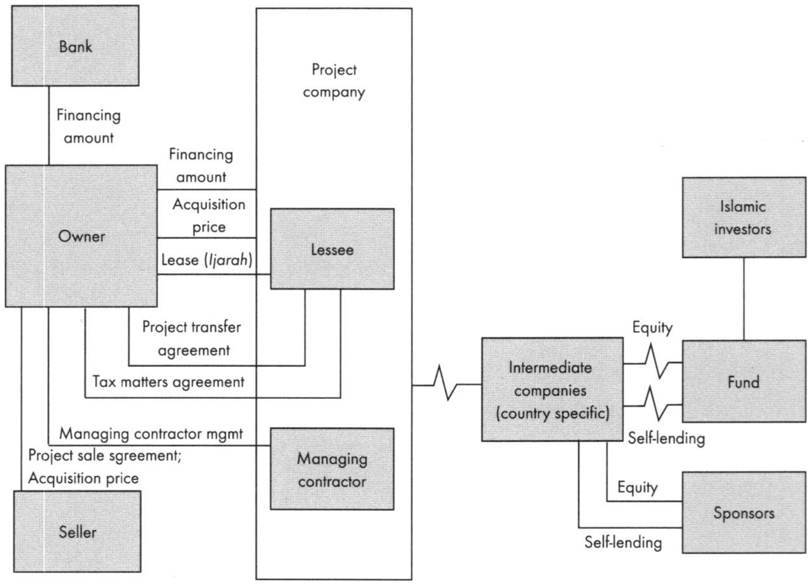

Source: Michael J.T. McMillen, 'Islamic Financing Products in the United States: Structures and Current Developments', International Islamic Finance Conference – The Islamic Free Market Institute Foundation, Capitol Hilton, Washington, D.C., 26 September 2002.

Securitisation of real estate

One area of innovation that is expected to take place in the Islamic real estate finance world in the near future will be the development of the *Shari'a*-compliant real estate securitisations in key markets such as Saudi Arabia described below. Securitisation is an asset monetisation technique that sits well with the principles of *Shari'a*. As mentioned in the introduction to this chapter, real estate is the asset class that Islamic investors most favour; as a consequence, financing real estate through securitisation is likely to gain immediate favour with Islamic investors. Please also see Chapter 10, 'Opportunities with *sukuk* and securitisations'.

Securitisation as a financing technique is particular well-suited to situations where certainty and matched funding are required. In principle, securitisation makes a real asset monetisable based on a regular future cash stream. As a result of the construction boom, liberalising views about property ownership, and the expatriate influx across the Middle East, the mortgage market in the region is developing rapidly. In common with more developed markets there are two main providers of mortgages – banks (which fund mortgages primarily from customer deposits) and independent mortgage originators (or installment companies, as they are referred to in certain regions across the Middle East). The latter form of institutions is generally not able to accept customer deposits so they need to secure alternative financing sources to fund the mortgages that they originate. Securitisation may be one such option; after all securitisation offers access to cheaper, match-funded, long-term capital markets funding. Provided that the mortgages offered by these installment companies are compliant with *Shari'a* an Islamic securitisation may be structured.

More legislation needed through the Middle East region

The basic securitisation structure has been adapted to fund mortgages in a number of jurisdictions. In July 2005 Amlak issued a US$200 million *sukuk* that will be used to fund the issuance of Islamic mortgages. Other mortgage originators across the Middle East are establishing Islamic securitisation programmes to fund their long-term capital requirements. A key market for such securitisation programmes must be Saudi Arabia where all of the key players, as well as new market entrants, are working to formalise *sukuk* rules and launch such programmes. But, like most jurisdictions in the emerging markets, important challenges revolve around the question of a true sale of the underlying property, a necessity for a successful securitisation; then the applicability of such a sale, through the securitisation, to non-Saudi Arabian investors. Trust laws used in the Anglo-American context are absent. The various elements of a successful real estate mortgaging and securitisation process relating to hypothecation, notarisation and whether or not cash can be swept offshore have been addressed in one-off transactions applying clever structures. But, the new Saudi Capital Markets Act merely addresses bonds and the sale of debts in a traditional sense and the legislative authorities have not yet expanded the act to embrace both mortgaging and securitisation of either traditional or *Shari'a*-compliant mortgage alternatives.

Saudi real estate securitisation

At the time of writing, there is a total prohibition on the issue of debt securities by a Saudi Arabian corporate and the sale of securities in Saudi Arabia is prohibited by anyone other than a regulated banking institution. However, such a restrictive legal framework has not prohibited the market from developing – the Caravan I transaction (*Shari'a*-compliant vehicle finance securitisation) was closed in 2004. Judging by the 'big-ticket' Islamic structured financings that have recently emanated from Saudi Arabia over the 2004 (most notably the US$1.2 billion *Eti-salaat* financing) and the considerable interest that new Capital Markets Act has generated, it is foreseeable that the domestic securitisation market in Saudi Arabia may rapidly develop.

A significant amount of resources have been invested to decipher how an Islamic securitisation may be structured in respect of Saudi Arabian assets. The following section illustrates some of the considerations that need to be borne in mind.

Overview of Saudi Arabian legal regime

The paramount body of law in Saudi Arabia is the *Shari'a*. In addition, there is legislation enacted in various forms, the most common of which include royal decrees, royal orders, Council of Ministers resolutions, ministerial resolutions and ministerial circulars. All such laws are ultimately subject to, and cannot conflict with, the *Shari'a*.

Saudi Arabian adjudicatory bodies are required to interpret secular legislation in line with *Shari'a* principles. The legal regime in Saudi Arabia hence incorporates *Shari'a* principles that are often expressed in general terms, providing a Saudi Arabian adjudicatory body with considerable discretion as to how to apply such principles. It should also be noted that previous decisions of Saudi Arabian adjudicatory bodies are not considered to establish binding precedents for the decision of later cases; the principle of *stare decisis* is not applied in Saudi Arabia. In addition, the various legislation and other pronouncements of official bodies in Saudi Arabia having the force of law and the decisions of the various Saudi Arabian adjudicatory bodies are not generally or consistently indexed and collected in a central place or made publicly available.

Issue of securities

Currently there is a total prohibition on the issue of debt securities by Saudi Arabian corporations that are not classified as joint stock companies (namely Saudi Arabian banks). The issuer in a Saudi securitisation structure must be located off-shore. The sale of securities in Saudi Arabia by anyone other than a regulated banking institution is prohibited. However, in the latter case both investors and arrangers of securities have adopted a pragmatic approach to this restriction.

The new Capital Markets Act provides for the issue of bonds and *sukuk* by Saudi Arabian companies and liberalises the rules relating to the sale of securities in Saudi Arabia. However, the implementing regulations that will flesh out the provisions of this new Act have yet to be published.

The Saudi Arabian regulator has taken the approach that any securities (including those issued by an off-shore vehicle) that are denominated in Saudi Riyals will fall under the ambit of its regulation. To avoid the additional administrative burden that will result, it is suggested that the securitisation structure incorporate currency- hedging techniques (whilst complying with the stringent *Shari'a* requirements in this area) so that any issuance is made in US dollars. As the Saudi Riyal is tied to the US dollar (and this is not expected to change), rating agencies may take the view that the US dollar/Saudi Riyal exchange rate is unlikely to fluctuate and permit spot currency exchanges on specified dates to be incorporated into the structure without affecting the rating.

Establishing the SPV

Every securitisation structure will envisage an on-shore vehicle purchasing the underlying assets from the Originator and transferring certain rights in the underlying assets to an off-shore vehicle which will then issue *sukuk* certificates. However, Saudi Arabian legislation does not recognise the concept of an orphan SPV. To mimic the operational effect of an SPV, a Saudi Arabian limited liability company (the 'Saudi SPV') may be used and the operation of the Saudi SPV is limited as follows

- The shareholders and directors of the Saudi SPV enter into a restrictive covenants agreement that prevents the Saudi SPV from taking any action that is inconsistent with the rights of the *sukuk* holders.
- The articles of the Saudi SPV will be drafted to only permit activities (that are not specified in the securitisation transaction documents) to be taken with the unanimous consent of the shareholders – one of which will be the Issuer's Agent.
- The management of the Saudi SPV will be delegated to the Issuer's Agent.

The minimum share capital requirement for a Saudi SPV is SR500,000 (US$1=SR3.75) which must be fully paid up on incorporation. A large part of this amount may be returned to the shareholders shortly thereafter.

The Issuer (as it is not domiciled in Saudi Arabia) may not own shares in the Saudi SPV, without prior approval of the Saudi regulators (and it is not certain whether such approval will be given). Consequently, it is suggested that the majority of shares of the Saudi SPV are owned by the Originator and a minority of the shares being held by an agent of the Issuer that is domiciled in Saudi Arabia (the 'Issuer's Agent'). The role of the Issuer's Agent is to protect the interests of the *sukuk* holders.

True sale

Saudi legislation does not formally recognise the concept of true sale. Local counsel will ordinarily set out the characteristics of a true sale in the transaction opinion and conclude that the sale/assignment conforms with such characteristics. Regional rating agencies are comfortable with this approach, and the Saudi legal regime in relation to bankruptcy laws (including claw-back risk and set-off) and consolidation risk.

The originator may be appointed as servicer of the underlying assets without affecting the categorisation of the sale/transfer. Providing the underlying agreements do not specifically contain a prohibition on assignment, the underlying obligors neither need to be notified nor consent to the assignment.

Security

The Saudi SPV may not grant 'conventional' security over the underlying assets to the Issuer - this is a corollary to the prohibition of foreign ownership in respect of assets domiciled in Saudi Arabia. This will not be as problematic as may first appear as a modified security structure is frequently used for such assets.

The security package will include the Issuer's Agent being delivered the title deeds to the underlying assets (for the duration of the financing) and the Saudi SPV granting an irrevocable power of attorney to the Issuer's Agent that will permit the Issuer's Agent to convey the underlying assets to itself or a Saudi domiciled third party (that is, it may sell the assets for valuable consideration). The Issuer's Agent will be able to effect such a conveyance without the need for the Saudi SPV to take any additional action. This power of attorney will be deemed irrevocable for the duration of the financing and this will be stated in the transaction opinion.

In addition, security over the Saudi SPV's bank accounts or collection accounts in Saudi Arabia may not be granted to the Issuer (or any off-shore entity). It is suggested that as far as possible all monies should be swept off-shore on a daily basis. Security over these amounts may then be readily granted to or by the Issuer in the usual manner. The advantage of structuring the security package in this manner (that is, a grant of power of allowing and entrusting the title deeds to the Issuer's Agent) is that sufficient rights in the underlying assets will have been transferred to the Issuer for the *Shari'a* scholars to issue a fatwa that the *sukuk* certificates may be freely traded in the secondary market.

The security package described in this section has been tested in relation to real estate assets that are located outside the Holy Cities of Mecca and Medina. The Saudi Arabian regulator takes a much more stringent approach to real estate assets in the Holy Cities and it is suggested that the views of the Saudi Arabian regulator should be obtained if a significant percentage of the underlying assets are located in the Holy Cities.

Taxation

There is no stamp duty or VAT chargeable in Saudi Arabia. However, in respect of certain income that is generated in Saudi Arabia, Zakat (a religious tax – current rate 2.5 per cent) may be payable. In addition, 'interest equivalent payments' (this is one translation of the term used in the Saudi Arabian tax regulations) that flow out of Saudi Arabia may be subject to withholding tax. The regulations relating to withholding tax were amended in 2003 and there is still some uncertainty as to their application. If applicable (and there is no double taxation treaty of which an investor may take advantage) the standard withholding tax rate is 15 per cent.

Bearing all these above parameters in mind Exhibit 8.8 is a suggested structure for a Saudi Arabian real estate securitisation transaction.

Remarkable potential

When one examines the depth of opportunity of the Saudi Arabian market, important socio-economic needs, and the rising leaders in the banking and securities regulatory regime, it is clear that Saudi Arabian authorities are addressing these questions in a systematic manner. Once achieved, the shifting from innovative and high profile, but complex, programmes such as the Munshaat *sukuk al intifa'a*, will be made to the adaptation of *ijarah* or *musharaka* models for the mass market as in the UAE and, in turn, their ultimate securitisation. Should the market regime further liberalise to embrace property ownership by non-nationals, an explosive growth in property values and securitisation of real estate assets may be expected. Indeed, if the liberalisation expanded to the Holy Cities or nearby points of access, the breadth of this opportunity and the benefits it would bring to the national economy defy imagination. Such thoughts were once considered unimaginable, but are now contemplated to varying degrees in official and non-official circles throughout the GCC including Saudi Arabia.

Exhibit 8.8 **Recent cross-border securitisation of Saudi Arabian real property assets**

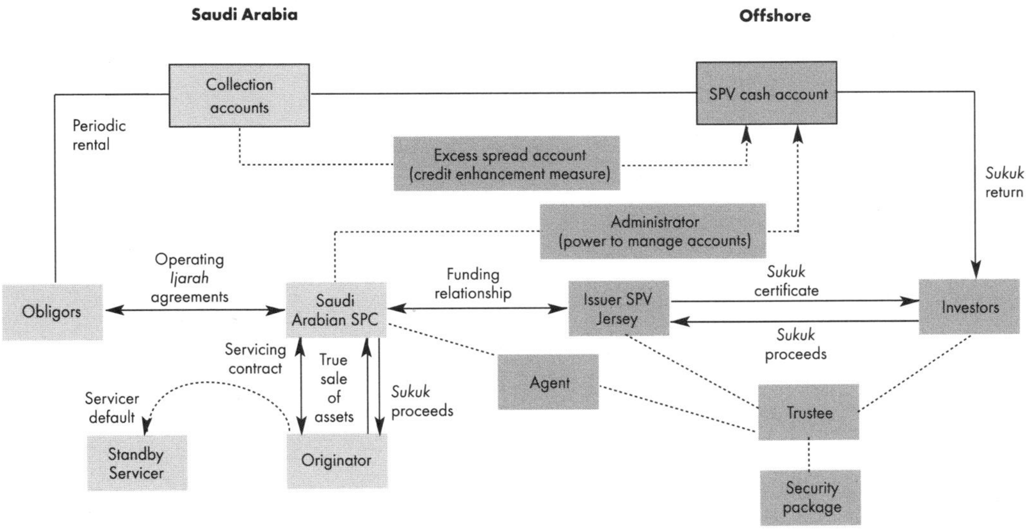

Source: Author's own.

Conclusion

The nature of property finance is directly influenced by local taxation, local real estate customs, and the sophistication of local real estate financiers. There are multiple *Shari'a* approaches which may be followed allowing the Islamic investors to participate in global markets. As we have seen, the regional markets in which Islamic rules are meant to prevail often are more complex than western markets.

Unfortunately, the single most complicating issue is taxation. And this issue will not go away. Petroleum surplus countries seeking to invest in US, European and Asian real estate are moving from low or no-tax environments to medium or high-tax countries, with which their governments do not have tax treaties. As a result, this sub-segment will be subject to high degrees of structuring. In GCC countries, however, the impediments to property transactions and securitisation are likely to be legislated away in order to facilitate the growth of Islamic finance as is consistent with most regional government goals.

Islamic asset management

9

Stella Cox and Lawrence Oliver with Abdulkader Thomas[1]

Introduction

This chapter looks at the development and growth of Islamic investment funds through the prism of several key asset classes. In the course of the chapter, past, existing and recently innovated investment products provide a template for understanding the Islamic asset management process. Islamic banking emphasises profit share related to risk assumption, and the total prohibition of exposure to interest-based financial instruments and transactions. Equity investment has blossomed since the mid-1990s, and *sukuk*, covered elsewhere in this book, have achieved a place of significance in the market.

The product examples illustrate the ways in which the development of the Islamic fund management capability has benefited the entire Islamic financial sector. Is there a greater opportunity for efficient portfolio diversification, and if not, why not? What has impeded development, and what is the extent of those impediments? This chapter aims to offer an insight to these issues and, hopefully, the solutions. Equity investment, as a key topic in this chapter, provides an interesting illustration of Islamic fund structuring and also demonstrates one or two of the elements that have consistently been proven critical to the successful launch of an Islamic investment fund.

Islamic principles

The mainstream financial system is familiar with money itself being the commodity, and income returns are correlated merely to the time value associated with the investment. The development of the Islamic financial sector has been based upon the productive use of money for the growth of the economy and the benefit of the community. It is an asset-based system. If money is to be invested, it should be through physical ownership of tangible assets with an income stream that may be attributed to the economic use of the asset.

Creating an Islamic asset base

Until relatively recently, much of the product innovation within the Islamic financial sector was primarily engineered to meet the specific investment risk and return criteria of the Islamic commercial banks. From the mid-1970s onwards, Islamic banks were able to enjoy increasing success in the retail market, thereby mobilising significant deposits and simultaneously generating a requirement for short-term investment assets so that obligations to retail customers were assured. The international trade and commodity markets initially became the principal focus of Islamic finance, largely due to the huge turnover in physical assets and the short-term profile of the trade flow. A variation of short-term financing techniques were implemented to deliver Islamic finance to the market place.

Islamic fund management

For many years, Islamic banks relied on structured finance contracts to support the delivery of asset-based investment funds. These primary level financing products have, in many ways, been responsible for generating momentum within the Islamic financial sector. They have played a significant role in promoting Islamic fund management, too. More recently, traded and securities-based opportunities have underpinned the majority of today's Islamic investment funds. Some of the newer, increasingly popular asset classes once enjoyed limited acceptance and investment funds.

After a slow start the momentum within the fund management sector has increased dramatically and, since the mid-1990s, it has become a hugely fashionable industry, attracting the involvement and participation of a number of the largest global banks and blue chip fund managers. It has also served to support the emergence of several, sophisticated Islamic investment banks.

Islamic investment pyramid

Previously, the provision of diversified investment opportunities that combined potential for enhanced yield with a regular and liquid redemption profile had been limited. Furthermore, because these limitations were a feature of the market for 15 or more years it did little to encourage the

Exhibit 9.1 **Islamic investment product pyramid**

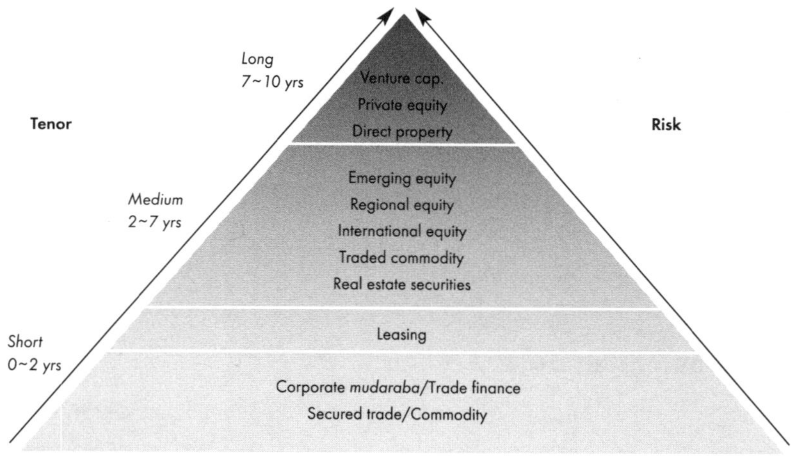

Source: Stella Cox and Lawrence Oliver.

Exhibit 9.2 **Product matrix**

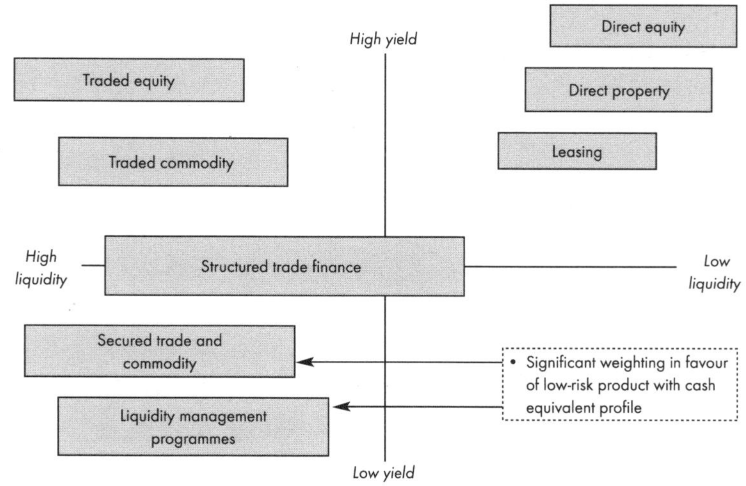

Source: Stella Cox and Lawrence Oliver.

substantial private investor. The concerted effort of both Islamic and mainstream banks to originate new and more sophisticated investment opportunities has increased the choices available to all investors. Meeting the requirements of the high net worth and private client, so as to realign substantial, conventional portfolios, became one of the challenges for the Islamic fund manager and the demand has still been only partially satisfied.

Asset management tool matrix

As is well known, construction of a balanced portfolio requires access to a range of asset categories and investment horizons and a professional, portfolio manager will seek performance through prudent and diversified allocation. This clearly requires more than the cash and bond equivalent investment structures. Numerous initiatives by major firms have recently encompassed real estate (both direct and securitised), traded commodities, global, emerging and regional equities and even some direct equity investment programmes in an endeavour to appeal to the more adventurous, yield-conscious client (see Exhibit 9.2).

Simplified *murabaha* trade financing and *mudaraba* funds

Amongst the matrix options, the *murabaha* contract quickly dominated as a money management tool. Trade finance facilities were structured and extended to companies on a full commercial risk basis or, at the request of the investor, incorporating third-party security in the form of a standby letter of credit or guarantee that was usually issued by an agent bank that may also have structured the transaction.

As the requirement for Islamic investment product increased dramatically during the 1980s, the bilateral financing concept was built upon by a number of Arabian commercial banks that established *mudaraba*s, or unitised portfolios, that could invest as funds. Retail depositors acquired the units of the *mudaraba*s and capital was then allocated to individual *murabaha* trade investment opportunities by the manager, or *mudarib*.[2] The objective of the *mudaraba*s was to invest in bank-secured trade transactions that generated profits more or less equivalent to those available through placing deposits in the international money markets. The *mudarib* was then able to take a pre-determined share of the profits before distributing the balance (effectively dividends) to investors.

The principal sponsors of the early trade and commodity funds were the Saudi commercial banks, with Samba launching its US dollar and Saudi riyal trade portfolios as far back as 1986. Products were structured to deliver retail investment opportunities to local customers, deemed likely to become increasingly attracted to the *halal* investment opportunities offered by Islamic financial institutions. The *mudaraba* concept was both efficient and economical for the sponsor, who retained discretion over investments. Somewhat ironically, the trade funds also benefited from wholesale investment by the Islamic banks, which were attracted to the short-term, low-risk investment profile and were hungry for asset diversification.

The Islamic financial sector has yet to complete the establishment of its own financial market infrastructure. Much of its liquidity is dependent upon structured investment solutions. The operational procedures and systems that will allow investment assets to be traded through a regulated secondary market environment have not yet been fully implemented.

Murabaha has been a remarkably dependable contract and a mainstay for Islamic banks seeking short-term investments with a similar risk-return profile to the interbank deposit. There is a valid argument that there has been over-dependency on the *murabaha* contract, which has impeded the development of other liquidity management products.

The counter-argument is that as well as enabling the Islamic banks to manage and derive profit from short-term cash balances, the wholesale *murabaha* trade and commodity-based structures have served to expand the investment asset base of the Islamic banking sector. The contract has certainly provided an asset stream for the *mudaraba* portfolios, which have been an undoubted success and aggregate funds invested run into billions of dollars. The *mudaraba* investment product is widely adopted by both Islamic and conventional banks. Some might say that the *mudaraba*s, bearing many of the features apparent in mainstream mutual funds, laid the foundations of the Islamic fund management industry. A trade *mudaraba* has some issues to deal with in managing the positions so that it is not a fund that trades in debt. Ideally such a fund should be a closed-ended fund to avoid trading in debts.[3]

Commodity investment funds

Market-traded commodity funds became an innovation of the early 1990s, when there was still very limited *Shari'a* endorsement of investment in the international stock markets. The traded commodity funds were intended to capitalise on the experience of the earlier bank-secured commodity investment structures based upon trade finance. The sponsors' objectives were to deliver a higher-yielding, relatively liquid, investment to institutional and private investors seeking portfolio diversification. The investment bankers sought to provide clients with exposure to commodities via physical trades transacted through international commodity exchanges and other suitable trade-based investments.

Setting yield objectives was challenging. An Islamic traded commodity portfolio cannot be measured against a mainstream benchmark, such as the Goldman Sachs Commodity Index, as typically the benchmark would include an excessive component of prohibited commodity contracts, as well as a futures bias that is still generally unacceptable to Islamic clients. In order to develop confidence in their products, investment bankers such as Kleinwort Benson, in partnership with the Islamic Investment Company of the Gulf (IICG – now part of Shamil Bank), established a track record for their respective commodity funds with their own seed capital. This approach – whereby the manager demonstrates a sustained or consistent on-target performance during a suitable period of incubation – is an alternative method of establishing that the manager's performance objectives are viable.

Both the Kleinwort and IICG funds were launched during the 1990s amidst sustained growth in the international equity markets. So, somewhat ironically, both products were adversely affected by a downturn in the commodity markets at the time of their launch. If they were criticised for under-performing it was probably more a matter of them under-performing client expectations. Despite careful market positioning, both were expected to achieve performance in line with the global equity markets rather than the commodity sectors that they invested in!

A commodity fund must own the commodities that it sells; *salam* and *istisna'a* may be used as forward strategies; and the underlying commodities must be permissible. The fund must have physical or constructive ownership of the underlying commodities in order to be traded[4] and the price of the commodity must be known.

Ijarah lease finance and funds

The subsequent desire to extend investment horizons directed market focus towards financing a greater percentage of non-trade assets. From the early 1990s, leasing, or *ijarah*, increasingly has become a preferred contract for offering medium to long-term structured finance. Through the extension of medium-term leases to investment grade lessees, investors can generate rental streams comparable to corporate bond yields within the framework of an enormous and diversified global leasing market.

There are many similarities between an Islamic and a conventional lease that provide considerable incentive for a conventional user of Islamic finance. There are also a number of features of the *ijarah* contract that have found particular favour with *Shari'a* scholars and, because of this, some innovative lease funds have been structured around it.

Exhibit 9.3 ***Ijarah* fund structure**

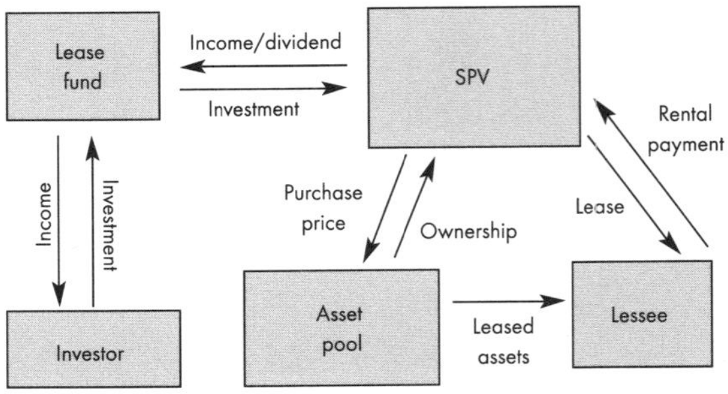

Source: Stella Cox and Lawrence Oliver.

An *ijarah* contract incorporates a fixed-term, or periodically re-fixed, income stream, or rental, from the economic use of a physical underlying asset (see Exhibit 9.3). Outside of Malaysia, the majority of scholars concur that once an asset has been purchased and sold, any further trading in the income stream (receivables) is deemed to be trading in debt. For this reason, the *murabaha* contract, with an asset that is purchased and sold immediately under deferred payment terms, is not appropriate for securitisation. Lease income can be readily securitised without the infringement of *Shari'a* because the investor retains title to the leased asset throughout the investment period and the security attaches to the asset, carrying the proportionate rental stream with it.

Ijarah funds have been incorporated to capitalise on the availability of a broad spectrum of international investment opportunities. Most Islamic lease funds invest in pools of suitable leased assets (examples), which may be sold to a special purpose vehicle (SPV) owned by the fund. The fund manager may choose to evidence holdings to investors by issuing certificates that represent their ownership of, or title to, a percentage of the asset pool and, thereby, a pro rata share of the income stream. Theoretically, as the certificate (a *sakk*), or security, evidences title to an asset holding and thereby entitlement to the associated income stream, it may be traded. Although we cannot claim that there is a true secondary market as yet, fund sponsors have often injected liquidity by purchasing certified holdings from their investors.

The leased assets must have a beneficial use; be permissible; lessor must take ownership risks; and rent must be set according to Islamic rules. The manager's fees may be a portion of the rental. The basis of the *mudaraba* in these funds is approved in the contemporary environment based on the classical Hanbali support for *mudaraba* to be applied to services and leasing as well.[5]

International equity investment

Although the first Islamic global equity products were launched in the mid-1980s, the origination of Islamic equity funds became a focus of our marketplace during the second half of the 1990s. The concept and acceptability of Islamic investors actively participating in the international equity markets has long been debated by both market practitioners and *Shari'a* scholars. Even now, some still remain uncomfortable about the impact of a company's non-*Shari'a*-compliant financial activity on share price movements and investment dividends. In the 1980s, general opinion rejected the concept of stock market investment.

A classical concern of many Muslims and scholars is that the modern corporation is analogous to a *shirkah* or partnership. Thus, each investor is a partner and party to the company's decisions, whether permissible or not from a *Shari'a* perspective. But, a growing number of modern scholars disagree with this perspective as the decisions are predominately taken by the majority and the individual shareholder is incapable of vetoing an impermissible action.[6] This transformation of Muslim views allowed the first significant experiments in equity investing in the global capital markets.

The first Islamic international equity funds were launched in the 1980s on a stand-alone basis by international banks. The first two were sponsored by the London fund management operations of Kleinwort Benson and UBS in 1986. The funds appointed independent *Shari'a* supervisory counsel to provide structuring guidance and give final endorsement to their investment strategies but were not able to find co-sponsorship from any of the Islamic institutions. These early equity products were successful in as much as they offered a much-needed opportunity for portfolio diversification and began to introduce the international equity markets to investors previously wary of mainstream involvement for reasons of *Shari'a* compliance. The products performed competitively, although their potential was restricted by the absence of consistent *Shari'a* endorsement of global equity investment and limitations in distribution.

The initial experience apparently deterred other promoters and the Islamic financial sector did not refocus on the international equity markets until the mid-1990s. The re-emergence of Islamic equity funds followed the successful launch of the National Commercial Bank and Wellington fund. The success of this fund broke down the primary barriers relating to the screening of the underlying securities and defining them as permissible for Islamic investors. Acceptance of the asset class is far more widespread with products launched by international banks, fund managers, Islamic banks and joint ventures of every permutation.

Screening equity securities

Jabir b. Abdullah reported that the Prophet Mohammed (PBOH) forbade the sale of wine, [swine] carcass, swine and idols.[7] This *hadith* sets the standard that the main business of the target company must not be impermissible. After that, a qualitative process is applied to screen or 'purify' a stock universe so that it will conform to *Shari'a* stipulation. The process of purification is not dissimilar from the selection processes followed by the socially responsible asset manager universe.[8] Purification may be taken from the dividend or gains upon sale. Some scholars feel that the purification is solely applied to income since the gain on sale is not a function of the impermissible elements, notably interest income.[9]

Analysts must conduct a review of individual stocks at a number of levels. These are contained within two general screening procedures.

Exhibit 9.4 **Screening stocks at the industry level**

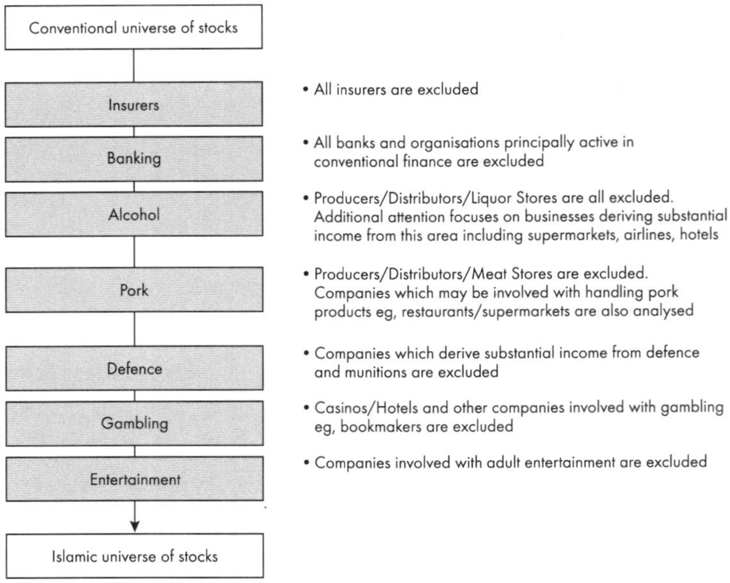

Source: Stella Cox and Lawrence Oliver.

One screen is applied at industry level (see Exhibit 9.4) and the other from a financial perspective. From a *Shari'a* perspective, this screening prevents Muslims from acquiring wealth in a way that violates the rights of God, contracting parties and third parties. Foremost, in asset management, this means avoiding the forbidden areas which include *riba*, gaming, and the like as shown in Exhibit 9.5.[10]

Exhibit 9.5 **Screening process – Stages 1 and 2**

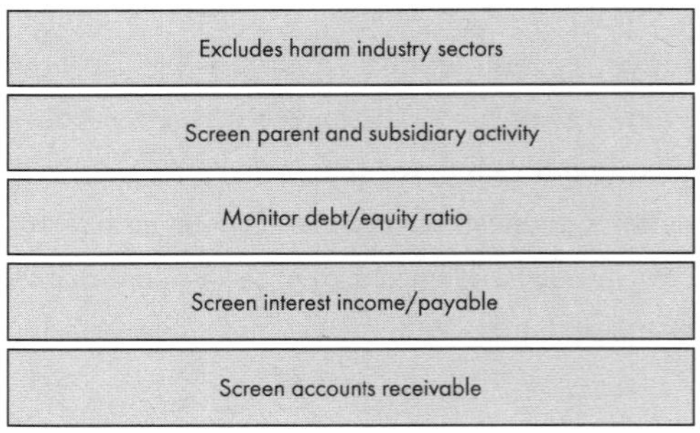

Source: Stella Cox and Lawrence Oliver.

Although it is relatively straightforward to identify *haram* or non-permissible industries, there has been an inconsistency of scholarly opinion relating to the financial ratios that may be applied: for example, in determining the correct formulae for the acceptability of debt, for cash-plus-interest-bearing securities and even for receivables.

The basic view of Islamic scholars has been to limit an equity company's exposure to interest income to 5 per cent of the company's income. This has no basis in either the *Qur'an* or *Sunnah*, and is the result of the collective *ijtihad* of modern Muslim scholars. The basis for this judgement is that the modern corporation, unlike a true *musharaka*, does not entail the direct power of one shareholder to veto the decisions of the company, rather if a shareholder objects to a policy that generates incidental income, all other income being permissible, then that shareholder must consent to refrain from that income.[11]

Exhibit 9.6 **Screening process – Stage 2**

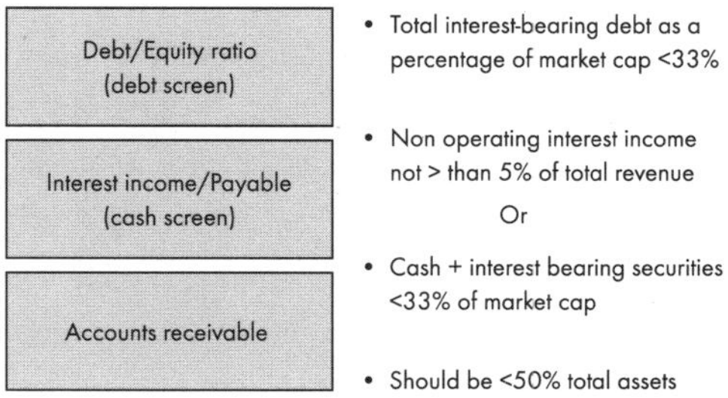

Source: Stella Cox and Lawrence Oliver.

When it comes to the screening of debt, the question of what is incidental is derived from a specific *hadith* in which the Prophet Mohammed (PBOH) stated that 'one third is big or abundant' and this, combined with the rule of the *khluta* or mixture, leads to the rule of mixing borrowed funds with non-borrowed funds in a company's capital structure. As a result, Islamic scholars conclude that: 'the majority deserves to be treated as the whole thing.'[12] The inconsistency with respect to some ratios is that some scholars have given a temporary approval for the rule of *khulta* to be suspended given the shortage of permissible assets, and receivables or debt elements are periodically allowed to comprise up to 50 per cent. Unfortunately, many bankers believe that this is a permanent condition, and do not realise that as the universe of alternative assets such as *sukuk* or admissible companies increases, the exemption is meant to be revoked.

It is interesting that the basic screening procedure is largely unchanged since the 1980s. Greater acceptance of the new wave of international equity products has been attributed to a number of factors. They include:

- competition between Islamic institutions seeking to gain additional clients and secure market share;
- an increasingly pragmatic approach to international equity investment and stock selection procedures by *Shari'a* advisers. This positive development is largely due to enhanced communication and information flow between scholars and investment executives, some of whom benefit from lengthy previous career positions in the international capital markets; and
- sustained total market growth and escalating demand from an increasingly discerning Islamic investor base and, particularly, private sector clients seeking portfolio investment opportunities.

Islamic indices

Initially, performance of Islamic equity funds tended to be benchmarked against conventional indices such as the Morgan Stanley Capital Index (MSCI) with certain weighting adjustments that were necessitated by the exclusion of *haram* stocks, such as mainstream financials, brewers and distillers and companies with non-conforming financial statements. Some managers considered it inappropriate to measure Islamic portfolios against mainstream alternatives, citing it as being, effectively, a comparison of apples with oranges.

Islamic indices have subsequently been launched. Dow Jones sponsors its own index range with its own *Shari'a* committee. The other is a joint venture by FTSE under the guidance of The International Investor. Managers have been able to acquire commercial licence to these indices, and the information flows available from their promoters and the Dow Jones Islamic Market Indexes have become quite solidly established during the past few years. Some managers prefer to use them solely as an indicator, or reference, for the performance of their universe. Others still compare with mainstream benchmarks as they consider that they are more relevant to the investment objectives of their clients. RHB Unit Trust Management in Malaysia was the first to provide an alternative benchmark for the Malaysian market through the creation of the RHB Islamic Index, based on KLSE main board companies.

The Islamic indices have assisted in defining the *Shari'a* as a systemic and methodical approach to organising money and defining investment parameters. This has been helpful to investment managers and securities regulators in permitting and engaging constructively with Islamic investors and managers.

Fund performance – acknowledging the risks

Amongst the most frequently promoted features of Islamic funds are, quite obviously, *Shari'a* compliance and also the benefits of offering greater diversification for portfolio investment. The issue of liquidity has always been of primary importance to the Islamic investor, and one that has regularly affected final investment and allocation decisions.

Although most of the funds that invest in regulated capital markets do incorporate a regular redemption facility (usually monthly or quarterly), nonetheless, they are suitable only for those with medium to long-term investment horizon years. Their primary purpose is to provide portfolio diversification for investors willing to assume risk on their investment capital. They are not suited to risk-averse investors, with short-term investment horizons or those that prioritise capital preservation.

Fund managers will endeavour to minimise the adverse effects of market volatility through diversification of country risk and industry sectors. In the Islamic fund management industry it has been shown that performance swings are more acute in products with a specialised or narrow focus. In simplistic terms, one assumes potentially higher risk and greater volatility investing in a narrow sector, such as US technology, than when allocating funds to a globally diversified large cap portfolio. If the depth of the technology universe is then further reduced by the *Shari'a* purification process it may feasibly restrict avenues of allocation and increase the risk again.

Numerous regrettable events in the international financial services arena have led to derivatives being perceived as high-risk instruments of speculation and, consequently, the acceptance by *Shari'a* scholars of conventionally recognised hedging techniques is still very limited. Some progress is being made in the application of derivatives to mitigate certain risks in currency and equity exposure and, incidentally, commodity transactions. The concept remains controversial, the use of futures and short positions are widely rejected and not acceptable hedging instruments for Islamic fund managers. The application of stock options, however, does feature in the management of Islamic equity investment products. Chapter 12 goes into detail relating to the challenges of the derivative markets.

Capital-protected equity funds

In the 2000s, the first capital-protected funds were launched for the Islamic marketplace by National Commercial Bank of Saudi Arabia with Deutsche Bank and Shamil Bank in conjunction with Banque Nationale de Paris. Subsequently, such funds have proliferated. In Islamic finance, structures tend not to be entirely uniform and will differ, depending upon *Shari'a* and commercial stipulation. The management strategy of the capital-protected equity funds generally calls for the majority of the funds' assets to be placed in a fixed-term *murabaha* transaction supported with a third-party guarantee issued by an A1/P1-rated institution. The invested amount plus the realised profit on the deferred settlement date will ensure that the fund is able to return all capital invested. A lesser element of the portfolio, perhaps as little as 5 per cent or so, forms an advance payment on a basket of acceptable shares that may be delivered at a mutually agreed forward date for a pre-determined consideration. The investor has the choice of taking the delivery and paying the balancing amount or forgoing the delivery at the expense of his advance payment. Although there is similarity to conventional options, under an Islamic structure the advance payment must form a part of the total purchase price and cannot be paid as a premium outside of the main contract.

There are always lessons to be learned and for the Islamic asset management industry it has been that capital protection, 100 per cent performance participation, and liquidity are very difficult to achieve in one product. This in-built assurance through the Islamic contract of *urboun* is of great comfort to investors but, whilst the structuring innovations have not been widely disclosed, it is accurate to say that the capital protection has been incorporated at the expense of redemption frequency.

Fund of funds

There is certainly ample evidence that the Islamic investment fund universe has been significantly strengthened. The development and origination of new funds has been accelerating, with sponsors keen to address ever more complex and sophisticated opportunities, particularly in the equity investment arena. The fund of funds concept is an interesting one for the Islamic asset management sector. It has already been introduced to Islamic investors through the launch of AlFanar Investment Holdings, sponsored by SEDCO and managed by Permal Asset Management. Mainstream fund of funds managers tend to invest with hedge funds with bidirectional (long/short) strategies. To ensure *Shari'a* compliance Al Fanar selects long-only managers that are willing to adapt their management style to conform to the *Shari'a* stipulations relevant to the product. The objective is to maximise performance and minimise volatility, through asset allocation to proven managers rather than individual securities. Clearly the ability of the sponsor to monitor products and managers closely through avenues of proper disclosure is a critical factor in its implementation.

Despite continued endeavours to design and deliver Islamic hedge funds, this has been a fairly contentious subject for the past couple of years, with sponsors striving to be first to launch a viable, *Shari'a*-compliant product. In October 2004 Permal announced the launch of a US$20 million equity hedge fund with the endorsement of its joint venture partner, SEDCO, and their *Shari'a* advisers. Although an Islamic hedge fund is prohibited from taking short positions in a conventional sense, through the Islamic contract of *salam* it can again make advance payments against forward share purchases.

International private equity

Despite the natural conservatism of Islamic investors, the asset class has begun to develop. The Islamic investment banks have already been innovative, with Arcapita making sizeable cross-border acquisitions in the United States and Europe.

Emerging markets

Direct equity investment opportunities in the Muslim countries have also been discussed at length and a number of organisations are seeking to establish products for Islamic investors. From an Islamic perspective, these focus on the benefits of equity investment in the local economy, the potential for creating new companies and developing industries in the Muslim world and the opportunity to invest in fledgling businesses that are, again, relatively untainted by conventional debt, with little or no leverage.

Most certainly there is a huge requirement for private equity investment, but products must be properly positioned by skilled managers with potential investors that are both knowledgeable and willing to assume the risks of making illiquid investment in fledgling markets in very uncertain global conditions.

For fund managers, the principal difficulties lie in achieving satisfactory diversification in markets that may not be truly open to external investment, and whose credible information flow does little to assist in the preparation of analytical data and research.

Structure, marketing and distribution

The Islamic investment fund market has never been huge and has experienced an element of product crowding here and there, for example in the global equity sector. There are four or five Islamic funds that probably account for over 50 per cent of total assets invested in Islamic equity product, so it is not surprising that quite a few funds have struggled to raise a viable level of assets under management. As a result, promoters try to include additional features to appeal to the target audience and differentiate their product from others. *Shari'a* compliance, competitive performance and client support are all critical elements, but distribution remains the final determinant of success. A substantial number of Islamic investment funds have been delivered by mainstream institutions that have the benefit of both market awareness and large-scale resources.

Conventional banks including BNP Paribas, UBS and Citibank are widely known to possess multi-product Islamic expertise and have shown long-term commitment to the Islamic financial sector and its institutions. UBS, Noriba and Citibank have established Islamic bank subsidiaries in Bahrain; other institutions have rounded businesses of their own, enabling them to enjoy significant participation in the marketplace without incorporating an independent, *Shari'a*-compliant subsidiary. Whichever route is selected, commitment is important because it can be challenging for a conventional organisation to deliver its own, Islamically authenticated fund or financial product. However established the organisation, the issue of credibility usually has to be addressed.

International fund managers have long been involved in managing substantial, specialised portfolios for clients. The top firms have often enjoyed mandates from private and professional investors that provide their own matrix for *Shari'a* adherence. These have greatly broadened client investment opportunities and have also been immensely valuable in developing investor confidence.

The major Arabian commercial banks have, more recently, actively originated new Islamic investment funds. Many have appointed third parties to manage, but others have been able to combine international asset management capability with the strength of their distribution capability in their local market to satisfy client demand.

Alliances

The Islamic institutions have often preferred a joint venture approach, appointing conventional fund managers on the basis of their long-proven ability. The Islamic investment banks have regularly implemented this approach. Benefiting both from substantial shareholders and private clients, they have also recruited experienced executives to identify and monitor appropriate fund managers. Independent *Shari'a* supervisory committees enable them to assume active responsibility for matters of *Shari'a* compliance. Although some Islamic institutions are not, presently, resourced to manage funds in-house, they have developed brands and identities that enable them to deliver products to shareholders and significant, local private clients, and to form regional and international alliances for effective distribution.

In many instances, the alliance has been sealed with the deployment of seed capital by both sponsors. Each gains additional status and offers comfort to prospective investors by becoming a core or lead investor. The global equity fund launched by the Islamic services division of National Commercial Bank, and managed by Wellington Management, has capitalised on a combination of highly rated management expertise, strong brand and excellent distribution network to raise more assets under management than any other Islamic equity fund product.

A number of institutions are seeking to establish independent, Islamic fund management companies and successful, individual product offerings are leading to potential for long-term alliances. Probably the first, cross-market joint venture was Al-Bait, which was jointly financed in the late 1990s by The International Investor and Pictet & Cie. Its Al Dar umbrella fund was listed on the Luxembourg Stock Exchange and the first six product offerings reportedly raised in excess of US$100 million. Each had a different risk/return profile, including three equity products, a real estate and a leasing fund. These products were designed to be offered on a franchise or white-labelled basis to other institutions seeking to distribute Islamic investment funds to their own clients.

Online distribution

An interesting development that emerged alongside the dot.com technology boom was the establishment of several new online distribution ventures that intended to offer *Shari'a*-compliant investment services through the internet. Whilst endeavouring to weather the turbulence in the dot.com technology market, each of these initiatives had to develop its own business. Clearly, any online distributor must work hard to achieve its customer base as well as authorisation by the various international regulators. Simultaneously there is a need to access sufficient volume of diversified, eligible investment product that can be offered on a broad scale to retail investors. Although, ultimately, there will almost certainly be strong demand for online financial services, challenging markets have limited the commercial viability of these initiatives in the short term.

Jurisdiction of registration and regulation

Islamic fund managers have been absolutely resolute in their intention to align to *Shari'a*-compliant investment strategies; initially the only disincentive was the lack of opportunity to diversify. Generally, investors have been able to maintain their exposure to the international capital markets as it has been possible to combine *Shari'a* stipulation with established asset allocation practice.

Sponsors have sought to register and obtain authorisation for their funds in international regulatory jurisdictions including Ireland, the Channel Islands and Luxembourg and the Caribbean jurisdictions. There has also been a certain presentational appeal to listing Islamic funds on international and regional stock exchanges. It has been important to demonstrate to investors that *Shari'a*-compliant products can achieve the endorsement of international regulators. The incorporation of Islamic funds in international jurisdictions has also brought Islamic asset management to the attention of a global audience.

Many investors restrict their investments to securities with a stock exchange listing as they consider that a listed fund is better regulated and liquid. It should be emphasised, however, that listing itself does not provide liquidity for either Islamic or conventional products. Investment liquidity only exists through a genuine, open, secondary market environment.

Disclosure

We will touch briefly on the matter of disclosure, which has been an ongoing issue in the Islamic financial sector as a whole, and nowhere more so than in the area of managed funds. Outside of regulatory requirements, relatively little is revealed by some managers, on a regular basis, about ongoing performance, patterns of funds under management and so on. Part of this is due to the manager's or sponsor's reticence to make public details of a product to which they have committed huge resource and substantial capital outlay. Others feel reluctant to expose themselves to external criticism, whether of performance in volatile markets or, more importantly, of the *Shari'a* stipulations to which they adhere. Whatever the reason, the Islamic asset management sector needs to properly disclose information if it is to progress, and develop the regulatory and investor comfort levels to which it aspires.

Islamic global asset management

Research on the breadth and depth of the Islamic financial sector is only now becoming substantial. Accurate historical figures about the level of investment in *Shari'a*-compliant funds are difficult to access, and then to validate. This is because fund advisers and managers have disclosed information with different levels of regularity and detail. Such variability is the result of both the newness of this market and its concentration in emerging markets. Nonetheless, the market is building an infrastructure replete with standards that bodes well for the future.

A snapshot of market development as of 31 December 2004 (see Exhibit 9.7), shows two of the most powerful trends in the sector. Equity funds have become significant with up to US$6 billion now deployed since 1995; and *sukuk al ijarah* issuances, following GCC standards, have in just a few years equalled the equity fund deployment.

There is little argument that, because of an initial period of accelerated growth, the Islamic fund sector has been overcrowded with global equity product, and a proportion of funds have not raised sufficient assets under management to sustain them. However, others have enjoyed significant success, demonstrating that the right blend of manager, sponsor and founder investor is a winning combination.

Not all Islamic funds have performed well, but some have achieved performance in line with, or better than, both international and Islamic benchmarks. Those with more diversified investment strategies have faired better. Performance swings have, as has been mentioned, been more acute in narrowly focused products.

Exhibit 9.7 **Development of Islamic global asset management, as at 31 December 2004**

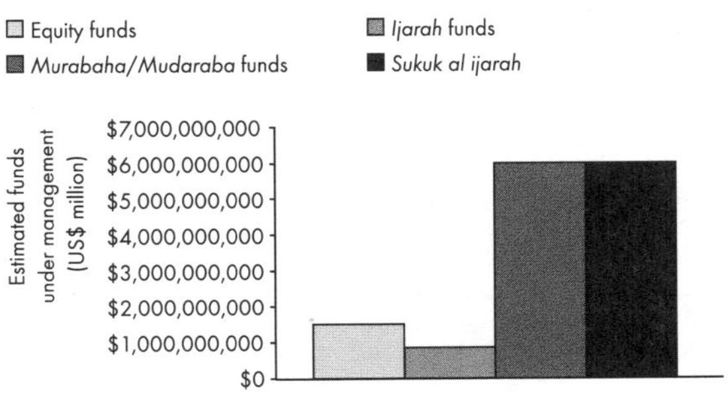

Source: Islamic Banker and AJIF.org, LLC.

Other than equity, approximately US$856 million, or 10 per cent, was invested with the sector's 15 lease-based funds, and a further US$3.94 billion, or 47 per cent, with 26 *murabaha* and *mudaraba* funds with a cash equivalent risk/yield profile. Outside of the international sector,the Malaysian domestic market offered 26 unit trusts aggregating a further US$780 million of client investments.

Apart from the obvious benefits of increasing choice and opportunity for asset diversification, a positive feature of the ever-increasing investment fund universe has been an overall reduction of the sizeable fees sometimes levied by product originators. The heavy management fee (that was initially a feature of most Islamic funds) is likely to have been substituted with a lesser-fixed charge and, in some instances, a bias towards performance-related remuneration.

Addressing the issues

Islamic fund management clients themselves are seeking more than diversified investment opportunities. Investors need to be confident that funds can be redeemed as well as placed, that *Shari'a*-compliant financial instruments are properly structured and transparent. In common with the majority of Islamic investment products, Islamic funds have not typically been rated despite the fact that international rating agencies have indicated their willingness to review this position on a number of occasions. Any concerns have usually been levied at the lack of transparency in investment structure rather than strength and reputation of the relevant sponsor and manager.

Structured finance has again taken the lead and it is encouraging to note that *Shari'a*-compliant bonds issued by the Governments of Malaysia, Bahrain and Qatar have attained internationally accepted ratings. The *sukuk* or bond issue by the Islamic Development Bank was given a AAA rating. This was a first for any Middle Eastern issuer. Such growing transparency is certain to enhance confidence in and growth of the Islamic asset management universe.

Conclusion

Through working closely with both Islamic scholars and regulatory authorities it appears that solutions can be found to the problems that have previously inhibited the development of new investment products, and the choice available to investors is increasing rapidly. The Islamic financial sector is a cautious one and a few fund sponsors have failed to identify the cost and lead-up time required to develop product and subsequently to win the approval of potential investors post launch! Whatever the objective of the product, it requires recognised *Shari'a* authentication and a winning combination of sponsor, manager and back office support. Identifying genuine customer demand is another essential component and sought-after clients are rightly demanding in their expectations, seeking products that are properly structured and managed and realistically priced.

A broad range of asset-based investment opportunities has been considered and increasingly complex asset classes reviewed. The demand for new products and innovations is ever increasing. Islamic financial institutions are still being established and they are continuing to grow in size. But having an enormous capital base is not much use if those assets cannot be managed and invested!

Certainly, the Islamic financial sector is young and is endeavouring to develop expertise that has taken centuries to evolve in mainstream financial practice. However, the momentum must be maintained as it is simply not efficient practice for its largest banks and institutions to be limited to a choice, albeit wide, of privately sponsored products that require separate, detailed review and due diligence. It is critical for Islamic institutions to possess the ability to allocate and redeem funds efficiently, through widely accessible and standardised products, thereby improving the likelihood of deriving profits to be shared with depositors and a good return on capital to shareholders. It is essential for Islamic investors to understand fully the nature of their investment risks and exposures.

The private sector investment fund products have been crucial to the development of the market and will surely continue to play a pivotal role in offering portfolio diversification opportunities. Nobody expects these initiatives to substitute the ease and comfort that is derived from recourse to standardised market practice, but the innovation and development of a broad range of *Shari'a*-compliant investment funds has created a wide-ranging, asset-based platform from which to support the market-building process.

---

[1] Based on the Stella Cox's presentation at Euromoney's 3rd Annual Islamic Finance Summit Pre-Conference Workshop: 'An Introduction to Islamic Banking, Finance And Investment Management', January 2003 and adapting various speeches, writings and presentations on this topic.

[2] Elgari, Dr Mohamed, unpublished interview by Omar Fisher for *The American Journal of Islamic Finance* on 24 January 1997.

[3] Usmani, M.T., *An Introduction to Islamic Finance*, (Karachi: Idaratul Ma'arif, 1998), p. 216 and p. 218.

[4] Usmani, Muhammad Imran Ashraf, *Meezan Bank's Guide to Islamic Banking* (Karachi: Darul Ishaat, 2002), pp. 219, 220. Also see Usmani, M.T., *An Introduction to Islamic Finance*, *op. cit.*, p. 215.

[5] Usmani, M.I.A., *op. cit.*, p. 219. Also Usmani, M.T., *op. cit.* p. 214.

[6] Usmani, M.T., *op. cit.*, pp. 205, 206.

[7] Siddiqi, Abdul Hamid, tr. Sahih Muslim, Vol. III (Lahore: Sh. Muhammad Ashraf, 1992), p. 830. Also see Khan, Dr Muhammad Muhsin, tr., Sahih Al-Bukhari, Vol. III (Beirut: Dar Al Arabia, undated), p. 233-6 and 241.

[8] Elgari, Dr Mohamed, unpublished interview with Omar Fisher for *The American Journal of Islamic Finance* on 24 January 1997.

[9] Usmani, M.T., *An Introduction to Islamic Finance*, *op. cit.*, pp. 210, 211.

[10] Iqbal, Munawar, 'Wealth Creation: An Islamic Perspective', presented at a seminar on wealth creation at Durham University, July 2003.

[11] Usmani, M.I.A., *op. cit.*, pp. 211, 212.

[12] Ibid, p. 214, 215. Also see Usmani, M.T., *op. cit.*, pp. 208, 209.

10 Opportunities with *sukuk* and securitisations[1]

Abdulkader Thomas, with appreciation to Mohammad Asaria and Tamara Box

Sukuk – legal structure

Sukuk (plural of *sakk*) are frequently referred to as 'Islamic bonds' but a more accurate translation of the Arabic word would be 'Islamic investment certificates'. The distinction being that, at its simplest, a bond is a contractual debt obligation whereby the issuer is contractually obliged to pay to bond holders, on certain specified dates, interest and principal. In comparison, under a *sukuk* structure the *sukuk* holders each hold an undivided beneficial ownership in the underlying assets (the '*sukuk* assets'). Consequently, *sukuk* holders are entitled to share in the revenues generated by the *sukuk* assets as well as being entitled to share in the proceeds of the realisation of the *sukuk* assets. The legal structure and format of *sukuk* certificates may be considered analogous to US trust certificates and *sukuk* certificates may be listed and rated. Under modern Islamic jurisprudence, investors may receive periodic payments under a *sukuk* issue that are benchmarked to Libor. Hence *sukuk* certificates are frequently priced using identical pricing technology as conventional Eurobonds.

To date, the majority of *sukuk* issues are full originator recourse structures and are structured around the *sukuk al ijarah* concept, illustrated in Exhibit 10.1.

The market trend is for *sukuk* issues to be more highly structured. An example is the US$200 million DMCC (Dubai Metals and Commodity Centre) *sukuk*, which was arranged jointly by Dubai Islamic Bank and Standard Bank. In this transaction, *sukuk* holders were able to elect to receive the periodic payments payable under the *sukuk* certificates in either cash or gold bullion. This transaction was

Exhibit 10.1 ***Sukuk al ijarah* structure**

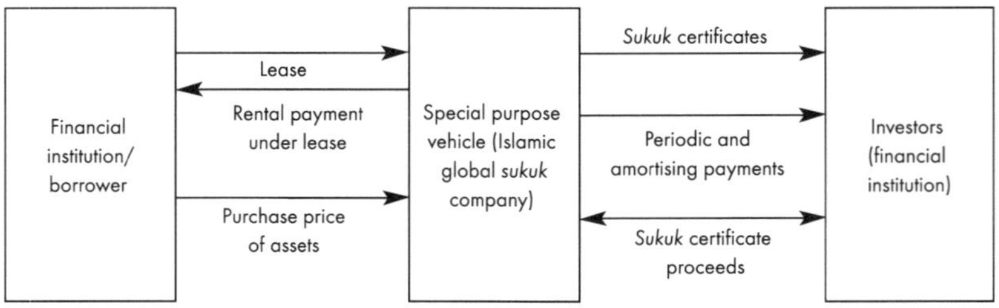

Source: 'Sharia'a, Sukuk and Securitisation', Lovells, September 2004.

also one of the first public *sukuk* issues emanating from the Middle East to be structured around *musharaka* principles.

The Emirates Airlines *sukuk*, issued in 1995, was structured around similar principles.

Emirates transaction

The structure of the Emirates transaction is illustrated in Exhibit 10A. *Musharaka* at its simplest may be described as an Islamic partnership. One party (the originator) makes a contribution in kind (be it expertise or some other form of tangible asset) and the other party (the investors) contributes the capital required for the venture. Although, by its very name *musharaka* implies some form of equity participation, in actual fact the risk profile of these certificates are similar to fixed-income investments.

Exhibit 10.A **Structure of the Emirates transaction**

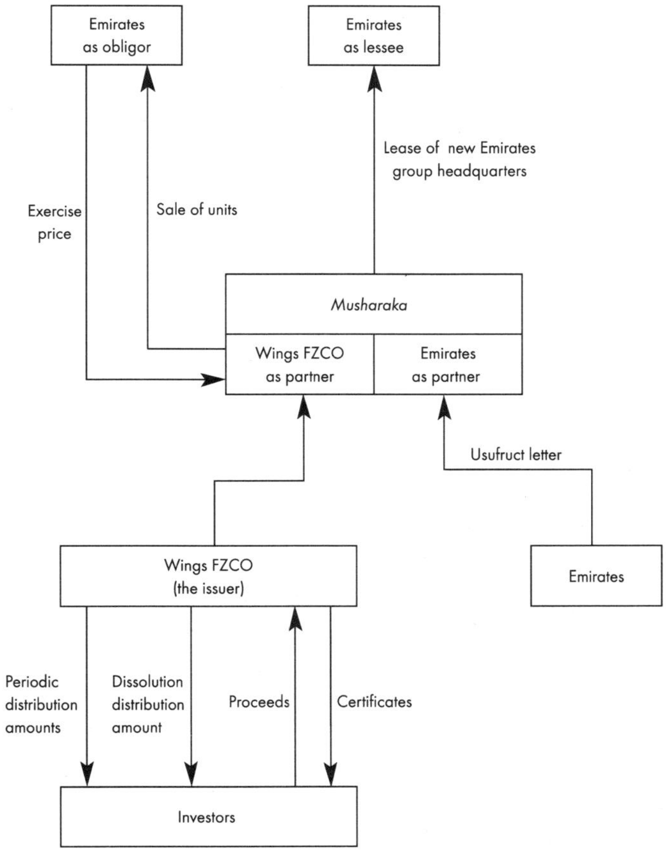

Source: Wings FZCO Offering Circular.

- Emirates and the issuer of the *sukuk* certificates, Wings FZCO, entered into a *musharaka* whereby both Emirates and Wings had undivided ownership of the *musharaka* assets (which on the closing date were the capital contributions raised from the issue of *sukuk* and the contribution in kind of the relevant piece of real estate from Emirates [as evidenced by the usufruct letter]).
- At all times after the closing date the *musharaka* assets were taken to constitute all revenues and assets acquired from the application of the *musharaka* capital (ie, rental income generated from the development of this piece of real estate).
- On entry into the *musharaka* agreement, Emirates and Wings entered into an agreement detailing how revenue would be distributed.
- On the issue date of the *sukuk* certificates, Emirates and Wings' participation in the *musharaka* is represented by a specific number of units. During the life of the transaction, Emirates is obliged to purchase units from the issue which reflects the amortisation schedule of the *sukuk* certificates.

From a *Shari'a* perspective, the rationale for incorporating the *musharaka* structure is that the *sukuk* certificates that are issued may be freely tradeable in the secondary market prior to the real estate being fully developed, and being able to be traded which may not necessarily be the case in the traditional *istisna'a/ijarah sukuk* real estate development structure.

In the structures above, the *sukuk* holders have had recourse against the originator. As the financial infrastructure and education in the industry increases and pools of assets that are suitable for securitisation develop (such as consumer finance assets), market participants are looking to structure non-collateralised, non-recourse, *Shari'a*-compliant securitisation transactions.

Sukuk securitisation

Shari'a-compliant securitisation structures

Unlike the conventional securitisation markets – which may securitise all forms of debt receivables, future flow transactions, and other non-asset-linked or whole business flows – Islamic securitisation will require a higher connectivity to the underlying asset and operating business. This relates, in part, to the fact that such transactions violate the Islamic restrictions on *riba*.

Even though the tools are distinctive, the process to achieve an Islamic securitisation is virtually identical to any conventional asset-backed securitisation:[2]

- mandate the arranger and set up the deal team;
- analyse the portfolio; historical data, price and repayment factors;
- issue the term sheet summarising the deal, describing the client, legal structure, cash flow, historical features and hedging, if present;

Exhibit 10.2 **Conventional skeleton securitisation structure**

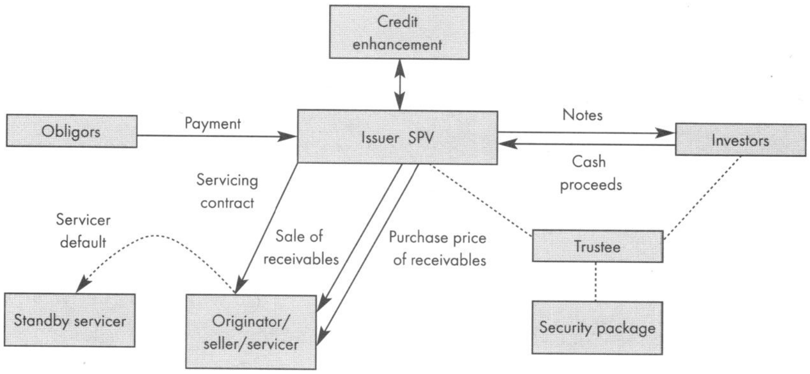

Source: Lovells.

Exhibit 10.3 ***Shari'a*-compliant skeleton securitisation structure**

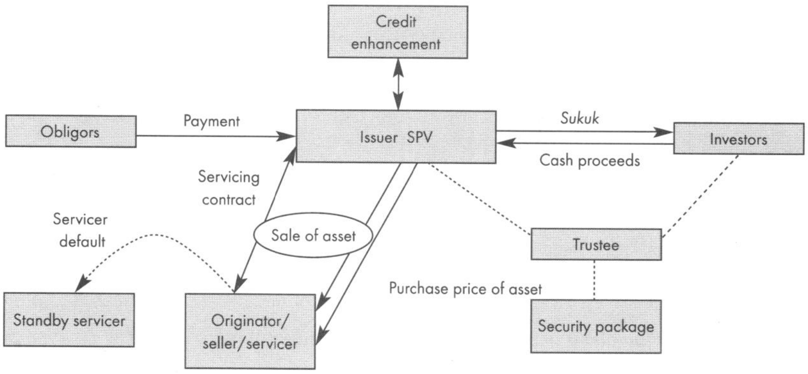

Source: Lovells.

- document the deal;
- accounting approval of off-balance sheet treatment, true sale;
- servicing analysis;
- rating;
- credit approval;
- finalise the sign-off;
- marketing – write the offering memorandum; and
- close the deal.

Exhibit 10.2 illustrates a conventional securitisation, the steps of which will be familiar to readers, and Exhibit 10.3, the base structure of an Islamic securitisation.

Asset backing and liability

A key principle of Islamic finance is that financing schemes should be asset-backed. In a *Shari'a*-compliant securitisation structure, some degree of ownership in the underlying assets should be transferred to the issuer, rather than a mere assignment of the cash flows as permitted under a conventional securitisation.

A transfer of absolute registered title in the underlying assets is not necessary as this would prohibit securitisations of Middle East assets. This is because legislation in a number of Middle East countries prohibits non-resident entities from purchasing or leasing certain locally domiciled assets and local entities from issuing debt securities. The transfer to the issuer (from the originator) of a collection of 'rights akin to ownership' that allows the issuer to participate in the revenues generated by the underlying assets is sufficient to satisfy the constraints of *Shari'a*, provided that the *Shari'a* scholars are satisfied that the risk and reward associated with the *sukuk* assets is vested with the issuer of the *sukuk* certificates. Alternatively, the *fatwa* may be qualified and state that the *sukuk* certificates may not be traded in the secondary market at a premium or discount to their face value.

When considering a *Shari'a* mortgage securitisation, an unqualified *fatwa* permitting the *sukuk* certificates to be freely traded in the secondary market will only be obtained provided the underlying mortgage pool comprises at least 51 per cent of *ijarah* mortgages (the typical Islamic mortgage structure), and up to a maximum of 49 per cent *istisna'a* mortgages (mortgages over properties that are being constructed). The rationale for this prohibition is that the *Shari'a* scholars classify *istisna'a* mortgages as merely receivables.

Credit enhancement

Shari'a-compliant securitisation structures may incorporate credit enhancement techniques providing that the underlying assets are not recharacterised. First-loss accounts, non-interest bearing liquidity facilities (although these may be structured as *murabaha* arrangements so that the finance provider may realise a profit on such facility), over-collateralisation and, arguably, tranching, may be incorporated into a *Shari'a*-compliant securitisation structure. As more issuers seek to tap the market this is an area that will clearly develop.

Securitisation's potential

As of late 2005, only a handful of true Islamic securitisations have come to the market, but this is a rapidly expanding structure. The *Shari'a*-compliant consumer finance market (including residential mortgages) across the GCC region and western Europe is growing at an aggressive pace. In addition, for some Arab States export-finance securitisations of oil and petrochemical receivables provide a potential pool of assets to securitise. The Global Oil case study, below, provides a good example of this.

Structures previously considered not compliant with *Shari'a*, for example future flow securitisation transactions, are being reconsidered by *Shari'a* scholars. Traditionally these had been rejected, as it was felt by scholars that there was insufficient certainty as to the regularity of the payment streams and that assets backing these transactions were not 'real assets'. Market participants are investing time and resources in an attempt to modify the structure of traditional future flow securitisation transactions so that they may comply with *Shari'a*. If these discussions yield a positive outcome, this is a sector with enormous growth potential – airline ticket and toll road revenues may all be securitised in a *Shari'a*-compliant manner.

Receivables securitisation

Case study: securitised *murabaha* for Global Oil – Malaysia[3]

In 1989, Global Oil Corp. (60 per cent), a major Japanese contracting company (20 per cent), Malaysia's national oil company (10 per cent) and the local government (10 per cent) formed a joint venture to construct Middle Distillate Synthesis plant to produce diesel, kerosene, naphta and wax. The RM1.9 billion plant was to come on line in 1993. The financing was funded from three distinct sources.

1. An equity injection of RM1.275 billion from the shareholders (up to RM475 million was raised by Global Oil internally.
2. RM500 million conventional fixed-rate debt arranged by a major local conventional bank.
3. RM125 million Islamic debt syndicated by Local Islamic Bank (LIB).

Global oil's decision basis

The project proved an economic success for Global Oil and it was keen to expand its funding base in Malaysia and was open to overtures to structure a portion of the Sarawak plant finance according to *Shari'a*. Global Oil instructed its primary advisers to carve out an asset universe for the proposed syndication in order to facilitate the local variant of long-term sales contract or *murabaha* called *bai' bithamin ajil*. The syndicate purchased specific equipment and building materials for the Sarawak plant. These were then sold to Global Oil for a specific mark-up under an Islamic deferred payment scheme. The universe of assets was divided into a RM50 million group with the deferred payment contract terminating in eight years and a RM175 million group due in five years.

The structure of payments for deferred sale or *bai' bithaman ajil* may be analysed from the point of view of gross amount over extended period to determine yield. For the five-year tranche, Global Oil's mark-up translated into a 7.5 per cent annual return to LIB. For the eight-year portion, the yield was 7.75 per cent. At the time, the pricing was competitive when compared with yields obtainable in the local Malaysian market.

Although LIB and its Islamic insurance subsidiary Local Syarikat Takaful invested RM30 million, they could not prudently take down the full amount. Therefore, LIB invited Tabung Haji,[4] a major Japanese bank, the national oil company pension, as well as several local banks and companies to participate in the syndication. The originally planned syndicate was for RM100 million, but it was oversubscribed and the final agreement was for RM125 million. A landmark for this deal was that it was the first corporate syndication to or from Islamic structures (outside of syndicated commodities sales). Although a few European banks had participated in the commodity syndications, this was the first major transaction to serve a major multinational industrial company as client and include a major Japanese bank.

This transaction was not simply syndicated: the ultimate receivables were securitised. LIB applied the concept of *bai' al-dayn*, which is uniquely permissible in the Malaysian context. This entails the trading or discounting of trading promissory notes. In essence, LIB, on behalf of the syndicate, would sell Global Oil's debt in the domestic Malaysian secondary market to institutional and individual investors.[5] The result is an Islamically permissible instrument that is similar to a corporate bond. What makes the traded debt distinct is that it is like a revenue bond based upon a true underlying transaction in which goods or services are traded and a commercial risk is realised. In other words, the Malaysian practice would not admit of general obligation, general purpose or other unsecured working capital bonds.

Rating and market acceptance

The Global Oil transaction was a landmark. Following the first Global Oil issuance, Bank Negara and the Securities Commission unrolled an aggressive Islamic finance framework. This brought depth to the instrument choice and the local private debt securities (PDS) market, notably for Islamic instruments, gained prominence and preference among local institutions and companies following the 1997 Asian financial crisis. Total funds raised through the Islamic debt securities in Malaysia, as at 31 August 2000, stood at RM6.1 billion or 40 per cent of the total funds raised in the financial system. This increased to 64 per cent of new issuances by 31 August 2004. This success rested on the growing universe of Islamic instruments and funds willing to purchase them in order to diversify their portfolios.

Outcome

The importance of the initial transaction was threefold. Foremost, LIB demonstrated the depth of its corporate finance skills and its ability to innovate to meet the needs of a major multinational corporation. Secondly, although one may presume that Bank Negara encouraged Global Oil to pursue the deal, Global Oil did so enthusiastically, facilitating whenever possible. Finally, this transaction, applying a modernised approach to classical Islamic tools, succeeded in bringing Muslims, Japanese and Europeans into a single modern corporate finance deal whilst creating a tradeable security. As a result, this transaction set the stage for Islamic institutions to broaden their clientele and market role. The chairman of Global Oil's Malaysian subsidiary noted: 'The securitisation of payments under an Islamic purchase and sales agreement makes Islamic financing an exciting and viable alternative to other ways of raising investment capital.' The broader Malaysian framework of 'Islamic debt' financing took off, based on the initial *bai' bithamin ajil* deal.

Rating *Shari'a* securitisations[6]

Criteria

Rating agencies will not per se apply a different ratings criteria to an instrument just because it is *Shari'a* compliant. Since 2002, the ratings agencies have begun to integrate *sukuk* into their analytical frameworks. The main approach to determining the strength of an issuance is the same as for traditional transactions, including:

- the financial position of the issuer;
- the liquidity position of the issuer or the underlying assets;
- whether or not any hedging of specific underlying risks has been put into place;
- if the issuer is a financial institution, its capital adequacy;
- the response of the assets or issuer to stress tests; and
- if it is an asset-backed portfolio: the portfolio's uniformity, measurements, characteristics, and response to stress tests.

In order to appeal to a global investor base and secure a diverse universe of investors with distinct domiciles and broad asset diversification goals, the Islamic investment banking business must engage the ratings agencies. Such interaction is critical for the long-term evolution of the *sukuk* markets.

The rating agencies' analysis will take into account the specific nuances of the legal regime in which the *sukuk* assets are located, and there have been some concerns about the legal precedents in some Muslim countries, such as Saudi Arabia.[7]

Historical data

As Islamic markets are new, the risks will be perceived to be above average. As *sukuk* are predominately asset-backed bonds, using ratings in their true function as credit risk analyses is critical. Asset-backed bonds are distinct in the conventional market since the bond maturity and underlying pool performance may vary from an underwriter's assumptions. This could cause a significant difference between *expected* and *final* maturity. These precise distinctions apply to Islamic pools as well. *Sukuk* are fundamentally asset based, connecting directly to the assets and not simply the cash flows.[8] In some cases, over-collateralisation may also be used as a tool to manage reinvestment risk due to early redemption, as was the case in the Auto Leasing Hanco case in Chapter 5.

Rating agencies look to historical data relating to the performance of the underlying assets. Default analysis is a core element of the historical analysis. The *ijarah* MALT™[9] securitisation case, described below, illustrates the issues raised by investment bankers and ratings agencies in learning about the new Islamic asset structures. As we see in the closing case of the Qatar global *sukuk*, the absence of specific rules in some Islamic sovereign markets makes assessment of risks a major challenge. Even in the case of the *ijarah* MALT™, some investors felt concerned about the SPV structure.

Rating risk

The *ijarah* MALT™ and Qatar cases illustrate the problem of rating risk: pre-payment risk, reinvestment risk, and repricing risk.[10] To date, all Islamic *sukuk* have been priced off conventional interest indices. For instance, the *ijarah* MALT™ case deals with transactions priced off the 10-year US treasury note. The Qatar case is priced off Libor. In the *ribawi* capital markets, mortgage-backed bonds are approximately 25 per cent of the total asset-backed bond markets (up from 15 per cent in 2001).[11] Since Islamic alternatives to conventional mortgages are priced off the same indices, there may be a risk of convexity as with conventional mortgage-backed securities (MBS): when market rates fall, underlying obligors will replace their existing obligations with more attractive ones, putting pressure on investors to replace the mortgage instruments with dissimilar securities bidding down the yields on those same securities, even though the market as a whole may be undergoing a rising rate trend. The paucity of Islamic MALT™ issues probably mitigates this risk in the short term.

Historical data and rating risk

Case study: *ijarah* MALT™ securitisation

When considering the elements of asset acquisition and evaluation, more historical data for either a class or a specific pool leads to better, finer pricing and higher rating. Less history means wider spreads to comparable pools, which would influence Boutique Investment Bank's (BIB) offer to Michigan Bank for MALT™.

The Michigan Bank pool comprised an average level of asset leverage of the portfolio of 83 per cent: 65 per cent of the portfolio was leveraged more than 80 per cent and the 35 per cent was leveraged well under 80 per cent, skewing the average. The highly leveraged segment enjoyed 25 per cent first loss insurance purchased by Michigan Bank from Global Risk Insurance (GRI). Therefore, the high leverage was mitigated by built-in enhancement.

The US mortgage market allows a variety of low document and no document approvals based on consumer credit scores or downpayments. The Michigan Bank pool was a full document pool meaning that strict underwriting was performed on every deal with full consumer documentation obtained to verify credit quality. The methods of consumer and property underwriting were standard and conformed to market practices. The portfolio also documented total credit exposure of Michigan Bank to each consumer, supplementing the bank's existing proof of total consumer credit access based on stringent full document underwriting.

BIB priced the pool at 93 instead of par or a premium, arguing that the consumer pricing was below market for 'non-standard' transactions utilising SPVs. BIB's pricing did not account for a number of critical underwriting risks, including the risk of rising consumer interest rates. Although none of the Michigan Bank transactions was delinquent, indeed, certain transactions were pre-paid up to six months in advance, BIB worried that, since their introduction in the US banking market in 1996, no Islamic transactions had been tested in court. Therefore, there was no final proof of whether any Islamic mortgage alternative transaction was enforceable.

In the midst of the BIB offer, two distinct insurance issues arose. First, a consumer elected to secure casualty insurance independently of the bank. Could the consumer actually secure a traditional homeowner's coverage? All of Michigan Bank's consumers had done so, but one underwriter denied that local law and practice permitted it. Therefore, the portfolio coverage had to be changed to protect from asset loss. Second, the title insurance was an owner's policy with some parties using lender's policies and some using direct consumer endorsements. BIB objected and the portfolio was rewritten with an owner's policy and leasehold endorsement.

This left BIB's final concern that the portfolio had above-average risk, thereby mandating below-average pricing. But, BIB did not accept for the purchase by Michigan Bank of portfolio level insurance from GRI for an additional 25 basis points. One reason for this decision may have been an undisclosed choice by BIB to create a first loss provision and hold the excess cash in its own account for its own benefit.

Liquidity

The ratings agencies have some difficulty evaluating liquidity with *sukuk*. The vast majority of *sukuk* are held and not traded, therefore, the risks are less well understood with respect to price volatility and pricing efficiency. Typically, ratings agencies look at the depth of the secondary market, yet the *sukuk* markets do not yet have any secondary trading depth outside of Malaysia.

Shari'a risk

The universe of supervisory risks typically associated with securities issuances include accounting, regulatory, and compliance risks. *Shari'a* risk is not taken into account by the key western ratings agencies. Failure to comply properly with regional *Shari'a* standards may result in a pool, deal or instrument being deemed impermissible, and it is therefore most properly a part of regulatory risk.[13]

Rating a sovereign ijarah *transaction*

Beginning with Malaysia's June 2002 US$600 million global *sukuk*, there has been a string of sovereign *sukuk* offerings, including:

- two Kingdom of Bahrain issuances in late 2002;
- the Islamic Development Bank US$400 million offering of August 2003; and
- Qatar in September 2003.

These and subsequent corporate issuances were rated by Standard & Poor's, Moody's and Fitch Ratings in addition to other agencies.

In specific sovereign *sukuk* cases, the agencies are prepared to issue ratings which may be higher than those of the lessee, corporate issuer, or sovereign subject to specific mitigants. Likewise, when there are material government risks, as in specific jurisdictions, then the rating may be less than the lessee's rating. For most agencies, the key guidelines require a thorough analysis of lease and acquisition payment obligations in order to ensure that they have the same credit quality as the lessee's conventional debt obligations.

Beyond ownership structures, the agencies will look to servicing issues. These, in turn, bring the analyst back to the primary question of whether or not cash flows are sufficient to govern payment.

Finally, with sovereign issuers, the agencies will look to whether it is committed to *sukuk* at the same level as conventional debt, or more. In the case of Qatar, the government agreed to strong covenants which are more common with unsecured international sovereign bonds and included retaining the State's credit rating, continuing membership in the International Monetary Fund, and other actions which speak to the maintenance of a good credit history and rating, but are not specific to the transaction. The Qatar *sukuk* have an irrevocable undertaking of Qatar to purchase the parcel at term or under specific events of default or dissolution of the trust. This confirms both the commitment of Qatar to support the growing Islamic finance field as well as the critical nature of the asset, at least for national prestige. The country has put its entire long-term credit access on the line to support this transaction.

Legal and regulatory issues with *Shari'a*-compliant securitisations

In the sophisticated capital markets, the decoupling of asset credit risk from the issuer's credit risk requires a true sale. A true sale is necessarily subject to specific warranties, which if breached would allow an asset put back. Within large markets such as the United States, this may be relatively straightforward, but it is not where transactions cross multiple borders. Novation is less well understood, even not permitted in many emerging markets, in contrast to UK and US law which allow the substitution of creditors by the novation of contract rights and obligations with the consent of all parties. Novation best fits with transferring assets in securitisations.

For a successful securitisation, assignment must be absolute and with notice to the debtor. Equitable assignment, in which there is no notice and partial transfer, is common with whole business securitisations and large unit transfers. Neither of these are well established in emerging markets. The method of assignment pursued in some jurisdictions is to transfer the assets in equity to avoid stamp and transfer taxes.

When security is granted, there is a difference between floating and fixed charges; and charges which cover all assets and those which cover specific assets. The former has less priority in bankruptcy. Securitisation – Islamic and conventional – hinges on achieving a true sale of the assets. But, if the sale is recharacterised as a loan or a fixed charge is recharacterised as floating, the nature of the transaction may be completely changed with the rights of the investors jeopardised. The risk of recharacterisation may be significant since some transaction organisers try to arbitrage closely the differences between loans and asset sales.

Tax and accounting issues

The selection of the jurisdiction governing the SPV will determine the tax position: tax neutral, taxable or limited taxes. Securitisation is most affected by the following taxes:

- withholding taxes on dividends or interest;
- transfer taxes on the asset sales;
- SPV-level corporate taxes;
- withholding taxes on SPV-issued securities;
- VAT on SPV fees due;[14] and
- taxes on any hedges.

The choice of jurisdictions will influence a large number of underlying structuring decisions, which in turn drive the end-investor's profit extraction issues. The tax treaty countries often have rules structured to give interest payments preferential treatment, leading to structuring arbitrage between loan and sale; resulting in decisions that prefer either whole loan sales or partial assignments as forms of tax management.

Ultimately, these decisions are driven by accounting. National standards such as UK GAAP, US GAAP, and MASB govern national transactions. AAOIFI and IASB are best practices, but not obligations. Accounting treatment may take three paths:

- separate presentation – measurable and connected, with the originator retaining significant benefits;
- derecognition – no ongoing significant connection to originator; and
- linked – originator has significant benefits, but limited risk exposure.

Each method has a specific possible outcome. For instance, issue credit guarantees could end delinkage. And, the termination of delinkage may have substantial tax impacts depending upon the jurisdiction.

Jurisdiction and trustee issues

Jurisdiction is prospectively a huge issue since trust law is particularly a creature of the English common law and the other laws that have evolved from it (US, Malaysia, Australia and so on). In contrast, countries applying the Napoleonic code or adaptations thereof, including most of the GCC states, lack a true trust law or regulation, creating a major challenge for securitisation, both conventional and Islamic. Thus, *sukuk* issuances by Qatar, Caravan I and Saxony-Anhalt (Germany) have all required an awkward structure whereby the asset must be transferred out of a state lacking trust laws to a state with a suitable trust law infrastructure.

The fundamental concept of trust is that ownership may be segregated into two classes: legal and beneficial. The former has title; the latter merely has some of the benefits that would normally be associated with legal ownership.[15] The rights of a legal owner cannot be restricted by general operation of law. Trust law therefore is exceptionally complicated. The concept of legal and beneficial ownership is recognised in *Shari'a*, and Islamic jurists have found that trust structures make *sukuk*-like bond issuances more efficient.

If a trust is chosen, there is a difference between a note trustee, who manages the payments, and the security trustee who controls the tool of enforcement. The trustee's role with regard to the issuer is to ensure compliance, which may be seconded to an independent servicer. In troubled times, trustees are meant to protect investors and ensure promptness of either collection or enforcement.

Separate from the trustee, or hired by the trustee, there are a number of critical parties who facilitate *sukuk* and bond issuances:

- paying agent or servicer: provides administrative support to the issuer to pay;
- common depository: for Eurobonds, Euroclear and Clearstream are the most frequent choices to hold the instruments;
- custodian: holds the collateral on behalf of the investors; ensures settlement is executed correctly; maintains a clearing account; and provides corporate information and execution of corporate actions such as payments; collections and tax claims;
- listing agent: applicable for exchange-listed transactions;
- back-up servicer: supports primary in event of servicing failure or default; and
- cash manager and bank account.

Shari'a securitisation opportunities

United Arab Emirates

The real estate market in the UAE (particularly in Dubai) has grown at one of the fastest rates across the world over the last couple of years. A securitisation transaction was arranged by Barclays Capital in 2005 backed by payments under real estate finance arrangements and long-term leases in respect of properties located on one of the Dubai Palm developments. Although this transaction was fully collateralised it was aimed to kick-start the market. Once investors and market participants become comfortable with local laws there is nothing to prevent true securitisations emanating from this jurisdiction in the near future. With the current trend in Dubai to convert existing conventional residential mortgages into *Shari'a*-compliant mortgages, it is thought by many commentators that a true *Shari'a* securitisation of this asset class will emanate from the UAE in the near future.

Kuwait

Attempts have been made to structure a securitisation transaction in respect of Kuwaiti assets. So far the Kuwaiti regulator has distinguished between conventional assets securitised as *sanacat* and securitisable Islamic assets deemed *sukuk*. The former have specific rules, but the latter were, as at mid-2005, the subject of as yet uncompleted rule-making at the central bank of Kuwait. Privately placed *sukuk* issuances have been allowed with tight restrictions pending the formalisation of *sukuk* rules. There is huge potential in this market and it is likely that some of the first public securitisation transactions that will emanate from Kuwait will either be linked to commercial property or auto-finance contracts.

Qatar

Qatar has seen tremendous growth in its Islamic finance industry and a large amount of Islamic capital has flowed into Qatar. The majority of these funds have been invested in *Shari'a*-compliant project finance transactions (mainly in the oil and gas sector). The funding provided by both Islamic and conventional banks for these transactions will likely require refinancing (these transactions by virtue of their sheer size are a significant drain on bank liquidity) and may be refinanced through a *Shari'a*-compliant securitisation.

Indonesia

Islamic financing is taking root in this market and the first cross-border Islamic financing transaction was structured in 2005, for Pertamina (the state oil and gas company). Judging by the rapid development of the Islamic consumer finance industry (auto-finance and micro-finance in particular) in Indonesia, and the vast natural reserves that exist in Indonesia, it is far from a remote possibly that a *Shari'a* securitisation of either of these two asset classes may be completed in the near future.

Malaysia

Arguably the most active Islamic finance market in the world is Malaysia. Malaysian Islamic bankers have spent significant resources developing the Islamic capital markets. In 2005, Time Engineering Bhd. issued a RM556 million (US$150 million) five-tranche *Shari'a*-compliant securitisation. This offering was considered a true securitisation under Malaysian guidelines and is backed by payments due from the Malaysian government to the originator under contracts to supply teaching equipment and training to state schools. In addition, CAMAGAS (a Malaysian government-controlled secondary mortgage company) launched a *Shari'a*-compliant mortgage securitisation that was arranged by HSBC Amanah. These transactions are not in isolation and are part of a cogent plan for the expansion of Islamic financial transacting within the local and regional markets.

In the early phase of the development of the Islamic capital markets it was thought that certain Islamic financing techniques considered permissible by the Malaysian *Shari'a* scholars would not be acceptable to the Middle East scholars (Islamic jurisprudence is divided into four main schools of thought and the school of thought that is prevalent in the Middle East differs from that in Malaysia). However, recently there seems to be a convergence of opinions between the Malaysian and Middle East *Shari'a* scholars regarding certain concepts such as *ijarah* that are particularly relevant for the further development of the Islamic capital markets. It is hoped that the growth of the Malaysian *Shari'a*-compliant securitisation market will catalyse the growth of the Middle East market.

Continental Europe, the United Kingdom and the United States

There is no reason why an Islamic securitisation may not be structured utilising assets in a non-Islamic country. In fact, the attention of Islamic investors and conventional investment banks is being focused on such jurisdictions – especially in the field of commercial real estate. If the underlying leases/transaction arrangements are structured in accordance with *Shari'a* (to do so should not be a considered a major departure from conventional practice) a *Shari'a* securitisation may be structured with little difficulty over such assets. For example, in 2004 US government-regulated mortgage funder Freddie Mac securitised US$200 million of certificates relating to residential transactions applying the declining-balance partnership method. Judging by the affinity that Middle East investors have for European and US real estate it is likely that there will be significant demand for such securities. Bearing in mind the overall demand for *sukuk* certificates, there is a possibility that these instruments may provide a more competitive cost of funding than similar conventional instruments. This will certainly be a growing area in the near future.

Conclusions and challenges for *sukuk* and Islamic securitisations

Increasingly *sukuk* linked to assets based in the United Kingdom, Continental Europe and the United States are being structured as Islamic investors wish to include securities with these risk profiles in their portfolios. In addition, non-Islamic issuers are seeking to take advantage of the increased liquidity that is currently being enjoyed in the Islamic world. A clear example of this trend was seen when the German Federal State of Saxony-Anhalt issued a US$100 million *sukuk* in 2004. The regional finance minister stated that the rationale for issuing a *Shari'a*-compliant instrument was twofold:

> 'On the one hand [for] economic reasons. There are investors out there and it makes sense to provide them with a product. On the other hand it is a matter of international courtesy. We want to send out a message of respect for other cultures that have different regulations on investing.'

The demographics of investors in *sukuk* certificates are varied with non-Islamic investors increasingly participating in these instruments. For example, in a 2005 *sukuk* issue, 48 per cent of the issue was subscribed for by conventional investors, of which 11 per cent were fund managers, 24 per cent were institutional investors and 13 per cent were central banks and government institutions. It appears that Middle East credit risk seems to have become more appealing for European investors.

The greatest challenges to securitisation in the Islamic markets include limited enabling legislation, restrictions on foreign ownership of assets and enterprises, limited enabling infrastructure such as SPVs and trusts being permitted and methods for setting these up or allowing them to cross borders. As with standard securitisations, homogeneity of assets and stable cash flows make for the most successful issuance.

For banks, there is always a regulatory-induced impetus to securitise if local law allows it. A flat 8 per cent charge on private sector claims under Basel I gives banks an incentive to move high-quality assets off their balance sheets, a form of capital arbitrage, through securitisation. That leaves banks with lower-quality assets and no fundamental reason to re-evaluate their operational complexity.[16] This is true whether one is dealing with an Islamic bank or a conventional bank. Basel II eliminates this one-size-fits-all element, but does not reduce the drive to monetise assets and disperse risk through securitisation.

---

1 For a more in-depth look at *sukuk*, see Adam, Natif J., and Abdulkader Thomas *Islamic Bonds: Your Guide to Issuing, Structuring and Investing in Sukuk* (London: Euromoney Books, 2004).

2 Husain, Syed Tariq, 'Securitisation' at The International Islamic Finance Forum, Dubai, 17–19 March 2002.

3 Based on 'Al-Bai Bithaman Aill: Deferred Payment Financing in Al-Islam: The Shell Oil, Bank Islam Transaction' and 'Interview: Dato Abdul Halim Ismail, Managing Director of Bank Islam Malaysia' from *The American Journal of Islamic Finance* (vol. I, no. 2, Dhul Qada 1411).

4 The trust fund and savings programme for Malaysians seeking to make their required pilgrimage to Mecca.

5 A special permission of Bank Negara, the central bank was obtained for this purpose. Malaysian scholars have permitted this practice based upon their interpretation of certain rulings during the evolution of classical Islamic law. The consensus of scholars outside of Malaysia is that the underlying rulings were ultimately overruled. The concept does not include discounting according to a fixed rate of interest. But, it may include a negotiated change of price adapted to reflect either an increased (decreased) likelihood of collection.

6 See Mark Fisher and Zoe Shaw *Securitisation 2nd edition: For Issuers, Arrangers and Investors* (London, Euromoney Books, 2003) Module 2, 'The rating agency's approach', Helene M. Heberlein of Fitch Ratings provides an excellent overview of the important considerations for rating agencies to which this sub-segment owes a debt.

7 See *Securitisation and Shari'ah Law* (Fitch Ratings, Emerging Markets Special Report, March 2005).

8 Conversely, conventional asset securitisations may separate an asset into multiple cash flow strips including rent and capital only, whereby the cash flows are stripped from the original asset. Strips, themselves may prove highly volatile in a changing interest environment.

[9] 'MALT' meaning 'mortgage alternative' is a registered trademark of SHAPE™ Financial Corp.

[10] Mardam-Bey, Ibrahim et al, 'Islamic Securitization', presented at Terrapinn Securitization World MENA, 12–15 April 2005.

[11] Bacha, *op. cit.* In the Malaysian context, Bacha notes the strong link between interest rates and Islamic yields. In a Granger Causality Test, Bacha determined that Islamic instruments are subject to the same rate movement exposure as conventional debt instruments.

[12] Hughes, *op. cit.*

[13] Bacha, *op. cit.*

[14] VAT is difficult to avoid or recover in Europe.

[15] Fisher and Shaw, *op. cit.*, p. 193.

[16] Hasan, Maher, 'Overview of the Capital Adequacy Standard Practices for IIFS' presented at Asian Islamic Banking and Finance Workshop on 'Implementing Islamic Money Market: Issues and Challenges', 23 September 2004.

Liquidity management: developing the Islamic capital market and creating liquidity[1]

11

Stella Cox with Abdulkader Thomas

Introduction

This chapter focuses on the development of the Islamic capital market and reviews the progress that has been made in developing its infrastructure with respect to creating liquidity for investors and Islamic banks. It surveys what the market has to offer and considers how the direction of Islamic asset origination has been shaped by the environment within which it works. It should be emphasised that the successful management of liquidity has been among the greatest challenges for Islamic financial institutions and investors.

Liquidity management and mainstream financial services

Whatever the financial requirement, a multitude of short-term investment and funding products are available within the mainstream financial sector.

Accessing the services of banks, financial institutions and fund managers is a ready solution for the retail and corporate marketplace. Larger corporations, banks and financial institutions have recourse to the international money markets and to the capital markets. They can place deposits and raise finance on either rolling or fixed terms that range in duration from overnight to many years.

Nowadays, the ability both to access liquidity and invest flexibly through the conventional financial marketplace can be taken for granted. Within the Islamic financial sector the situation is somewhat different and requires that products are asset-based. Investment should therefore be effected through physical ownership of tangible assets (or part thereof) with an income stream that may be attributed to the economic use of the asset.

Challenges of Islamic liquidity operations

Religious jurisprudence has excluded Islamic banks from the natural benefits of mainstream financial practice such as recourse to the institutional money markets, certain international capital market products and, according to general perception, to a lender of last resort. Despite this, for the past three decades, Islamic banks have had to conform to regulatory stipulations more commonly applied to an interest-based banking environment. They have been required to comply with mainstream capital adequacy and liquidity ratios and have had to find alternative, *Shari'a*-compliant solutions to the regular, interest-based deposit reserve requirements that satisfy their regulators. Progressively, Islamic financial institutions have applied *murabaha*, *salam*, *tawarruq*, *sukuk* and derived applications of each to manage their excess liquidity. One of the challenges is that, outside of Malaysia, there is no true money market structured to serve Islamic banks. This chapter examines each of these methods and a offers a number of examples as illustrations.

Murabaha as a liquidity management tool

The *murabaha* contract has been dominant in Islamic finance. It has enabled Islamic banks to extend trade finance facilities to a range of international counterparties on deferred payment terms. Commonly, wholesale *murabaha* transactions are credit enhanced, with the beneficiary asked to support its payment obligations by arranging for a third party bank to issue a letter of credit, or other appropriate security, in favour of the financing institution. In simple terms, the profile of the investment becomes broadly comparable to that of an interbank deposit, namely short-term bank risk with fixed maturity. As a result, it has enabled Islamic institutions to assure their own regulators of their recourse to sufficient wholesale liquidity on demand.

The traditional path of a commodity *murabaha* is for the Islamic bank to buy a non-*ribawi* commodity from a broker, typically one active on an exchange such as the London Metals Exchange (LME). The Islamic bank then arranges for the broker to sell the commodity to a third party on deferred payment terms. Transactions have durations that range from one week to one year and have yields similar to money market yields, or similar duration short-term deposits.

Conducted correctly, the sale is a true sale and not a deposit. Therefore, it cannot be unwound. This requires either the process (discussed later) of *tawarruq*, or a parallel *murabaha*. In the latter case, the Islamic bank will approach the broker to engage in an equivalent purchase on the bank's behalf whereby the bank buys the commodity on deferred terms from one party and sells it spot to another. The end-result is the equivalent of breaking a time deposit. But, the transaction has more steps and may prove costly compared with a traditional deposit termination. Alternatively, if the Islamic bank has made appropriate arrangements it may utilise *salam* as a means to fund out the deposit; but this too requires an extra step as the bank must source the commodity at term to close out the *salam*.

During the first Gulf War, some international banks, fearing the consequences of maintaining exposure in the GCC, refused to roll over their *murabaha* placements into new transactions. This caused several Islamic banks to find themselves struggling to place funds productively in the absence of local Islamic interbank markets. The experience has proven to be an important influence on several central banks to develop *sukuk*, *salam* and other tools that move the interbank transacting closer to home.

The international metals trade has been an important means for Islamic banks to manage their liquidity. But, it has been criticised in some Islamic circles on three grounds: the trade is not a 'true' trade with the commodities moving from a supplier to a user; the Islamic market drives commodity trades above the underlying commercial trade; or the trade may be 'faked' with the result that the purchase and sale may be between the same party, a disguised *bai' al-'inah*. Over the years, almost all Islamic banks have successfully driven out the disguised *bai' al-'inah*; but challenges relating to 'true trade' and volumes are more difficult to deflect. Nonetheless, the position of most scholars is that once a sale is independently and freely agreed and the elements of *'inah* are absent, then the sales transaction is valid.

Murabaha – asset or liability?

There has been much criticism of the *murabaha* contract in recent years, particularly by commentators who fairly point out that it is limited in application. Critics have also harboured very real concern that dependence on the contract has actually impeded research and development of other *Shari'a*-compliant instruments that might be securitised, and would therefore be better placed to support the development of the Islamic capital market.

However, considering the various customer and regulatory demands placed upon the Islamic banks helps to balance the argument. Just imagine what would happen in the mainstream financial environment if the international money markets became inaccessible for a week, or even a day? The market would probably collapse. For three decades Islamic banks have managed to exist, grow their client base, make profit distributions and satisfy their local central banks, but to do so they have been obliged to maintain an exceptionally high level of liquidity at all times.

Example: Global Oil Malaysia – growing the business

Global Oil Malaysia was pleased with the outcome of its long-term Islamic debt issue. This caused it to return repeatedly as a client of Local Islamic Bank (LIB). 'Overall, this has been a rewarding and challenging experience and we have been impressed by the sophistication of both the Islamic and conventional banking and financial systems, in balancing the varying concerns of industry and commerce,' evaluated Global Oil's chairman. As a result, Global Oil Malaysia was a willing partner in the development of new concepts as brought forward by the domestic Malaysian Islamic finance industry.

For instance, Global Oil Malaysia has continuously expanded its Malaysian investment plans. In 2001, the oil giant committed up to RM20 billion over the next five years to expand its oil and gas operations. The company's treasurer noted that the company would be looking at all financial instruments available in the Malaysian capital markets, including the offshore centre Labuan, to raise funds. He did not hesitate to emphasise his willingness to apply Islamic methods.

Subsequently, LIB lead and underwrote a *musharaka* note issuance. The transaction included the securitisation of promissory notes (*shahadat al-dayn*). As the two issuances traded in secondary markets, the foundations of an Islamic bond market was established. The debts, in the view of Malaysian authorities, are Islamically permissible to be traded since they are not interest-based.

As Bank Negara Malaysia (the central bank) began to offer new financing options, Global Oil became a strong supporter of new products and services. Thus, when the plant required supplies, Global Oil entered into *murabaha* contracts with LIB.

With specific buyers, Global Oil sold against letters of credit. When the bills of exchange were received, Global Oil would discount them to LIB making them into 'Green BAs' or Islamic bills acceptable for discounting in Malaysia. In this approach, Global Oil contributed its credit to the market creating a tradeable instrument with an attractive rating whilst supporting smaller suppliers in the regional markets.

The natural progression was for Global Oil to structure a *murabaha* notes issuance facility, or MUNIF programme. This facility was essentially a *bai' al-'inah* working capital facility in which Global Oil isolated specific assets to sell to LIB, and then at a future date agreed to buy the assets back. This facility allowed Global Oil to monetise assets subject to a lien for working capital purposes.

Salam

A number of Islamic banks have also used *salam* as an element of strategy that also applies *murabaha* in order to manage liquidity. Again, the *salam* strategies require a relationship with commodity brokers, typically in international commodity trading centres such as London. There have been fewer counterparties for *salam* transactions since these contracts have features that are not the same as ISDA or other formats that are preferred, even mandated, in western markets. In 2002, the Bahrain Monetary Authority (BMA) entered into a cooperative arrangement with the LME in order to facilitate the liquidity management needs of Islamic banks.

Tawarruq

Maintaining sufficient liquidity flows is still essential to the market and the development of *tawarruq*-based products has been a strong initiative of recent years. Previously, Islamic institutions have allocated short-term liquidity through deferred settlement *murabaha* transactions. Reciprocal requirement has often been dependent upon reverse *murabaha* solutions. The term itself means 'turning something into paper' and its validity requires true sales to an independent party. [2]

Exhibit 11.1 ***Tawarruq* transaction**

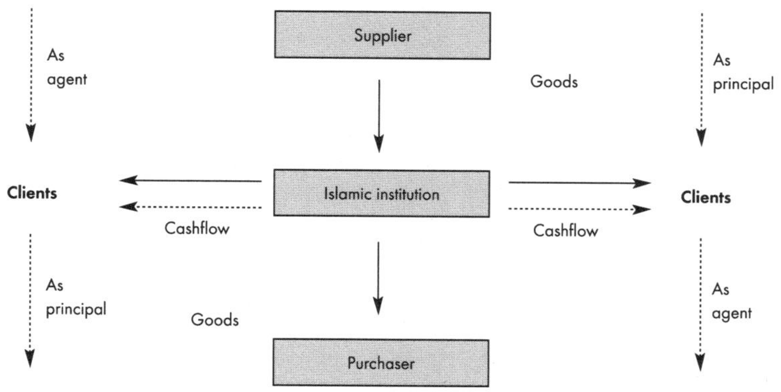

Source: Stella Cox.

In the expanding universe of *tawarruq* transactions, the common formula is for an Islamic bank to establish a set line with a commodity provider at a specific value. This line could be reciprocal. When the Islamic bank has funds to place, it advises the broker who draws against the line to buy commodities on a deferred basis. As the broker wishes to repay or the Islamic bank seeks repayment, then the goods are sold by the broker to a *bona fide* third party and the proceeds applied to settlement of the original commodity-deferred sales transaction (see Exhibit 11.1).

In a new era of cooperation, the major Islamic banks are exerting greater direct control over the management of their own liquidity. Spot value purchases and sales of assets are supporting the facilitation of wholesale *Shari'a*-compliant, interbank transactions. The Islamic banks interface as direct counterparties with asset brokers, merchants and each other, thereby avoiding unnecessary and costly intermediation by third-party banks. Further structuring developments have enabled *tawarruq*-based financing products to be offered at a retail level by a growing number of Islamic and Arabian banks. Such has been the growth and demand for the structure, that our esteemed scholars have been called to review its merits on a number of occasions.[3] It is likely that the principles of the process will require further definition but it is to be hoped that parameters can be established for ongoing development with full *Shari'a* endorsement. Although new to the market, already we have seen unprecedented levels of standardisation in the operational and administrative procedures that support delivery of this product. It has served to facilitate dependable liquidity.

Tawarruq is distinct from *bai' al-dayn* transactions as practised in Malaysia. This is because the *tawarruq* transaction entails the purchase of a non-monetary object and its sale. But the *bai' al-dayn* transactions are the result of a completed sale, and the end sale of the debt certificate.

Islamic 'debt' securities

A review of the audited financial statements of many Islamic commercial banks reveals that regularly, more than 70 per cent of the balance sheet is still invested in *murabaha* structures. In both *murabaha* and the similarly constructed *al bai bithaman ajil* contract favoured in Malaysia, the underlying asset is purchased and sold at inception with deferred payment consideration. The Malaysian market has developed a procedure for securitisation of the *bai' bithaman ajil* contract, but the resultant *bai' al-dayn* securities (sometimes referred to as Islamic debt securities) have proven contentious in the Arab World. Within the Malaysian money market umbrella, interbank trading (government investment certificates, Islamic bankers' acceptances and Cagamas *mudaraba* bonds), *mudaraba* certificates, and Islamic cheque-clearing are key components. All turn fundamentally on the sale of debt concept following the execution of a permissible sale with a receivable. The government investment certificates pay a yield based on economic performance and inflation, adjusted to comparable instruments.[4] Uniquely, the *mudaraba* certificates represent a pure negotiated approach to profit-sharing between surplus and deficit banks for short periods of time.

Outside of Malaysia, the majority of *Shari'a* scholars concur that any further trading in the income stream will be trading in debt because the receivables are no longer directly attributable to an asset to which the investor retains beneficial title. Similarly, the *murabaha* contract may not be securitised, as it would amount to securitisation of debt rather than assets.

Defining liquidity strategies

In defining the investment strategy for an Islamic fund, the manager has to consider how his recourse to, and investment of, liquidity might affect the performance and/or the *Shari'a* endorsement of his product. Most investors seek the comfort of knowing that they can exit a fund if necessary, but equally important is the manager's need to identify appropriate structures for the deployment of his fund's own surplus liquidity. Historically, managers of Islamic funds have been challenged by inadequate access to acceptable short-dated placement outlets, which can be described, at best, as limited.

It has been a feature of the funds of the Islamic sector that the investment exit strategy is generally dependent upon the product sponsor, or a nominated liquidity agent, who must acquire the asset holding from the investor. Success is often determined by the investor's perception of the strength of the promoter and the liquidity agent, or guarantor. Furthermore, established liquidity management structures, such as *murabaha*, may not be classified as interbank deposits or freely transferable securities and are therefore ineligible investments for certain international fund structures. A number of fund managers have admitted to leaving short-term cash balances on current account; not particularly effective, as cash can represent a substantial, defensive element of an Islamic portfolio in volatile market conditions.

Short-term liquidity programmes

Among new products which have been developed, the AlFanar Murabaha Fund is a short-term investment product allocating to low-risk *murabaha* transactions involving obligors with minimum single A ratings. The fund is sponsored jointly by Permal Asset Management and Jeddah-based SEDCO.

Overnight investment programmes

As of mid-2005, the only fund in the market offering an overnight investment solution was ABC Islamic Bank's Islamic Fund and Clearing Company. ABC offers a blend of trade and lease-based assets, pooled to generate very short-term investment opportunities that can also be secured through a guarantee issued by the parent bank. The ABC programme has played a valuable role in providing placement opportunities for both asset-hungry, liquidity-conscious Islamic institutions and mainstream, international fund managers seeking to off-lay the short-term cash element of the portfolio or fund.

Ijarah lease finance

During the past 15 years the Islamic financial sector has made progress in extending its investment horizons. Investor demand for a combination of enhanced performance plus risk and asset diversification has resulted in the financing of a greater percentage of non-trade assets. *Ijarah*, or leasing, has become a preferred contract for offering medium to long-term asset-based finance. An *ijarah* contract incorporates a fixed-term, or periodically re-fixed, income stream, or rental, from the economic use of a physical underlying asset. Lease income can be readily securitised without the infringement of *Shari'a*, because the investor retains title to the leased asset (or a part thereof) throughout the investment period.

Ijarah funds

These have been incorporated to capitalise on the availability of a broad spectrum of international investment opportunities. Lease funds tend to invest in pools of suitable leased assets, which may be sold to a special purpose vehicle, owned by the fund. The fund manager may choose to evidence holdings to investors by issuing certificates that represent their ownership of, or title to, a percentage of the asset pool and, thereby, a pro rata share of the income stream. Subsequent sale of certificates releases liquidity.

Creating liquidity

Most sponsors of Islamic lease funds now incorporate periodical redemption facilities as a feature of their product. Whilst invaluable, historically the investment exit strategy has been underwritten by the product sponsor, who will acquire asset holdings from the investor or arrange asset sales on a 'best effort' or matched basis. Amongst the first to implement the concept were the Islamic Development Bank and the Al Tawfeek/Al Amin companies of the Dallah Albaraka Group. As investors had the right to redeem their funds by selling back holdings to the sponsor, these funds became the first to address the issue of in-built liquidity.

Undoubtedly, the long-held aim of some of the larger Islamic lease funds has been the securitisation and subsequent trading of the asset portfolio within a regulated market environment. Product sponsors have grappled with the challenges of obtaining regulatory approval and the prospects of achieving international ratings, but it has been impossible to move speedily without an established market infrastructure.

Nevertheless, there has certainly been progression and more recent initiatives have included liquidity provision by third-party facilitators with their own investment-grade ratings.

Short-term investment programme

Example: Arcapita Islamic *Ijara* Liquidity Program

In 2000, Arcapita Bank (formerly First Islamic Investment Bank) in Bahrain launched its own Islamic Ijara Liquidity Program, illustrated in Exhibit 11.2. Its objectives were to provide consistent income, whilst preserving investment capital; to meet the liquidity and short-term investment needs of Islamic institutions (although one-month was the shortest-date investment as at mid-2005); and to offer risk-adjusted returns comparable to those available through the traditional money markets.

To achieve this, the bank established a special purpose company to acquire a pool of leased assets in the United States. Investor funds acquire a percentage of ownership of the leased asset pool through a subsidiary of the bank. The subsidiary then issues uncertified securities – *sukuk* – to investors in the Islamic financial sector. They confirm their fractional ownership interests in the underlying assets. Investors have monthly access to liquidity through a *sukuk* put option. This enables them to put their *sukuk* back at face value on any given redemption date after a minimum one-month holding. The difference here is that the redemption procedure is not dependent upon Arcapita, as the programme sponsor. The *sukuk* may be put back on a third-party liquidity provider which, in this instance, is Société Générale. A profit return is attached to the *sukuk* which is advised to the investor at the time of investment and re-fixed on a monthly basis. Arcapita's product is a particularly interesting initiative as the *sukuk* concept was innovated in Malaysia and this was the first example of its application by a Gulf-based Islamic bank.

Exhibit 11.2 **Arcapita (FIIB) *Ijara* Liquidity Program**

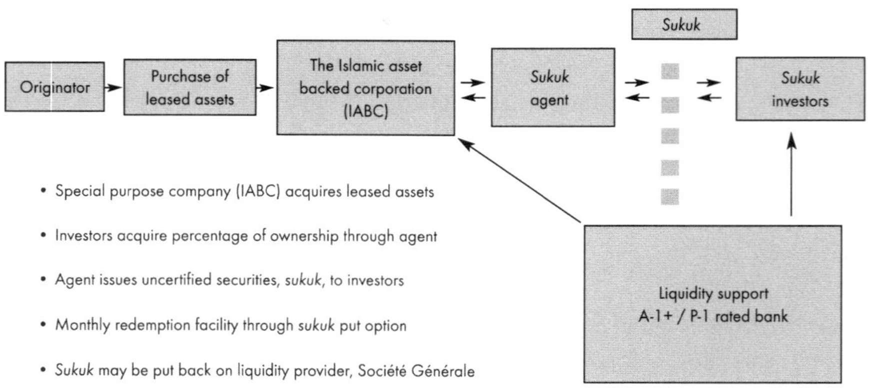

Source: Author's own.

Islamic investment asset base

Although there have been successful initiatives, it has proven difficult to originate sufficient volume of assets that are both eligible for securitisation and are *Shari'a* compliant. The global market has offered asset supply, but also presented structural and taxation issues that have proven challenging. Nonetheless, ongoing demand has supported the growth of the Islamic fund management sector, where activity has increased dramatically and the international capital markets have served to deliver allocation opportunity. Construction of a balanced investment portfolio requires access to a range of asset categories and investment horizons and a professional portfolio manager will seek performance through prudent and diversified allocation.

In recent years, it is actually the international equity markets that have been a focus of Islamic asset management with equity funds representing more than 65 per cent of the total Islamic fund universe. Although encountering initial reservations from the *Ulema*, sponsors persevered with initiatives to launch equity products. Of course, the investment universe of each fund and the resultant dividends or income must always be screened or purified in accordance with prevailing *Shari'a* stipulation (see Chapter 9: Islamic asset management). Every Islamic investor prioritises *Shari'a* compliance, but its delivery in combination with investment exposure to established, regulated and liquid capital markets has provided a compelling story for fund managers to offer to their clients. Certain Islamic equity funds have been listed on both international and regional stock exchanges. Again, that listing may give added respectability and demonstrate a product regulatory endorsement, but does not mean that liquidity is automatically available unless there is a genuine secondary market.

Disclosure, regulation and rating

Investors are increasingly sophisticated. Those unwilling or unable to assess the merits of Islamic financial products will look to accredited rating endorsements. Until now, there has been little to assist Islamic investors in determining whether or not their risk is investment grade. Islamic investment products have not, until recently, been rated by the international agencies who have previously suggested that both levels of disclosure and reporting standards within the Islamic financial sector need to be improved. Achieving authorisation in international jurisdictions has necessitated the implementation of improved management and reporting systems as both regulators and prospective investors demand more accurate information about structure and performance.

Rising to the challenge

Accelerating the origination of instruments to support the Islamic capital market infrastructure and inject liquidity is always central to the industry debate. However, the sector is young and is endeavouring to develop expertise that has taken centuries to evolve in conventional financial practice. Mainstream capital market development in the Middle East is, itself, at a relatively early stage. Even large projects have typically been funded through informally raised private equity combined with local bank debt. The pace of change has been dependent upon government perspectives, improvement of the legal infrastructure and the gradual opening of markets to inward investment. Progression in these areas enhances prospects for external assessment and rating of individual investment opportunities.

Formation of Islamic capital market infrastructure

Unresolved operational and procedural issues have affected the emergence of the Islamic capital market. Progress in standardising products and systems has been gradual. It has proven difficult to advance without consensus and consistency of opinion amongst the esteemed *Shari'a* authorities; at times there has been insufficient cooperation between the Islamic banks themselves. Although there is no doubt that the Islamic financial sector needs, and its participants want, the market to evolve, establishing sufficient numbers of founder participants willing to invest in it and support it on comparable terms has not been easy. Strong and, ideally, centralised regulation has always been a prerequisite and, for many years, there were unanswered questions as to who might provide it.

Malaysia

During the mid-1990s, with considerable encouragement and support from its government, Malaysia made rapid progress in implementing a dual banking system in which the Islamic banking sector operates in parallel to the conventional sector. As a result, the Islamic interbank money market is already in place and the Islamic capital market has evolved. In summer 2002, Malaysia issued a US$600 million Islamic sovereign *ijarah sukuk*, lead managed by HSBC, with a five-year maturity profile. Heavily oversubscribed, the *sukuk* was awarded a BAA2 rating by Moody's and a BBB rating by Standard and Poor's. Fifty-one per cent of investors were from the Middle East.

Middle East

Encouragingly, the Middle Eastern authorities are becoming increasingly involved. The Islamic financial sector has recently benefited from the launch of a series of Islamic bonds, or *sukuk*, that have been developed with the proactive support of the BMA. These include short-term financial paper, issued as *sukuk al salam*, and longer-term *sukuk al ijarah* extending to five years. In October 2004, the Government of Bahrain announced the latest US$250 million *sukuk* issue, lead managed by Citi Islamic Investment Bank. This offer has taken Bahrain's issuance of *Shari'a*-compliant short and medium-term instruments during the past three years to US$1 billion.

The undoubted strength of the sponsor and the premium on return over comparable risks in the international marketplace have been very positively received by investors. In a new development, the most recent issues have been rated A- by Standard & Poor's, distributed in the international marketplace and listed on the Bahrain Stock Exchange.

In October of 2003 the Government of Qatar issued its own *sukuk*. Lead managed by HSBC and QIIB, at US$700 million, it is the largest single issue to date. The issue was rated A+ by SSP.

The International Islamic Financial Market

The Islamic world is extremely diverse and the emergence of the Islamic capital market has always been dependent not only upon the satisfaction of *Shari'a* stipulation at a very broad level, but also the ability to accommodate the regulatory and financial accounting standards of jurisdictions stretching from the Middle East to Africa, Asia and beyond. Recent, new direction appears to be stemming from international cooperation and shared intention to deliver.

In April 2002, the Labuan Offshore Financial Services Authority (LOFSA) signed a memorandum of understanding with the Bahrain Monetary Agency (BMA) and the Islamic Development Bank to support the establishment of the Islamic capital market. The resultant, multinational International Islamic Financial Market (IIFM) is now headquartered in Bahrain. Its membership now extends to the Central Bank of Indonesia, the Central Bank of Sudan and Ministry of Finance of Brunei. Its primary purpose is to provide a cooperative framework for the market infrastructure.

Islamic capital market – multinational institutions

The Liquidity Management Centre (LMC) has been established in parallel with the IIFM, founded by the Islamic Development Bank, Kuwait Finance House, Dubai Islamic Bank and Bahrain Islamic Bank. It has taken a proactive role in the *sukuk* issuance programme. Ultimately, the LMC will be well placed to perform as liquidity manager for the Islamic financial sector. This is extremely important because whilst there are a number of new initiatives taking place, most presently address investment of liquidity rather than the ability to access funding. Bahrain is also the headquarters of the International Islamic Rating Agency (IIRA), established to bring consistency to the rating of Islamic financial instruments. To gain international credibility the procedures of the rating agency will need to be utterly transparent and there have been suggestions that it will work with the international agencies to achieve comparability. Finally, the Islamic Financial Services Board (IFSB) in Kuala Lumpur has been established to centralise the setting of prudential standards for the regulation and supervision of Islamic banking.

Ongoing development

Sukuk

The role of individual Islamic banks is also crucial, they have all-important credibility in their domestic environments plus the size and scope to anchor capital market initiatives. In April 2003, First Islamic Investment Bank (FIIB, now Arcapita Bank) launched its debut *sukuk* to finance the expansion of its European operations. The US$75 million medium-term issue was lead managed by The Securities House of Kuwait.

International banks have also played their part in the development of Islamic financial services and it is to be hoped that their commitment will extend beyond proprietary investment services. Certainly, there is great competition amongst the global investment banks to lead manage the new Islamic bond issues.

Additionally, their substantial balance sheets and long-term market experience can be harnessed to support the market-making capability and accelerate the volume-building process.

Issuance and secondary trading

Other Arab governments, banks and now large corporations are exploring *sukuk* issues. Corporate domestic issues in Malaysia aggregated US$3 billion in 2002 and represented 60 per cent of all bonds issued, but are not yet commonplace in the Gulf. However, the signs are encouraging: the Islamic Development Bank's debut international *sukuk* in 2003 raised US$400 million and was awarded a AAA rating[5] by Standard and Poor's. The Islamic Development Bank planned the *sukuk* in an effort to familiarise the international capital markets with the structure. Lead managed by Citigroup and co-led by Abu Dhabi Islamic Bank and Kuwait Finance House, 70 per cent of the issue was placed with conventional investors. Seventy per cent of the order book came from the Middle East, 14 per cent from Europe and 16 per cent from Asia Pacific.

In preparation for secondary trading, provision is being made to list and cross-list *sukuk* issues. For example, in September 2003, the Malaysian global *sukuk* was cross-listed on the Bahrain Stock Exchange. There is still some concern that *sukuk* are not actually being traded. This is certainly true, but the market was starved for so long of high-quality sovereign paper that investors have, thus far, been purchasing to hold. Aggregate international issues currently total less than US$3 billion. Market consensus suggests that there will be little evidence of appetite to trade before critical mass builds beyond US$10 billion.

Conclusion

There are still issues to resolve, but quality of asset origination is undoubtedly improved and the structuring innovations of recent years have served to strengthen the asset-based platform upon which to build. It seems that the foundations of the market are finally in place. The Islamic financial infrastructure should be greatly strengthened by its four new multinational institutions.

Improved cooperation, dialogue and direct interaction between the major Islamic institutions are enhancing their own contribution and beginning to create some standardisation of newer products and innovations within the market.

Ultimate success has, to an extent, always been dependent upon the proactive involvement of the central regulatory authorities relevant to Islamic financial services. The visible participation and support of Bahrain and Malaysia in innovating *Shari'a*-compliant bonds has enhanced product credibility and market profile. Subsequent sovereign issues are consolidating the position. Successful capital markets thrive on substance and security. Effective supervision and strong regulation helps to prohibit erratic behaviour by participants as well as serving to comfort investors. Independent rating endorsement allows objective assessment and, again, develops investor confidence. In turn, market confidence injects liquidity and helps build the critical mass that any financial market needs to flourish.

1 Based on the Stella Cox's presentation at Euromoney's 3rd Annual Islamic Finance Summit, London, January 2004.

2 Suwailem, Sami, *al-tawuruq wa al-tawuruq al-munathim*, unpublished paper August 2003 circulated on www.islamic-finance.net May 2005 and Khoja, Ezziddine, *al-tawuruq* available at www.islamicfi.com. These transactions are not free from criticism in the Islamic markets.

3 Usmani, M. Imran, 'Islamic Liquidity Management', presented at the Fifth Harvard Islamic Finance Forum, May 2004.

4 Arshad, M. Khairuddin, 'Design of Islamic Financial Instrument: Regulatory and Liquidity Devices of the Central Bank', presented at Central Bank of Kuwait on 25, 26 October 1997.

5 The first such rating for an Arabian issuer.

12 Risk management and derivatives

Abdulkader Thomas

Introduction

Perhaps, this chapter best starts with the International Swaps and Derivatives Association (ISDA) definition of a derivative:

> 'A derivative is a risk-shifting agreement, the value of which is derived from the value of an *underlying asset*. The underlying asset could be a physical commodity, an interest rate, a company's stock, a stock index, a currency, or virtually any other tradable instrument upon which two parties can agree.'[1]

Classically, there were two methods to manage risk. One is to form a pool with others facing a common risk to meet losses arising from a specific form of danger. In classical Islamic society, such pools were formed to provide risk mitigation from pirate attacks or loss due to weather or travel accident. Alternatively, one might form multiple partnerships with different parties aiming at the same trade in the same place, but altering timing and route[2] – effectively disaggregating the enterprise so as to disperse risk. From a practical point of view, the former bears less complexity. Unlike modern western risk management techniques, there is no upfront payment to a third party.

Islamic finance is still struggling to determine whether or not it has a parallel approach to western risk management. On the one hand, nobody wants to pay upfront for insurance and then worry that there is a product searching for a client. On the other hand, many western-style contracts applied to risk mitigation lack the obligatory properties of contract as defined by *Shari'a*. Structured systemic Islamic financial products require structured innovation within *Shari'a* confines. Derivatives guru Warren Edwardes isolates six primary zones of financial innovation (he calls them pillars)[3] as follows.

1. *Competitive:* This is the most tight and difficult zone in which to operate when seeking better solutions to existing problems. The challenge is to avoid fixing something that is not broken.
2. *Regulatory:* All new markets: the Eurobond market in the 1960s; the credit default swap[4] markets today; and the Islamic banking markets are all markets in which at some point the regulatory regime and the nature of the business are not yet coordinated. As a result, there is a possibility that regulatory rulings may force change to established practices; or to allow new practices.

3. *Accounting:* If interest is *riba*; is rent interest for tax purposes? Is there a possibility to arbitrage distinctive methods so that one meets the tax or regulatory rulings that govern one compared with another?
4. *Taxation:* Is the *riba*-free income equal to interest when it suits one's tax planning?
5. *Religious:* Is the structuring of *riba*-free deals susceptible to generating different risk profiles in finance; or creating artificial transactions with ungainly costs?
6. *Ignorance:* Buyers of innovation need to beware of needs created by the innovator which may prove independent of needs that one knows or understands.

The innovation zones presented are the areas in which the financial service industry seeks to manage complex risks such as currency risk, yield or rate risk, equity risk, commodity, and inflation risk. These risks, in turn, have sub-risks including transaction, translation, and economic.[5] But, Edwardes warns us that the combinations of risks are infinite, with some of the variations directly coming from the use and abuse of the very instruments meant to manage risk![6]

Perhaps the most important derivatives question made after an examination of the substance of the contract is whether it serves a public benefit or *maslahah* to such an overriding degree that it may be transacted.[7] In the case of *salam* and *istisna'a*, Islamic scholars from the time of the Prophet Mohammed (PBOH) have agreed that the public good outweighs the break from generally accepted contractual forms. This chapter examines how the modern thinking by contemporary Islamic scholars and bankers has yet to find a clear consensus.

Many Muslim market observers confuse gambling and speculation. This lack of clarity is a major problem when seeking to analyse hedging strategies, engage in structured arbitrage or develop derivative products.[8] Also note the concept that much of the content in this book is, in fact, about derivatives.

Takaful and insurance

This book does not cover *takaful* and insurance as a general topic. The primary reason is that *takaful* is emerging as a specific discipline with the same depth and diversity that conventional insurance has when contrasted to the other disciplines of finance. Within the context of derivatives and asset protection, *takaful* remains underdeveloped outside of specific markets such as Malaysia and Bahrain. But, the rapid uptake of Islamic finance in markets such as the United Arab Emirates, Saudi Arabia and Kuwait has caused a renewed and deeper attention to core *takaful* products for asset protection. Outside of the primary Islamic markets, *takaful* is not fully developed and in some markets *takaful* programmes were developed ahead of the primary Islamic investment modes, resulting either in business failures or very slow business growth.

The word *takaful* means 'solidarity'. The root applications are pre-Islamic and are based upon persons with a common 'insurable interest' pooling their funds to create a means for recovery of loss in the event of any loss. Modern *takaful* has branched in two distinct directions, each involving the same core *ijtihad* as Islamic banking to get to the new business result. One direction treats the premiums as contributions to a managed pool and the other treats the managed pool as a form of *mudaraba*. In both cases, the methods remind most observers trained in traditional insurance of mutual insurance.

The leading *takaful* products to date have been consumer and business asset protection oriented, or property and casualty delimited. Life *takaful* or family protection programmes have followed. More recently, innovators have been examining how the *takaful* business may mimic the monoline insurers who provide credit default and other forms of insurance to the securities industry. Such asset protection schemes are so far jerry-rigged using traditional insurers.

Derivatives

According to the former Federal Reserve Board chairman Paul Volcker: 'Derivatives by their nature do not introduce risks of a fundamentally different kind or of a greater scale than those [risks] already present in the financial markets.'[9] His statement turns on its head the primary hypothesis of a major book on Islamic finance, namely the idea that *gharar* is trading in risks.[10] If derivatives are no more risky than regular financial businesses, are derivatives permissible? Beyond the derivation of modern financial transactions from core Islamic contracts, and before the *halal* and *haram* of it all, we need to understand what derivatives are in the modern capital and financial markets sense.[11]

> 'A financial market derivative is indeed a financial instrument that is derived from a cash market or standard or "plain vanilla" financial market instrument. A cash market instrument is a financial market instrument that involves paying a principal sum upfront. For this, the buyer obtains the right to interest and return of principal after a period of time (a loan or a bond) or for part ownership of a company (a share).'[12]

Edwardes postulates that the financial markets are built up of four key instruments[13] which may be hybridised or reconstituted in multiple ways.

1. *Spot sale.* This is a sale that is concurrent with the delivery of the object and the payment for the object of the sale.
2. *Forward sale.* This is a sale in which the object is deliverable at a later date, but paid for at the time of contracting.
3. *Option to buy or sell.* This is a right, not an obligation to execute the sale of an object.
4. *Deposit or loan.* This is the placement of monies or an object in another's custody, typically with some form of payment for the period of custodianship or use of the monies (interest) or object (rent).

These instruments have clear *Shari'a* parallels which may be structured or hybridised in permissible or impermissible manners to create derivative transactions which may result in the dispersion of risk and its management at the financial institution or client level.

But, each step away from the key instrument that one takes creates a specific and new risk if the transaction unwinds prior to maturity. For instance, in the application of *murabaha* for liquidity management, the actual sale is difficult to reverse and is typically achieved by a parallel transaction. If the markets suffer any specific shocks, as with the 1990–91 Gulf War, then it may not be possible to execute the parallel transaction.

The pure application of derivative contracts and processes is to transfer or exchange risk profiles, a process called hedging. A financial or commodities investor who fails to hedge faces liabilities that run from capital loss to commercial negligence.[14] The conventional market buys and sells the tools and processes of hedging. The buyer's choice is defined by the buyer's appetite for risk and leads to pragmatic questions about whether or not it is better to buy an out-of-the-money or at-the-money or in-the-money option or derivative.

On the face of it, these hedging decisions appear completely opposed to the Islamic approaches discussed hereto in this book, which are fundamentally cash market instruments. Islamic cash market instruments are based upon the core concept of sale giving an equity right to asset ownership without income, unless it is connected to the asset through the operation of a business or letting of the asset. If one is to derive downstream processes to disperse or manage risk in the Islamic market, then, following the position of Professor Mohammad Hashim Kamali, one may find that the classical concept of *salam* is used to reduce risk in a manner that parallels practices in modern western futures and option markets.[15] The remainder of this chapter explores theories and methods relating to the actual and prospective application of derivatives as governed by Islamic contracts. We do not explore arbitrage as part of the practice of derivative structuring since there is no *Shari'a* objection to profiting from the price movements of the underlying commodities so long as the *Shari'a*-based rules of possession and sale are observed.

Futures and forwards

In his ground-breaking work on futures and options, Professor Kamali argues that modern, regulated practices governing the clearing of options and futures eliminate the risk of *gharar* and facilitate the clear transfer of title between legitimate buyers and sellers of commodities. This reality has a direct impact on the practice of engaging in a forward or future purchase, and it may marginalise the distinction between the formal Islamic process of *salam* and certain market practices of futures and options.

The issue of maslahah

In general, the clearing house functionality that characterises most modern commodities and derivatives markets removes many elements of *gharar* that once concerned Muslim scholars about certain types of transactions such as futures.[16] According to Kamali, futures allow better planning, risk management, cost efficiency, price awareness and, prospectively, price moderation.[17] Therefore, there is a *maslahah* with certain hedging transactions. For instance, a poor farmer may secure a certain and known buyer.[18] *Maslahah* means that an underlying process may have some problematic issues or prospectively harmful elements from a *Shari'a* perspective, but the good achieved by its application outweighs harm. In most *Shari'a*-driven analyses of futures contracts, the concern of Muslim scholars has been that the harm arises when transactions are akin to gambling or *maysir*. But, the statistical evidence from western futures markets, including Malaysia and Egypt, is that the moderating influence of futures on prices means that there is no evidence that the preponderant use is for the forbidden *maysir*.[19] The traditional western economic position is that futures market speculation provides the public good of market liquidity by ensuring that there are always buyers and sellers for the securities or commodities in question.

Possession

The position of the Hanafi School of Islamic *fiqh* is that the sale of an object which is absent at the time of sale is not susceptible to *gharar*, whether great or little, as the contract is not valid and complete until the object is inspected;[20] that is, the option of inspection does not go away unless mutually agreed. According to the Hanafi school, possession is not a condition of validity, but a determinant of the effectiveness of a sale.[21] This position undermines some of the scholarly complaints against futures contracts which are based on the fact that the seller does not possess the object of sale. It also addresses the concern of those scholars who wish to ensure that contracting parties can meet their obligations under ordinary circumstances. As a result, Kamali finds that the imputed prohibition against futures may not apply.[22] Nonetheless, Kamali points out that it is not entirely appropriate to draw direct parallels between conventional and Islamic futures and sales contracts.[23]

In the modern futures markets, the clearing houses ensure that the positions of all parties to a contract are met by absorbing the position of any party which terminates early. So, contracts are not truly, unilaterally cancelled, rather the contracting party is replaced. Moreover, the clearing house function of setting off debts removes *gharar* and facilitates the fulfillment of contracts by distant partners who do not know each other. Therefore, Kamali does not find this aspect of netting out obligations at an exchange or clearing house to be invalid despite its apparent transgression on the sale of a debt for a debt (*bai' al kali bil kali*).[24]

Stock futures

Western-style futures contracts are standardised in a way that works best for fungible commodities. This is exactly like *salam*, which is restricted to fungible commodities. Standardisation removes variability, diminishes negotiation, and eases settlement. These features are in distinction to forward contracts.[25] The challenge, however, arises with non-traditional underliers such as stocks or company shares. Stock futures do not admit of delivery in most markets which seems to make them impermissible. In reality, the approach has been for some Islamic fund managers to negotiate a specific *salam* agreement with their stock brokers. The former achieves futures contract execution because the latter interprets the *salam* as a form of futures contract, albeit non-ISDA compliant. Another challenge is that western market commodities futures contracts might conceivably be created infinitely, whereas Islamic contracts have specific time limitations, unless *istisna'a* is applied. The concern of practitioners is that *istisna'a* is not clearly applicable when the product, a security or commodity, is not susceptible to processing or manufacturing.

Margin purchases

Margin purchases, whereby one pays part, but not all of the purchase price, deferring the balance due to the future, seems necessarily a feature of western commodities futures. To some this is viewed as impermissible. Yet, the concept of *urboun* or 'earnest money' bears some analogy to margin deposits. Kamali discusses the *aqd al mudaff*, which is a contract in which delivery and payment are both specific but deferred to the future. This relationship is valid when ownership is not transferred. As a result, it works well for leasing and agencies. The historical concern of Muslim jurists is that when deferral is permitted in relationship to ownership, the risk of unwarranted speculation or gambling becomes too great. As noted early, the primary objections also include *gharar*: *istisna'a* is by consensus the permitted exception. Moreover, the concept when forbidden in sales does not seem to attach to the elements of condition that allow for *salam* and *istisna'a*, or conventional futures.

Salam

Since the time of the Prophet Mohammed (PBOH) in Medina, the capacity to fulfill future obligations has improved due to more efficient markets.[26] The great classical jurist Ibn Qayyim pointed out that 'parties may wish to postpone either the payment of the price, or the delivery of the object of sale, to a later occasion.'[27] Moreover, *salam* does not violate the concept of selling the unseen as it does not structurally cause unlawful consumption of one contracting party's wealth at the expense of the other.[28] And, there is a clear parallel to the futures markets where the objects of futures contracts, like *salam*, must be storable for a long period of time; salable by measure; and fungible. Ideally, it is best if these objects are available in large quantities.

Salam may be subject to negotiability if the underlying commodity is not a foodstuff and is not bought back or traded by the original *salam* seller.[29] 'Hedging is the common economic function of futures markets and the most common method of price-risk management.'[30] Although, 'Speculators are individuals who buy and sell commodity contracts without wanting to deal in the actual commodities,'[31] their function facilitates the market and may be a public good by increasing liquidity and facilitating the need of some parties to assume new risk profiles through a risk transference or hedging strategy.

Although non-conclusive, this segment is meant to show that there are strong reasons to believe that new, cutting-edge thinking on derivatives will cause either new instruments and approaches to emerge in the Islamic capital market, perhaps even for the more liberal Malaysian view on futures and options to prevail, perhaps with modification, across the Islamic markets. Whatever the new thinking brings, it is within the context that Islamic institutions and investors have the same obligation to manage, transfer and disperse risk as their conventional peers.

Options

An option is defined by ISDA as follows:

> 'An option is an agreement that gives the buyer, who pays a fee (*premium*), the right – but not the obligation – to buy or sell a specified amount of an underlying asset at an agreed-upon price (*strike or exercise price*) on or until the expiration of the contract (*expiry*). A call option is an option to buy, and a put option is an option to sell.'[32]

And by Kamali thus:

> 'An option is simply a contract entered into by two parties. The buyer of the contract is granted the privilege of buying or selling a security at a specific price, while the seller (writer) of the contract assumes an obligation to accommodate the buyer should the buyer exercise his privilege.'[33]

From a *Shari'a* perspective, there is a distinction between an option and the trading of the option: the former is permissible, the latter is not in the current view of Islamic scholars.[34] To the degree that a future contract is a form of option, it is not currently permitted by most Islamic scholars.[35] A warrant is a form of option attached to another security allowing, but not requiring, one to buy a specified amount of an asset at a certain price over a specified period of time.[36] An option can move one further from the underlying commodity than a future would. Under the *Shari'a*, there is a significant problem when one detaches the option from the asset, something that many Muslim analysts feel drowns the option in *gharar*. Kamali feels that the concept of 'option', both how the *Shari'a* treats the concept and whether the *Shari'a* embraces conventional options in any form, requires further research and analysis.[37]

An intriguing discussion on options takes place in the *Mejelle* (the civil code of the Ottoman Caliphate, and considered to be the first attempt to codify Islamic law). Although the discussion is inextricably linked to the rules of selling, the concept of the option as a right is clear. The discussion gives a sense of limited transferability and heritability depending upon one's position in the buy or sell side. This is not a discussion which lends itself to easy extrapolation, but it clearly demonstrates a set of principles that open the opportunity for debate. For instance, term, specificity, known counterparties are all defined elements of the option.[38]

Options trading

There is a difference between an option, a right to do something, and the buying and selling of that option or right.[39] Options represent *huquq*, rights, but do they represent benefits or *manfaa* and not wealth or *mal*? The general view is that rights are not tradeable at a price. But, *manfaa* is. When options result in physical delivery, they fit best into the established Islamic spectrum. But, cash-settled options involve the exchange of two money assets or netting of two payment obligations.[40] If monetary assets are exchanged at settlement, spot, but with a differential to the market price, many analysts feel that there is a clear element of *riba al-fadl*.

Embedding options

Certain authors[41] have proposed that many Islamic transactions are eligible for the embedding of options. For instance, a lease certificate could be convertible into shares of the lessee. Although there are no *Shari'a* objections to the concept, the primary problem is that this particular derivative speaks less to financial risk management and more to credit risk management. For instance, if the client fails on an obligation, then the financier can insert itself into the ownership structure and affect the affairs of the company.

Options are not the same as the option of stipulation – *khiyar al-shart* – approved of by the Prophet Mohammed (PBOH) to ensure that no fraud has taken place (a form of warranty). During this period, the *Shari'a* analysis of ownership is that it remains with the seller. But the holder may be responsible for loss if there is no fraud.[42] Other forms of stipulation provide clarity or benefit to the contracting party. Nonetheless, embedded options may follow the framework of *khiyar al-shart* as long as either or both parties to the option retain an option to confirm or rescind.[43] Embedded options seem to be a western concept. But, such options are built into a number of widely applied Islamic methods such as *ijarah-wa–iqtina'a* and declining-balance partnerships. Exit options may represent embedded accreting options. 'Accreting: denotes an increase in the underlying principal over the life of an instrument,' whereas 'Amortising: denotes a reduction in the underlying principal over the life of an instrument.'[44]

A number of Muslim thinkers have proposed *istisna'a* as a hedging tool due to the permissibility of delaying the payments and the delivery of the goods. In reality, this is the linkage of a financial hedging strategy to the production of a good or construction. The risk element delivered to the process would be elevated beyond reasonable pricing capacities. For a business manager, however, *istisna'a* with an imbedded call option may be an optimal means to manage currency or other cross-border risks. Khan gives the example of a developing country automobile manufacturer who has engaged a supplier in a developed country to manufacture parts for it. With an embedded call option, the supplier may elect, if there are adverse exchange controls or impositions, to take the delivery of cars in lieu of cash.[45]

Currency options

Currency options, which represent the payment of one currency now and receipt of its countervalue at a future date, are conceptually accepted by many scholars.[46] But, in the prevailing view, a currency future or forward is not agreed when the settlement on both sides is agreed for a future date. The structuring of a currency option by promise is permissible but non-binding, although there may be a charge to the promisee for facilitating the transaction. Obaidullah finds a distinction between fixed and floating exchange rates whereby the former may, in forward and future transactions, be susceptible to *riba*, but not the latter. The floating-rate analysis breaks down, according to Obaidullah, with the existence of global currencies such as the US dollar and the euro, which are used widely outside of their primary markets. Repo agreements clearly violate *bai' al-'inah* restrictions.

Urboun

The premium payable to buy an option does not constitute a downpayment the initial payment does under *urboun*. As a result, options are not the same as, rather prospectively they are similar to *urboun*. *urboun* is the earnest money paid by a buyer to a seller which will become part of the price if the sale is completed. Only the Hanbali School of *fiqh* allows for *urboun* to be kept by the seller if the buyer does not complete the purchase.[47] *Urboun* may be sold according to Hanbali *fiqh*, and this selling of *urboun* approaches more properly the concept of an option.[48]

In recent years, the *urboun* has been widely adopted in an option-like position with clients paying small downpayments or earnest money, which are forfeit if the buyer does not complete the purchase. The *urboun* may be structured with *murabaha* transactions. If the buyer completes the purchase, then the advance payment is applied to the settlement.

Principal

Kamali has listed the Islamic Fiqh Academy issues relating to options and futures:[49]

1. A contract must involve the transfer of ownership and possession of at least one countervalue at the time of contracting.
2. There must be an intention to take payment.
3. Netting of the settlement amounts appears to facilitate gambling and profiteering, particularly if the buyer does not intend to receive the commodity.
4. Western market options and futures do not follow the exact form of *salam* as known by the scholars.
5. The scholars are concerned that options and futures are tainted by the unlawful-like interest.
6. The option and futures contracts may revolve sale of what one does not own or does not exist.

To these Kamali offers specific thoughts from modern *Shari'a* literature to consider in contrast to the Academy's views, including that the Academy has so far declined to engage in, sponsor or encourage *ijtihad* on this matter.[50] The key considerations to consider in contrast to the Fiqh Academy position are:

1. The non-existence of the object is not precisely applicable to modern futures.
2. Modern market regulation and clearing methods reduce the amount of *gharar*.
3. Futures represent valid commercial speculation which the *Shari'a* affirms is not the same as gambling.
4. The linkage of the rules of possession as a protection against *gharar*, and the maxim 'sell what is not with you' is meant to prevent future disputes[51] and this risk is removed by modern clearing procedures.

5. The explicit contract lacks interest. And, the netting may not be an exchange of cash-for-cash in violation of the rules of *riba*. The *hadith* forbidding *bai' al kali bil kali* is more controversial than held out and *hawala*, which is permitted, seems to run against it. Unlike the restrictive view of the Academy, the transaction involves money as one value and the countervalue is a non-monetary object; the means of settlement is, in fact, its sale.
6. The tainting of the unlawful relates directly to the object, and shares in a company such as General Motors are tainted by its finance subsidiary; but copper does not have a tainting element.

With these contrasted positions, it is possible to anticipate that there will be a gradual development of new thinking on how *salam*, *istisna'a*, *urboun*, options and futures fit into the expanding constellation of Islamic financial practices when it comes to risk management.

Forwards

According to the ISDA definition, forwards are similar to futures, but are private market transactions:

> 'A forward is a customized, privately negotiated agreement between two parties to exchange an asset or cash flows at a specified future date at a price agreed on the trade date. Entering a forward contract typically does not require the payment of a fee.'[52]

The market practice of forward contracting is based upon notional capital and notional cash flows. This market approach moves us sufficiently far from the actual asset to prevent the Islamic capital market and its *Shari'a* advisers to currently feel comfort in these types of transaction.

For instance a forward rate agreement, a contract on a short-term interest rate calculated on a notional capital base and arbitraging the difference between the prevailing market rate and the pre-determined forward rate, involves multiple transactional elements that are objectionable from an Islamic perspective. The forward calculation is only based on a pre-determined payment obligation as opposed to the resultant income from business. The analysis of rate and agreement to pay is thoroughly de-linked from the underlying transaction. The actual transaction that relates to the forward is completely *ribawi* as far as one can determine.

Such a reality has implications relating to rate guarantees meant to protect financial institutions from rate, repricing, and basis risk. The capacity to structure caps, floors and collars for the Islamic market through tools that are bought and sold is not conceivable with today's level of research. The typical solutions applied today are embedded floors, caps and collars.

Swaps

ISDA defines a swap as follows:

'A swap is a privately negotiated agreement between two parties to exchange cash flows at specified intervals (payment dates) during the agreed-upon life of the contract (maturity or tenor). Entering a swap typically does not require the payment of a fee.'[53]

Islamic institutions lack the complex instruments and strategies that allow conventional financial institutions to hedge their rate or yield risks and currency exposures through swaps. A traditional swap is one option that is routinely applied in the global capital markets to restructure the nature of liabilities. In a vanilla swap, institutions with different risk exposures agree to *swap* their cash flows, allowing them to enjoy the risk profile that they desire; for instance, an adjustable or floating yield may be exchanged for a fixed yield over a similar period of time. Or, they may exchange their currency payment exposure. But, the Islamic approach views the exchange of cash flows as susceptible to *riba*, if not a *ribawi* trade in itself.

Frequently, Islamic institutions have executed swaps in the form of countervailing interest-free loans with each party taking direct currency risk per its view, but not paying a price or premium for the transaction. Likewise, some Islamic institutions have engaged in deposit exchanges that allow for a series of rolled over short-term interest-free deposits against a long-term interest-free deposit in the same currency reflecting different views on rate movements. In both cases, the simplicity of the approach is undermined by the fact that the deposits are not economically active and prospectively make this a costly hedging strategy. In the case of currencies that are not fixed, some Islamic analysts believe that *bai' as salam* may be used to manage currency exchange risks.[54] This is based on the concept of *thamania* or unique value, which is not correlated to the swap itself.

In a forward-thinking document produced by Tariqullah Khan[55] relating to risk management for Islamic banks, the author points out the clear distinction between *bai' al kali bil kali*, or the setting-off of debts, in contrast to *bai' al-dayn bil ayn*, or the settling of a debt with an asset. The discussion was prescient of the ongoing development of the *sukuk* markets because it relies upon the fact that properly structured *sukuk* are, in fact, assets and not simple monetary obligations (even though they may be structured to function as such for the purpose of securities and tax regulations). If adopted, these would replace with greater dynamism the old cash-and-carry models that rely on *murabaha*.

Since swaps are bilateral, negotiated exchanges or assets or cash flows, we are closer to identifying a tool that is Islamically permissible. For instance, the concept of *sukuk* allows for an institution to trade *sukuk* with distinctive characteristics. This is not yet fully feasible, because the universe of *sukuk* is not fully extended to include a large variety of short and long-dated, adjustable and fixed-rate instruments. An exchange of *sukuk* is similar to exchanging credit profiles more than simply exchanging income strips.

Credit derivatives

The logical, private sector extension of the function of government and multi-state export insurance agencies includes credit derivatives. These are meant to assist a lender or investor's risk through dispersion. Consider the two words 'credit' and 'derivative' in their original meaning. Perhaps the term 'credit derivative' is an oxymoron. Credit derivatives include portfolio swaps and total return swaps. In the latter, all fees and yield related to a portfolio, often an illiquid portfolio, are swapped for a fixed-income stream pegged to an interest rate. In credit default options, either the actual default or a deterioration in credit leads to a payment under a structured formula. Credit-linked notes are cash instruments based on derivatives. As a universe, these derivatives have greater asymmetrical volatility in the underlying instruments than marketable instruments such as bonds. Since these are all highly structured, negotiated bilateral transactions, they are not transparent. As a result, this market may be subject to a high degree of moral hazard.

Credit default of itself is a function of inefficient markets.[56] This is because one party knows more than the other. In this case, the bank knows more about the borrower than the insurer does. According to Fink, one problem with credit derivatives is that, like many derivatives, there is no formal oversight. From a *Shari'a* perspective, the lack of oversight and transparency points to an above-average risk of *gharar*. Moreover, is it feasible that such swaps could encourage a lender to liquidate a troubled company and collect rather than to restructure the company? The moral risks, *gharar*, and the linkage to a *ribawi* instrument mean that there is no comparable Islamic tool outside of an outright asset swap.

Synthesising derivatives or the effects

Generally, the financial risks facing an Islamic Bank, even if it resembles a merchant bank, are similar to those of a conventional financial institution. Thus the need to disperse these risks, even if they are not unique to an Islamic institution.[57] For instance, in a *murabaha* transaction most *Shari'a* scholars do not recognise a binding promise from the buyer until specific actions take place (see Chapter 3: Equity finance vehicles). Therefore, an Islamic bank may find itself holding assets with a lower disposal price than that promised by the defaulted or rejecting buyer. This brings on the problem of storage and distribution, a truly non-financial risk set.

The other core Islamic transactions also have a number of specific challenges. For instance, in the case of *salam* transactions, there is a price risk at the maturity. *Istisna'a* may have operational risks relating to delivery or quality of the delivered asset. *Mudaraba* and *musharaka* have non-traded or private equity-like risks: capital impairment, disposal price/fair value information and exit strategy. For deposits that run on *mudaraba* and *musharaka* lines, there are disclosure risks, co-mingling risks, and compliance (regulatory and *Shari'a*) risks.

For Islamic banks, market and credit risk are strongly bundled together.[58] Does this mean that Islamic transactions have above-average counterparty or moral hazard risks? Also what of the problem that penalty payments are not permitted except under strict conditions that are meant to ensure that the financier or investor does not profit from the payment?

Now that we have executed the *murabaha*, what are the risk factors?[59] The strategy pursued by some Islamic banks is a form of continuous sale, referred to as *bai' al tawrid*.

Exhibit 12.1 **Traditional *murabaha***

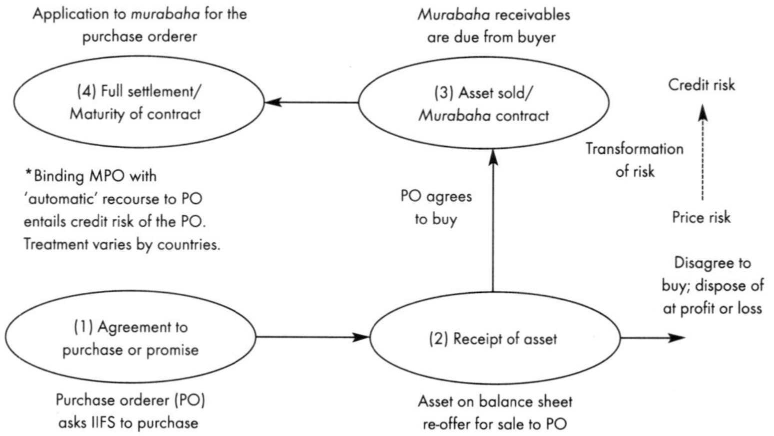

Source: BNP Paribas.

Exhibit 12.2 ***Murabaha* profit exchange**

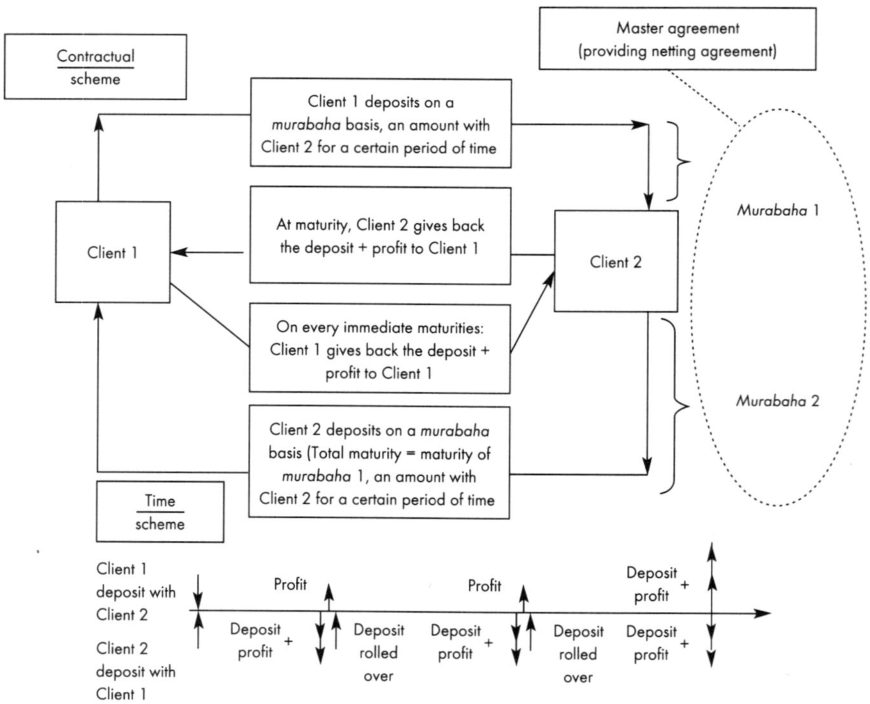

Source: BNP Paribas.

In the 1980s, Islamic institutions structured crude swaps which were not based on the cash flows, but back-to-back asset transactions in which the underlying *murabaha* transactions (see Exhibit 12.1) carried the relevant cash flows with them, synthesising the effect of a traditional swap. Recently, these methods have been revived and improved.[60] For instance, BNP engages in what they call a *murabaha* profit rate swap (see Exhibit 12.2), which allows contracting parties to exchange their risk profiles for a period of up to three years. One method to simulate a floating-rate transaction is for one party to the swap to engage in a series of serial short-term *murabaha* transactions. A key element is to make sure that the commodities underlying the distinct *murabaha* trades are not the same.

One problem with the synthesised costs is prospectively higher transaction costs as one is transacting more, there is a lack of ISDA or other standardised documentation, and there is an inability to properly calculate breakage if one party wishes to terminate early.

In the double currency swap,[61] *murabaha* is used to replace the interest-free deposits described above (see Exhibit 12.3). In this case, the counterparties execute opposing *murabaha* trades in different currencies, allowing an Islamic institution to hedge its exposure for as far as a counterparty is willing to execute a deferred-payment transaction on a commodity or asset sale.

Exhibit 12.3 **The double currency exchange deposit**

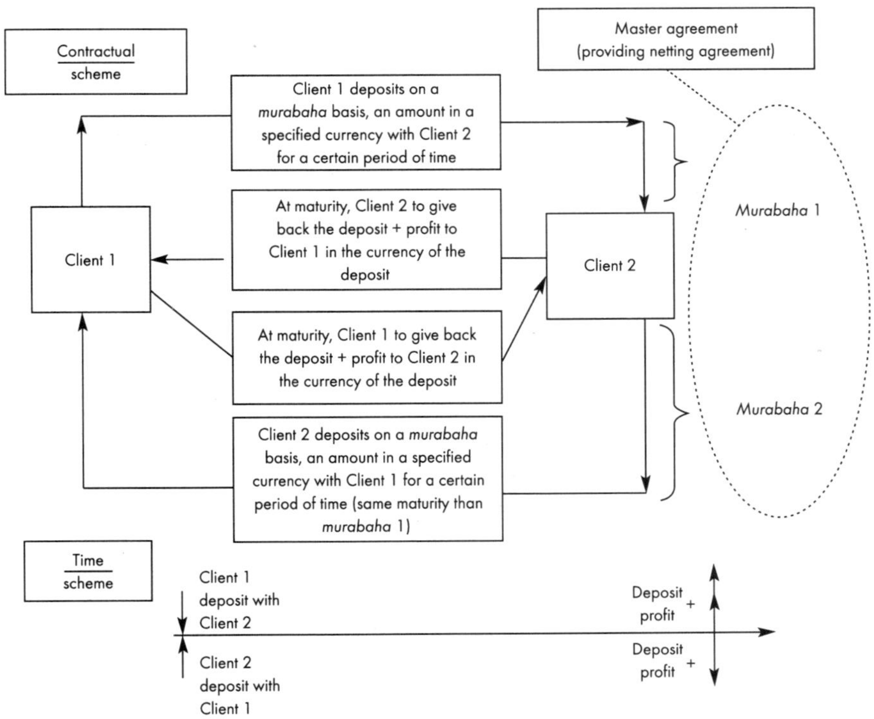

Source: BNP Paribas.

The *murabaha* profit exchange (see Exhibit 12.2) is currently able to synthesise structured flows for up to two years.[62] The limitation is based on the lack of sufficient terms available in the *murabaha* markets; but with the growth of *sukuk* issuances, one can imagine that the *sukuk* tenors of three, five, 10 or 30 years (based on US mortgage alternatives, for instance) will create the possibility of executing this form of exchange between short-term *murabaha* or short-dated tails on *sukuk* and long-term *sukuk*.

In capital-protected equity funds and guaranteed equity investments, the only way to achieve such protection is to structure an equity instrument with a derivative. For instance, the non-Islamic markets will match an equity portfolio with a zero coupon bond and an index option. But, the accretion of the zero coupon bond is correctly interpreted by Islamic scholars as interest, and thereby not permissible. And, the index option is not currently accepted as an Islamic instrument. As a result, some asset managers offering *Shari'a* funds that are capital protected may allocate 60 per cent of a portfolio to equity and 40 per cent to *murabaha* and now various *sukuk* instruments with longer maturities. In the worst case, the equity drops to zero, but the fixed-income instrument matures with capital and yield equalling the original investment.

Derivative market risks

The universe of risks addressed by derivatives also encompasses the risks that arise from the use of derivatives.[63]

- *Commodity and underlier risk:* The asset is not marketable or has unique credit or business risks of its own that are not correlated to the derived instrument.
- *Communication risk:* Disclosure of the nature of risks, the basis for counterparty performance, or third-party reporting relating to the underliers.
- *Convertibility risk:* Can the swap be executed and the transaction executed?
- *Currency risk:* How does currency risk affect the transaction and translation?
- *Liquidity risk:* Is there an active market to buy and sell assets?
- *Morbidity and mortality risk:* Are such risks calculated correctly?
- *Operational risk:* Does the business function, as promised; do the operations of the underliers or does their servicing meet cost effective standards?
- *Property risk:* What are the characteristics of the property, is it marketable and is it correctly measured?
- *Rating agency risk:* What will a downgrade do to risk if it happens?
- *Settlement risk:* Do the transactions have settlement risks which are unique or do they conform to market standards?
- *Systemic risk:* Is the transaction of a character that it can have a negative impact on the financial markets beyond a deal level failure?
- *Tax risk:* Are there tax risks that are not correctly defined, have they been identified?

- *Technology risk:* Is the underlyng transaction susceptible to unusual transaction risks?
- *Weather:* Can this affect the performance of the transaction?
- *Transportation risk:* Does this affect the settlement risk, asset performance?

Hedge funds

There has been a good deal of confusion with regard to a clear definition of a hedge fund: 'There is no agreed definition of a hedge fund. But in general, they are characterised as unconstrained, actively managed funds.'[64]

According to Kamali:

> 'A hedge refers to the concurrent holding of two opposite commodity positions, one in the cash market and the other in the futures market. A spread position refers to two concurrent and opposite positions, both are in the futures market.'[65]

Since the mid 1990s, the growth of hedge funds in the conventional markets has clouded the question of hedging. The confusion has spread to the Islamic market where the initial hedging endeavours have generated spirited debate as to the permissibility of both hedging instruments and hedge funds. A primary question has been about the permissibility of short selling, options and futures. Intriguingly, many of the debates in the Islamic market parallel debates about governance and best practice in the conventional markets.[66] What seems to be missing in this interaction is the view that hedge funds are the ultimate buyers of risk, in which market participants seek to lay off or hedge risk for a specific price and the buyer, the hedge fund, assumes a favourable arbitrage between the real value of the risk and the purchase price. Since hedge funds take the end-risk in the market, the last risk, they are distinct from arbitrage funds which seek to exploit price differentials between markets or between market participants. The rise in modern hedge fund complexity and their lack of regulation means that their capacity to introduce new systematic risks into markets is not measurable. On the one hand, the *Shari'a* favours the management and mitigation of risk. One the other hand, it does not favour the approach to risk dispersion that results in the aggregation of new, unseen risks.

As the buyers of residual risk, most hedge funds 'create risk using hedging instruments.'[67] This has prompted a concern among some analysts that the concept of an Islamic hedge fund is deeply troubling.[68]

The essence of this debate turns on core misunderstandings by both parties. Without hedge funds buying residual risk, and prospectively applying leverage to exploit an opportunity or maximise arbitrage to achieve the highest yields, there are no buyers of risk to allow others to exchange risk profiles, reduce risks, or otherwise smooth portfolio risks. As Edwardes adds, the fact is that, '... hedge funds ... [often] do anything but hedge. They deliberately take risks through futures markets to generate higher returns.'[70]

Alternatively, a long–short strategy is typically pursued by seeking a market-neutral position through buying an equal number of long positions to short positions. A long–short position's risk is correlated to the underlying securities. Long–short strategies require short sales, margin accounts, stock borrowings and interest payments. These tools are not specifically applicable in the Islamic market, but some of them may be replicated. For instance, *murabaha* has been applied to stock purchases in the GCC. Some scholars have permitted stock borrowings without interest. But, short sales have not yet been analogised to any form of permissible instrument, although some element of connection to *salam* may eventually be drawn.

Certain Islamic funds apply *salam* to hedge equity portfolios.[71] Leading scholars such as Dr Mohamed Elgari and Nazih Hammad have approved *salam* contracts for the purchase of equity securities. In this approach, a prime broker supporting the fund's trades pays cash to the fund for a basket of permissible equities; and the fund contracts to deliver the securities at a specific future settlement date. In the case of *salam* as approved by these scholars, there is no leverage and the primary position is maintained by the hedge fund. *Tahwil* or paying a third-party's obligations[72] has been raised in some literature relating to Islamic hedging and risk management as a reason to support the netting of obligations in a more aggressive *salam* strategy.

Legal

> '... Legal risk is the risk that a particular transaction does not produce the economic results that a party had bargained for, either because there has been a change in law or regulation or more usually because the party failed to appreciate or address one or more of the risks inherent in the transaction.'[73]

This definition applies beyond derivatives and is particularly apt in reference to the full Islamic market. Depending upon the deal type, each transaction has unique risks, including documentation risk, corporate culture risk, and – the primary issue in all transactions – counterparty risk. Each risk branches further. For instance, counterparty risk runs to *ultra vires* or operating with legal capacity and principal – agent risk. Product risks run to netting, settlement and collateralisation. There is also intention risk which speaks to gambling or business. The conventional derivatives markets have sought to address many of the legal risk challenges though common agreements such as the ISDA Master Agreement. The early stage of conceptualisation in the Islamic capital market for derivative and hedging products means that there is limited standardisation of non-*murabaha* transactions. When it comes to Islamic derivatives, the regulatory, tax and accounting management issues are at the precise same level as the legal ones, if not behind.

Conclusion

This chapter explores the still poorly developed field of derivatives applied to risk dispersion in Islamic finance. The two main challenges are that the market requires substantial research by Islamic scholars and jurists; and this research will necessarily inspire *ijtihad* with respect to the design and execution of new derivative instruments. The most promising areas are those involving *salam*, *sukuk* and options. A large number of reasonable interim solutions have been pursued applying *murabaha* and *salam*, but these are the beginning of the journey to develop replicable, scalable risk dispersion techniques that protect Islamic financial institutions and investors.

---

[1] From definitions posted at www.isda.org.

[2] Hanna, Nelly, *Making Big Money in 1600: The Life and Times of Isma'il Abu Taqiyya, Egyptian Merchant* (Syracuse, NY: Syracuse University Press, 1998), pp. 56, 57.

[3] Edwardes, Warren, *Key Financial Instruments: Understanding & Innovation in the World of Derivatives* (London: Pearson Education, 2000), p. 27.

[4] In a credit default swap, the assets are securitised, but the securitising SPV enters into a swap of risks with a counterparty whose default risk is preferred by the securities holders.

[5] Edwardes, *op. cit.*, pp. 35, 36. Some simple liberties are taken with Warren's paradigms as we shift to the Islamic.

[6] *Ibid*, p. 41.

[7] Kamali, Mohammad Hashimj, *Islamic Commercial Laws: An Analysis of Futures and Options* (Selangor, Malaysia: Ilmiah Publishers, 2002), p. 146.

[8] It may be surprising to some readers, but many of the modern financial applications of Islamic contracts are 'derivatives' of a sort.

[9] Edwardes, *op. cit.*, p. 42.

[10] Hayes, Sam and Frank Vogel, *Islamic Law and Finance: Religion, Risk and Return* (The Hague: Kluwer Law International, 1998).

[11] Edwardes, *op. cit.*

[12] *Ibid*, p. 7.

[13] *Ibid*, pp. 44, 45.

[14] *Ibid*, p. 110.

[15] See Kamali, Mohammad Hashim, *Islamic Commercial Laws: An Analysis of Futures and Options* (Selangor, Malaysia: IIM.I.A.h Publishers, 2002), p. 3.

[16] *Ibid*, p. 94.

[17] *Ibid*, see Chapter 2.

[18] *Ibid*, p. 16.

[19] *Ibid*, p. 20.

[20] *Ibid*, p. 103. Later, Kamali points out that other schools of Islamic law take the view of *salam*, and that its applicability to fungible goods also removes the elements of *gharar* (p. 105).

[21] *Ibid*, p. 113.

[22] *Ibid*, p. 23.

[23] *Ibid*, p. 22.

[24] *Ibid*, p. 130.

[25] *Ibid*, p. 24. Forwards are characterised by Kamali as privately negotiated documents which meet the needs of a futures contract, p. 25.

[26] *Ibid*, p. 115.

[27] *Ibid*, p. 107.

[28] *Ibid*, p. 91. Kamali cites Ibn Qayyim and Sanhuri relating to the lack of textual evidence forbidding the sale of non-existent objects.

[29] Elgari, Dr Mohamed, 'A Short Term Financial Instrument Based on the Salam Contract' in Khan, Tariqullah and Ahmad, Ausaf, eds., *Islamic Financial Instruments for Public Sector Resource Mobilization* (Jeddah: Islamic Development Bank, 1997), p. 253.

[30] Kamali, *op. cit.*, p. 38.

[31] *Ibid*, p. 40.

[32] ISDA, *op. cit.*

[33] Kamali, *op. cit.*, p. 184.

[34] Elgari, Dr Muhammad, comments as member of Shari'a Question and Answer Panel at 4th Annual Euromoney Islamic Finance Summit, London, 23 February 2005.

[35] Elgari, Dr Mohamed, Shari'a Question and Answer Panel, 4th Annual Euromoney Islamic Finance Summit, London, 23 February 2005.

[36] Edwardes, *op. cit.*, p. 233. Warrants are standardised options which can be traded on an exchange. The issuer may not be the issuer of the underlying shares.

[37] Kamali, *op. cit.*, p. 181.

[38] Tyser, C.R. et al, tr. *The Mejelle* (Kuala Lumpur: The Other Press, 2001), pp. 44, 45.

[39] Elgari, Dr Mohamed, Shari'a Question and Answer Panel, 4th Euromoney Islamic Finance Summit, London, 23 February 2005.

[40] Stewart, Glenn, *An Examination of Financial Derivative Products in Reference to Ahadith Literature and Fiqh* accessed at www.ajif.org on 28 June 2005.

[41] Khan, Tariqullah, *Financial Risk Management in Islamic Finance*, (Jeddah: Islamic Research & Training Institute, 2000).

[42] Kamali, *op. cit.*, pp. 195, 196.

[43] Obaidullah, Mohammed, 'Financial Contracting in Currency Markets: An Islamic Evaluation', *International Journal of Islamic Financial Services*, vol. 3, no. 3, 1999.

[44] Edwardes, *op. cit.*, p. 237.

[45] Khan, *Financial Risk Management in Islamic Finance*, *op. cit.*

[46] Obaidullah, Mohammed, 'Financial Contracting in Currency Markets: An Islamic Evaluation', op.cit.

[47] Kamali, *op. cit.*, p. 193. Kamali does not think that the purpose of the *urboun* and the option are the same and the analogy should not be brought too close.

[48] *Ibid*, p. 201.

[49] *Ibid*, p. 163.

[50] *Ibid*, p. 166.

[51] *Ibid*, p. 168.

[52] ISDA, *op. cit.*

[53] *Ibid.*

[54] Obaidullah, *op. cit.*

[55] Khan, *op. cit.*

[56] Fink, Ronald, 'Default Swap Faults', *CFO Magazine*, October 2004, pp. 39–42.

[57] Haron, Abdullah, 'Risk Management in Islamic Financial Institutions: Towards Developing Risk Management Standard,' presented at Asian Islamic Banking and Finance Workshop on 'Implementing Islamic Money Market: Issues and Challenges', 23 September 2004. Key elements of Haron's matrix of Islamic asset risks are reviewed in this sub-section as are complementary risks identified by Khan, Tariqullah, 'Unique Risks of Islamic Banks,' presented at Asian Islamic Banking and Finance Workshop on 'Implementing Islamic Money Market: Issues and Challenges', 23 September 2004.

[58] Tariqullah Khan, *Financial Risk Management in Islamic Finance* (Jeddah: Islamic Research & Training Institute, 2000).

[59] Hashim, Norsiah, 'Overview of the Development of the Capital Adequacy Standard Practices for Institutions offering Islamic Financial Services' at Asian Islamic Banking and Finance Workshop on 'Implementing Islamic Money Market: Issues and Challenges', 23 September 2004.

[60] Riegel, Jean-Marc, 'Islamic Hedging Instruments,' presented at Asian Islamic Banking and Finance Workshop on 'Implementing Islamic Money Market: Issues and Challenges', 23 September 2004. Also presented at 4th Annual Euromoney Islamic Finance Summit, London, 23 February 2005. Also see Iqbal, Zamir, *Financial Engineering in Islamic Finance* (Thunderbird International Business Review, Vol. 41 (4/5) 541-60 (July–October 1999), pp. 552–554 where Iqbal analyses a similar approach applying *salam* and *istisna'a* as well as *murabaha*.

[61] Riegel, *op. cit.*

[62] *Ibid.* Also, Riegel remarks at Euromoney 4th Annual Islamic Finance Summit, London, 23 February 2005.

[63] Edwardes, *op. cit.* Culled from multiple segments of this work.

[64] Burgess, Kate, 'Regulators test hedge funds' formula', *Financial Times*, 11 March 2005, p. 3. She goes on to report that the first real hedge fund was set up by a late 1940's short seller seeking to 'hedge' his exposure to the markets. The term was adopted to mean a form of insurance against a drop in the market. Arbitrage funds may be hedge funds, but are exploiters of price differentials in disparate markets.

[65] Kamali, *op. cit.*, p. 46.

[66] Burgess, op.cit.

[67] Warren Edwardes comment posted to ibfnet@yahoogroups.com on 31 May 2005.

[68] El-Gamal, Mahmoud, 'Near-fraudulent marketing of "Islamic Hedge Funds"' posted at www.el-gamal.com on 26 May 2005.

[69] *Ibid.*

[70] Warren Edwardes comment posted to ibfnet@yahoogroups.com on 27 May 2005.

[71] 'Alfanar Hedges its Fund in Difficult US Market', *Islamic Banker*, November/December 2003, vol. 94, 95, p. 7

[72] Khan, Tariqullah and Habib Ahmed, *Risk Management: An Analysis of Issues in Islamic Financial Industry*, (Jeddah: Islamic Research and Training Institute, 2001), p. 153.

[73] Levine, Iona, in Edwardes, *op. cit.*, p. 120.

13 The regulatory constellation and challenges

Abdulkader Thomas, with special thanks to Helmi Talib, Rifaat Abdel Karim, Umer Chapra and Tariqullah Khan

Introduction

In contrast to the western banking model in which banks segregate different financial business lines as well as differentiate between commercial and financial risks, Islamic banking does not necessarily segregate business lines. Islamic banking may not even distinguish between commercial and financial risk in the same manner. Such contrasts give rise to a newly emerging regulatory framework for Islamic banking. This framework is based upon the realities of Islamic banking, first, and then upon the real need of Islamic financial institutions to integrate into the global financial system and comply with specific standards. At this phase of development, the effort is very much directed at inclusion versus influence. Yet, the proactive approach taken towards Islamic banking by the UK's Financial Services Authority shows that the western markets are open to direct and well-structured input from the Islamic market and its regulators.

The traditional aims of western regulation include protecting consumers by ensuring that banks operate prudentially under the guidance of fit and proper managers, controlling system risk, and, more recently, making sure they do not lend themselves to abuse by criminals. Already in the ordinary course of business, criminal inquiries, increased as part of the so-called 'war on terror' have led to concern in the banking and import-export markets of transactions and wires being held up whilst authorities determine if the parties are behaving legitimately.[1] Successful propagation of an Islamic framework brings transparency to a world of suspicion in which some individuals confuse the differences in methods with facilitation of money laundering.[2]

Despite Dr Ahmed Elnaggar's aspirations, the Islamic Development Bank (IDB) did not become the central bank of Islamic banking, and as a result it did not become a lender of last resort. In fact, there is neither currently nor prospectively an Islamic lender of last resort. Nonetheless, some central banks are willing to discretely play that role for banks located in their home countries.

Islamic markets

With specific exceptions, the historical regulation of Islamic banking has been ad hoc. Only Malaysia launched its Islamic banking project within a defined framework under its established banking regulatory regime. And, only Malaysia pursued this process as part of the country's broader vision relating to its long-term economic and social goals. Iran, Sudan, Bahrain, Pakistan followed with detailed and comprehensive infrastructures.[3] OIC and other countries have taken the following approaches to incorporating the Islamic markets needs as follows:

1. ad hoc regulation for Islamic business lines, windows or banks;
2. permitting Islamic business lines, windows within a structured framework;
3. permitting Islamic banks within a structured framework; and
4. permitting all within a structured framework (Pakistan and Malaysia[4]).

Certain countries such as Pakistan and Malaysia have pioneered a central *Shari'a* board. In the case of Pakistan it is not restricted only to scholars but includes bankers, lawyers, accountants, and economists.[5] Most countries have not yet required such bodies and these may change the functionality of *Shari'a* committees at the bank level.

This chapter does not propose to evaluate and contrast the different countries and their Islamic regulatory systems. Rather the emphasis is on the issues defining the emerging consensus among these and other countries about the global Islamic regulatory framework and how that process allows Islamic financial institutions to interact in the global marketplace. The spectrum of financial and non-financial markets with influence on the financial sector includes money and foreign exchange markets, capital markets and commodity markets. The successful evolution of Islamic banking requires not only a global framework, but the commitment of a bank's primary regulatory body.

General supervisory standards

> 'Prudential standards developed for conventional banks do no necessarily foster the financial system stability in countries where Islamic banks operate.'
> (Dr Rifaat Abdel Karim, Euromoney 1st Annual Islamic Finance Summit, January 2002.)

On the one hand, the purpose of the Islamic regulators and advisory boards is to facilitate appropriate interaction with western regulators. On the other hand, the dominant and most authoritative western regulators are insisting that everyone plays with a similar playbook. This includes both traditionally unregulated entities such as offshore hedge funds finding themselves obliged to comply with specific US Securities and Exchange Commission requirements,[6] and non-traditional banking approaches, such as Islamic banking, being crammed into the Basel I and II accords.

Although general standards include the emerging anti-terrorism and anti-crime-related measures, these are not an emphasis of this chapter. A number of countries that formally regulate Islamic banking are fully compliant with key international standards.[7]

The existing standard is for Islamic banks to have *Shari'a* boards of prominent and qualified scholars. Malaysia has a centralised state-sponsored *Shari'a* board. A new approach has been suggested that the scholars represent both sides on a deal like lawyers and the opinion is validated by an independent body such as the International Islamic Financial Market (IIFM). This latter approach has been applied for a number of *sukuk* such as the Qatar global *sukuk* issuance. Elsewhere, a supreme state council as established in Malaysia, Pakistan and Iran sets standards and institutional level boards or representatives ensure business-level compliance.

A growing but still small number of countries have clear Islamic banking laws. The application of CAMELS, Basel I and II, compliance standards vary, and the GAAP/IASB/AAOIFI standards are applied variably. The general rule remains that Islamic banks are obliged to follow regulatory and accounting standards applied to traditional banks. These standards may encompass the familiar and govern the fitness and properness of a person to lead a bank. But, as this chapter emphasises, the core challenges are building up the correct analysis at the asset level.

Globally, the International Financial Reporting Standards (IFRS) promise to push a greater orientation towards market value. But, this type of analysis is difficult to determine with respect to Islamic finance. Even in the conventional markets, analysts fear that these rules will cause short-term volatility.[8] And this is where AAOIFI (the Accounting and Auditing Organization for Islamic Financial Institutions) and the IFSB (Islamic Financial Services Board) are playing a critical role harmonising standards and rules that are not precisely the same due to the lack of uniform approaches to value, risk and structure between Islamic and non-Islamic financial approaches. One example of the IFSB steps towards harmonisation is its work to incorporate Uniform Commercial Code (UCC) concepts into its regulations in a tabular form. The worst-case result of AAOIFI's and IFSB's work is to establish best practices.[9] Only Bahrain requires compliance with AAOIFI standards which are elsewhere best practice.

With the foundation of the Islamic Bank of Britain, as well as the exploratory efforts to establish new Islamic banks elsewhere in Europe, the role of European Directives as law will become increasingly important. On the one hand, these directives bring to the Basel accords the force of law. On the other hand, value-added tax and consumer protection laws may have deleterious meanings for Islamic banks wishing to offer *murabaha* sales as a form of consumer credit.

These observations define a patchwork that does not yet define a way forward to integrate Islamic banking into the global system.

Emerging Islamic network

Accounting and Auditing Organization for Islamic Financial Institutions (AAOIFI)

The first element of the Islamic supervisory network was the AAOIFI. The founding secretary general, Dr Rifaat Abdel Karim, is a member of the International Accounting Standards Board (IASB) and one of

Exhibit 13.1 **Regulations and issues**

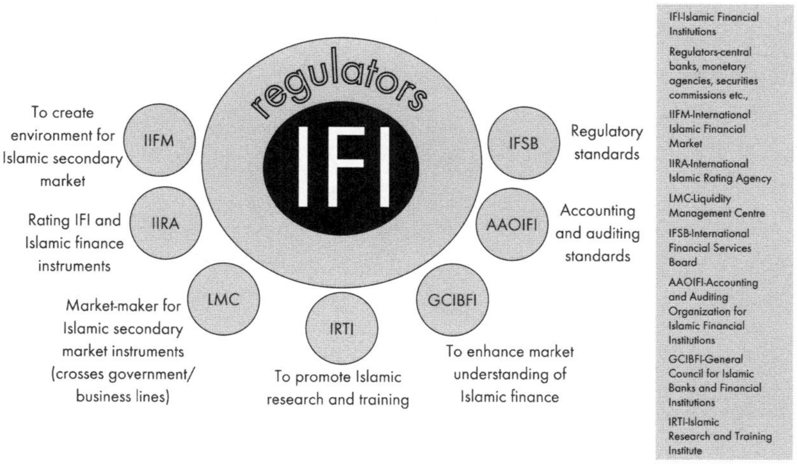

Source: Bryan Kraty.

the leading global authorities on accounting. Beyond the direct standardisation of Islamic standards, a key element of AAOIFI's work has been to achieve integration with global financial networks. AAOIFI's challenge started as the absence of generally accepted accounting, auditing and governance standards for Islamic financial institutions. Subsequently, AAOIFI has begun work on the development of prudential standards for Islamic banks.

Established in 1991, by Islamic banks and central banks from 24 countries, AAOIFI is a self-regulatory body. AAOIFI issues standards for Islamic financial institutions, which, as at mid-2005, included 22 on accounting; five on auditing; four on governance; two on ethics; and 18 on *Shari'a* standards. As a rule, AAOIFI has sought for the standards to complement IFRS standards for transactions, adapting them to the unique circumstances of Islamic financial institutions. The standard development process is also similar to the IASB approach. Its scope covers both Islamic financial institutions and Islamic insurance companies in a format that follows IFRS formats.

Since Islamic banking began to take root, each Islamic financial institution and regulatory authority developed standards, practices and regulations independently of others in the industry. Frequently, these standards were developed without any guidance by national banking regulators. As a result, the accounting practices applied by different Islamic financial institutions were inconsistent, and have remained so until recently. This means that financial statements are frequently non-transparent due to inadequate disclosures. Moreover, ad hoc regulations do not provide a 'level playing field' for all financial institutions. AAOIFI's efforts towards standardisation have moved the industry closer to achieving comparability and transparency of financial statements. AAOIFI's goal in this is to enhance confidence in the industry by achieving true and transparent disclosure that shows what Islamic banks actually do as opposed to cramming Islamic transactions into a conventional box.

Conventional accounting standards do not meet the specific requirements of the Islamic banking industry. AAOIFI has taken the strong position that Islamic accounting standards are necessary in order to provide sufficient, relevant and reliable information to the users of the financial statements of Islamic financial institutions and service providers. The approach taken by AAOIFI was to start with objectives established in contemporary accounting thought, test them against Islamic *Shari'a* and then accept those that are consistent with *Shari'a* and reject those that are not.

For instance, AAOIFI seeks to achieve representational faithfulness relating to the underlying Islamic transactions such as *murabaha*, *ijarah muntahia bittamleek* and so on. Such correct representation is needed in order to ensure comparability of financial statements.

Islamic Financial Services Board (IFSB)

Weighing in on these matters is the IFSB. This body was founded by the core regulators in both the primary Islamic markets, key minorities and multinational bodies such as the International Monetary Fund (IMF). Led by Dr Rifaat Abdel Karim (now in his role as secretary general of IFSB), the IFSB is focused on the structured regulatory convergence of supervisory standards. This international convergence is meant to achieve comparable standards of capital measurement and capital standards. Since 1988, the current Basel standards have provided a simple standardised approach to minimum capital requirements relating to five classes of obligors, but without any distinction between the relative degrees of obligor creditworthiness.

International Islamic Financial Market (IIFM)

The IIFM was established to facilitate secondary markets for Islamic instruments. Initially, there was some discussion that the charter of this central bank and IDB-supported body would be to act as a true secondary market purchaser. IIFM, however, was never capitalised for such a role and has settled upon two primary roles for itself: market education and *Shari'a* authentication. These roles take it out of the institutional supervisory and secondary markets role and move it more towards an independent *Shari'a*-compliance monitoring role with respect to Islamic securities. IIFM is likely to undergo changes as both the market and its board define a clearer space for it.

Liquidity Management Centre (LMC)

The LMC was formed to be an Islamic Fannie Mae-type entity, providing a secondary market buyer for *sukuk*. A public–private venture with commercial and central bank shareholders, the LMC has become more of a market-making investment banker than a secondary market resource. Like the IIFM, as the Islamic markets expand, the original mandate of the LMC to develop into a true secondary market buyer is likely to be fulfilled.

International Islamic Rating Agency (IIRA)

With the Basel II requirements in mind, the IDB and various central banks formed the IIRA. This body has yet to emerge as a ratings force, in part because the depth and availability of data in the emerging Islamic markets is insufficient in most cases to facilitate a home-grown ratings agency. Nonetheless, most OIC member states are following Malaysia's lead in establishing credit data capacity. As this data universe improves in size and quality, the viability of the IIRA will become more certain. Yet, as the data improves, global and regional private sector ratings bodies will also seek a leading role in rating Islamic securities and issuers. Already, all major international, all Malaysian, and the leading regional agency covering the GCC have begun to take seriously the Islamic financial markets. This may impinge upon the opportunity for the IIRA to grow into a significant and successful agency in its own right in the absence of sufficient resources.

Islamic Research and Training Institute (IRTI)

One of the treasures of the Islamic financial information constellation is the IRTI at the IDB. Not only have many of the leading thinkers in the field of Islamic banking spent time at IRTI, but the Institute has sponsored some of the most important analyses of products, concepts, regulation, supervision, development economics and risk management produced to date in the field. IRTI studies are typically published in Arabic, English and French.

Global Council of Islamic Banks and Financial Institutions (GCIBFI)

Since the inception of Islamic banking, there have been a number of industry groups. Until recently these were not properly funded, and they were frequently located away from the centre of the business. The GCIBFI is a promising relaunch of the concept of an industry group that facilitates the advancement of the Islamic financial sector through research, public relations and lobbying. Based in Bahrain but neutral to any one player and country, GCIBFI is making significant strides in lifting the profile of the Islamic financial sector.

As a whole, these institutions are significant and important to the future success of Islamic banking and finance. They remove the burden from individual banks, which in the global scheme are small, and present a coherent front relating to industry needs and objectives. This common approach is fundamental because of the misperceptions spawned in the global press relating to political events that mistakenly confuse 'Islamic' banking with informal money transfer systems such as the *hawala* systems or radical political movements that have appropriated the word 'Islam'.[10] More fundamentally and on a technical level, these bodies are necessary to ensure the proper integration of the emerging Islamic market into the global financial markets in an accurate and comparable manner. This last challenge is the most complicated due to the unique characteristics of both Islamic contracts applied to financial relationships and financial institutions specialising in these contracts.

Risk monitoring and measurement

Basel II

The new Basel accords bring a greater focus on risk measurement and control. These are based on the 'Three Pillars' concept of capital adequacy, supervisory review and market discipline. The Basel framework has traditionally been biased in favour of the internationally active banks from the G10 countries.

> 'Basle II Rules cannot create a perfectly harmonised banking regulation across all jurisdictions because different legal systems, market practices and business conditions would remain.' (Jamie Caruana, Chairman, Basel Committee on Banking Supervision.)[11]

The new Basel accords, therefore, do not directly address the specific requirements of Islamic banks. However, not all regulators of Islamic banking view this as a negative issue. 'Basle II will oblige Islamic banks to identify and unbundle the risks inherent in Islamic financial instruments,' commented Dr Zeti Aktar, governor of Bank Negara Malaysia.[12] These pillars are addressed by AAOIFI and are under analysis by IFSB.

CAMELS

Basel II reflects evolutionary CAMELS, which are the measuring tools applied since Basel I. CAMELS are meant to analyse the following factors effectively for the safety of the banking system, bank by bank:

- capital adequacy;
- asset quality;
- management/administration;
- earnings;
- liquidity; and
- sensitivity.

The core approach of two-tier supervision leads to expanded rights to do business as a function of good CAMELS results. The AAOIFI and IFSB approach is to allow the evolved CAMELS to adapt further to the realities of the business of an Islamic bank.

Pillar I: capital adequacy

External ratings-based

In order to calculate the risk, adjusted capital requirements have three options. The first option is to apply external ratings-based (ERB) methods to allocate risk weights. An ERB approach has an agency, public bias and is best suited to large banks operating in sophisticated markets with rich data and competing rating agencies. The ERB approach requires an experience-rich infrastructure and a full domestic capital market. Although this is very applicable to highly developed markets, only Malaysia truly qualifies to contemplate ERB application in its home market. But, the weakness of ERB is that it is deeply biased against small and medium enterprises as well as small transactions. This plays out in a systemic bias against small and medium-sized banks in any country, poor countries, and emerging markets.

Internal ratings-based

The second option is an internal ratings-based (IRB) approach. This has sub-branches of foundation-based methods – assigned by the regulator – and an advanced approach, whereby the central bank allows banks to apply their market experience and tested observations to the rating of client risks. IRB allows the banker to take into account a wider variety of commercial and market circumstances. The weaknesses of the method relate to its consistent application. The most important factor in its application is the obligation of the central bank to ensure that the implementation and oversight of IRB is independent from the bank's marketing. This approach is considered the most reliable in the current emerging market environment.

Models-based

The third option is a models-based approach. This is a refined version of IRB, but is portfolio and data-driven using sophisticated algorithmic tools such as the KMV model. Like ERB, this is an approach that requires a data-rich market. The models-based approach might be applicable in Malaysia alone among Islamic markets.

Pillar 2: supervisory review

Basel II's second pillar is supervisory review. The purpose is to evaluate the risk profiles of individual banks and to specify the need for remedial measures; the pro-active identification and management of problems before they become 'systemic'.

Pillar 3: market discipline

Basel II's third pillar is market discipline. This is meant to enhance the degree of transparency in public reporting by banks and their mandatory disclosures which lend improved insight into the adequacy of their capitalisation.

In order to comply with Basel II, banking regulators and bankers must have strong risk-identification abilities that allow them to measure, monitor and ensure ongoing management of primary risks. In the Basel II view, the primary risks are market risk and operational risk.

Market and operational risk

This is the risk of an unexpected loss to the bank's income due to unexpected changes in market prices. Some of the primary dangers include changes in the reference price (mark-up in *murabaha* or rental rate); changes in the prices of real assets and services; changes in the prices of financial assets; and currency exchange rates. While market risk is fundamentally related to the management of external variables, operational risk may be both internal and external as it relates to the loss resulting from inadequate or failed internal processes, people and systems or from external events.

Islamic banks have unique balance-sheet features that have a direct impact on their exposure to market risk. For instance, Khan points out that traditional banks face market risk mostly in the trading book. In contrast, Islamic banks face it in their banking book since instruments such as *murabaha, ijarah, salam, musharaka* and *mudaraba* all reflect a commercial risk that bundles market risk and credit risk.[13] The commercial aspects and underdeveloped secondary markets for Islamic instruments mean that the duration of the commitment ties the transaction strongly to the original reference rate.

Credit risk

When it comes to credit risk features, the primary issue is that the traditional banking market charges penalty interest. And, this is precisely *riba*. On the one hand, should the issue of collection arise, can an institution appoint and pay a third party to collect late or defaulted payments for a fee to be paid by the defaulting party? On the other hand, each Islamic process has a distinctive bundling of risks as identified by Khan.[14]

- *Mudaraba/musharaka*: These may be structured to approach loan-like conditions as with a declining-balance *musharaka*, but such transactions are not necessarily collateralised, and there is more variability in the definition of a default event.
- *Salam/istisna'a*: These clearly entail counterparty performance risk in a way that makes the separation of market risk from default risk difficult. In the case of catastrophic counterparty failure, the risk is high. *Istisna'a* also entails specific and unique sub-contractor and agency risks.
- *Murabaha*: Typically, this is collateralised, but the baseline default risk includes counterparty risk due to the fact that the client's promise to purchase is not always deemed to be a binding matter (a jurisdictional matter).

When risks are conglomerated, each Islamic institution has its own unique profile depending upon its distribution of assets across the different processes, and then to obligors. These lead to a potentially complex array of credit, liquidity, market and reputation risks.

Given the preponderance of Islamic banks in emerging markets, the small size of Islamic banks, and the unique risk profiles of their instruments, the most applicable system is the IRB approach. The localised and unique experience of each Islamic bank, its risk concentration in specific asset classes, means that it is more likely to adjudge, given the dearth of statistical data, the probability of a loss given default (LGD) of the facility or the probability of default (PD) of the obligor or both than either a ratings-based system or a models-based approach.

In the framework of Basel II, with the approval of supervisors, banks can use their own internal assessments of their asset risk components for meeting regulatory capital requirements. These components include

PD, LGD, exposure at default (EAD), and effective maturity of facility (MOF). The foundation IRB approach lets banks use their own PDs, but the supervisors assign LGDs, EADs and MOFs (see Exhibit 13.2). The advanced IRB approach allows banks to use their own PDs, LGDs, EADs and MOFs.

Exhibit 13.2 **Foundation IRB approach versus IRB approach**

Input	*Foundation IRB*	*IRB*
Probability of default (PD)	Provided by bank based on own estimates	Provided by bank based on own estimates
Loss given default (LGD)	Supervisory values set by the Committee	Provided by bank based on own estimates
Exposure at default (EAD)	Supervisory values set by the Committee	Provided by bank based on own estimates
Maturity (M)	Supervisory values set by the Committee or at national discretion provided by bank based on own estimates (with an allowance to exclude certain exposures)	Provided by bank based on own estimates (with an allowance to exclude certain exposures)

Source: Author's own.

The building of judgement-driven default probabilities requires bankers who are capable of detailed, thorough and independent analysis of financial statements of the client to assess its future cash flow and its ability to meet its contractual obligations. These are typically seasoned bankers. The analysis necessarily includes:

- debt service capacity of the client;
- liquidity of the client's balance sheet;
- historical earnings;
- access to sources of funds; and
- leverage ratio, etc.

The analysts must have access to peer group information, audit reports and, when available, external credit assessment reports.

Risk weighting Islamic financial transactions: a new proposal

Under the new Basel II rules, the risk weightings will become more textured and ratings-driven. Khan, in a ground-breaking study with Habib Ahmed [15] at IRTI, surveyed the risk perceptions at Islamic banks relating to the degree of risk per transaction type. They derived the following rankings with '1' not a serious risk and '5' a critically serious risk.

- *Musharaka* 3.69
- Diminishing *musharaka* 3.33
- *Mudaraba* 3.25
- *Salam* 3.20
- *Istisna'a* 3.13
- *Ijarah* 2.64
- *Murabaha* 2.56

Exhibit 13.3 **Risk weighting Islamic financial transactions: internal allocation of capital**

	Risk perception				
Modes of finance	*1 to 5*	*% of 5*	*Weight (w), Index Murabaha = 100*	*Capital needs $*	
Musharaka	3.69	73.8	144; w =1.44	288	Assumptions:Commitment (C) = $10,000; EAD = 50% (of C); LGD = 50% (of EAD); Minimum capital requirement = 8%; Weight (w) base = 100 Actual capital requirement = C*EAD*LGD*W*8%
DBM	3.33	66.6	130; w = 1.30	260	
Mudaraba	3.25	65	127; w = 1.27	254	
Salam	3.2	64	125; w = 1.25	250	
Istisna'a	3.13	62.6	122; w = 1.22	244	
Ijarah	2.64	52.8	102; w = 1.02	204	
Murabaha	2.56	51.2	100; w = 1	200	

C commitment, EAD exposure at default, LGD loss given default

Source: Tariqullah Khan.

Following this analysis – which took into account credit risk, rate risk, operations risk, market risk, foreign exchange risk, country risk and liquidity risk – they produced the following recommendation for risk weighting Islamic financial transactions (see Exhibit 13.3). This was submitted to IFSB which has recently published exposure drafts seeking to arrive at the correct analysis of the risks and the appropriate risk weights. Some accounting observers believe that, in the absence of regulatory obligation – that is, IFSB standards will be 'best practice' – many Islamic banks and windows will seek to arbitrage the most favourable weightings that their regulator will allow.

Khan proposes these weights for risk assets, and has had input into the AAOIFI and IFSB process. In the meantime, AAOIFI and the IFSB have agreed that not only do Islamic banks have to apply unique weights to measure risk assets, but they considered a formula for regulatory capital that applies the basic Basel definition, but considers:

- fiduciary (management delinquency) risk;
- commercial displaced risk;
- profit equalisation reserve; and
- investment risk reserve.

The risk-weighted assets exclude 50 per cent of the risk assets financed by profit-sharing investment accounts (PSIAs). The minimum capital ratio is the same as the Basel minimum. This conclusion, however, leads to a new problem: how does one analyse funds placed in an Islamic bank?

The analytical challenge of profit-sharing deposits

The problem is how to account for the conflicts between substance and form. For instance, consider the Islamic process of *ijarah-wa-iqtina'a*, which exemplifies some of these conflicts. Islamic bank accounting favours form, when contemporary accounting favours substance over form. The former treats the process as a lease which has a redemption feature. But, when the process is applied in US banks, it is accounted for as an interest-bearing loan since the redemption feature is viewed as contractual, even when it is a promise.

This challenge is exacerbated when considering a *musharaka* or *mudaraba* 'depositor' in an Islamic bank. In these deposit forms, the consumer is taking equity risk through this form of PSIA. Yet the shareholders are prepared to take a greater and infinite equity risk in the enterprise. PSIA account holders have only agreed to take a time-delimited equity risk, which may also be linked to a specific business line as opposed to the entire enterprise. The PSIA accounts may appear to have a negative affect on the credit, valuation and market risk of some institutions. However, this impact is often mitigated by risk-sharing contracted as an element of the account. These differences require an accounting treatment and disclosure that are unique to Islamic financial institutions.

In the AAOIFI approach, with respect to the restricted and unrestricted PSIA, capital is recognised when it is paid to the *mudarib*, the bank. The bank's share of profits is recognised at the time of liquidation if it is within a single period. If the PSIA continues for more than one period, then the profits are recognised on distribution. The *mudaraba* capital, if contributed in kind, is stated at fair value. Like the PSIA *mudaraba* accounts, the *musharaka* accounts face substantial challenges for integration into the conventional regulatory environment.

According to AAOIFI's FAS 6 relating to unrestricted investments and their equivalents, these are treated as elements of the bank's financial position, because they are based on unrestricted *mudaraba*. The accounts are not considered a liability of the bank, and they are not considered part of the bank's ownership equity because they lack certain ownership rights such as voting rights. The comingling of PSIA and shareholder funds nonetheless confuses the matter as to their characterisation.

Restricted investment accounts are not assets of the Islamic bank and should not be reflected in the bank's financial statements. This is because the bank does not have the right to use or dispose of these investments except within the PSIAs' contractual conditions.

PSIAs: risk capital or liability?

The challenge is whether or not PSIAs may be considered as constituting part of a bank's risk capital? Or are they pure liability? If it is capital, does the PSIA affect Tier 2 or Tier 3 capital? Moreover, are there specific risks to an Islamic bank's own equity in light of its accepting PSIAs? In this banking environment, there may not be an appreciable difference between unrestricted PSIAs and restricted PSIAs. But, is it possible to consider unrestricted PSIAs as a form of Tier 2, whereas restricted PSIAs are not part of a bank's regulatory capital? As we proceed with this chapter, these questions form a critical component of understanding the challenges of analysing the risks, and correspondent risk weights associated with Islamic banks.

Fundamentally, Islamic banking has primary problems with the treatment of PSIAs with respect to risk weighting and the definition of capital. Ostensibly, the assets financed by PSIAs do not affect a bank's risk-bearing capital because the commercial risk of these assets falls on PSIAs. In fact, there may be an inversion of the imbalance between PSIAs and risk assets compared with conventional bank deposits and risk assets as PSIAs prospectively take a greater asset risk: the risk assets may be less risky than the deposits.[16] Therefore, the AAOIFI Capital Adequacy Committee suggested that the risk-weighted assets financed by PSIAs should be excluded from the denominator of the capital adequacy ratio.

Fiduciary risk and displaced commercial risk

Beyond this, PSIAs raise issues relating to fiduciary risk, displaced commercial risk, and liquidity risk. For instance, the bank's capital has to bear fiduciary risk as the agent for managing the capital. Displaced commercial risk is the risk that the bank will either lose money on the investments underlying the deposits or the investments will underperform comparable deposits in the conventional market. Such circumstances may cause depositors to move their money to conventional banks. Because of this risk, AAOIFI has suggested that a proportion of the risk-weighted assets financed by PSIAs should be included in the denominator of the capital adequacy ratio.

This treatment applies to both restricted and unrestricted PSIAs. Since they bear commercial risk, they are akin to being a form of capital. But, PSIAs do not fall into any of Basel I or II defined Tiers. PSIAs may be close to Tier 3 subordinated debt, but their maturity is normally shorter than five years.

Liquidity risk

The liquidity risk of PSIAs is related to securing funding with maturities and rates that are suitable to the bank's business profile; and the risk of liquidating assets to support withdrawals in a timely manner and at reasonable prices to support the value of the investments. If the underlying assets are securities, they must be marked to market, further affecting the performance of such deposits.

According to Khan and Chapra, the factors complicating these risks include:

- incorrect judgement and complacency;
- unanticipated change in cost of capital;
- abnormal behaviour of financial markets;
- range of assumptions used;
- risk activation by secondary sources;
- breakdown of payments system;
- macroeconomic imbalances;
- contractual forms; and
- financial infrastructure deficiency.

Commercial risk

In terms of commercial risk, there seems not to be a reason to include PSIAs in the numerator or capital of the bank or PSIAs-financed assets in the denominator of the capital adequacy ratio. This is because

Exhibit 13.4 **Risk and contractual forms**

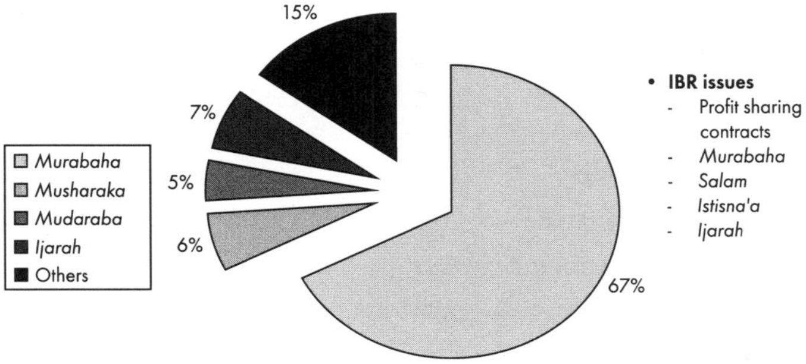

Source: Iqbal Munawar, Ausaf Ahmad and Tariqullah Khan (1998), *Challenges Facing Islamic Banking*, Jeddah: IRTI.

PSIAs appear to bear the risk of assets they finance. But, this is not necessarily the case by contract form, practice or regulation. When one takes into account the risk-asset side of an Islamic bank, some contracts, whose current applications among Islamic banks is shown in Exhibit 13.4, such as *murabaha, istisna'a, salam* and *ijarah* may require multiple steps which are not the same as traditional loans. These additional steps may increase transactional risk at the asset level, and later reach upwards to affect the viability of PSIAs. This leads to an argument that only the denominator of the Basel ratio is affected and PSIAs-financed assets should be excluded from the calculation.

With respect to both fiduciary and displaced commercial risks, a modification of the numerator of the Basel ratio in respect of PSIAs as part of capital was considered. But, these risks should be borne by the bank's own capital and not the PSIAs. For these specific risks, there is no reason to consider PSIAs as part of a bank's capital.

The regulatory capital equation

Basel II proposes a uniform definition of capital that varies the risk weights for assets and country risk. As a result, all banks in every country, conventional and Islamic, have the same minimum capital ratio to risk-weighted assets of 8 per cent. The components of capital under the standardised Basel proposals are:

- TIER 1 = (Retained earning + Share capital + Non-cumulative perpetual preferred stock + Reserves + Minority interests) – Goodwill
- TIER 2 = Supplemental capital instruments including: asset revaluation reserve, hybrid capital instruments, subordinated debt, intermediate term contract notes, and other reserves per central bank authorisation.
- TIER 3 = Subordinated term debt, usually with a minimum term.

The Basel formula for a bank's capital adequacy ratio (CAR) is:

Tier 1 + Tier 2 capital divided by total risk–weighted assets

Based upon their analysis of PSIA accounts, IFSB and AAOIFI believe that the CAR should be adjusted as follows in the case of Islamic banks:

CAR= OC/(WOC+I(OC+L)+(.5*PSIA)

where:

CAR = capital adequacy ratio

OC = Tier 1 and Tier 2 capital

PSIA = profit and loss-sharing deposits

W = average risk weight for PSIA-funded assets

L = non-PSIA deposits, true liabilities

The Islamic supervisory bodies allocate 50 per cent of the PSIA to the denominator, thereby accommodating their quasi-equity status. With the more complex risk weightings under development by IFSB, AAOIFI and analysts such as Khan, the reality is that Islamic banks will be asked to have more economic capital than their peers in order to adjust to the non-traditional risks embedded in specific Islamic financial processes.

This affects the risk-adjusted return on capital (RAROC) which is defined as:

(revenues – expected losses)/economic capital

Economic capital reflects the risk taken with a transaction, as capital calculated internally as an amount of own funds to cover losses with the confidence interval required for this activity. In most cases, economic capital is best viewed as the bank's book capital.

Securitisation

Dr Zeti's comments mentioned earlier are based on a view that securitisation, already well-developed in Malaysia's Islamic banking sector, will be a key element to the integration of Islamic banks into the Basel II regime. This has been echoed by at least one central banker in the GCC who thinks that Islamic banks should take less commercial asset level risk and more banking risk; that is, Islamic banks should hold the end securities from underlying Islamic transactions. But, Basel II does not fully deal with securitisation.

Basel recognises the risk dispersion role of securitisation whereby the ownership of assets is transferred along with credit risks associated with credit. Basel also understands that securitisation achieves risk diversification enhancing financial stability at the selling institution. But, securitisation turns on economic substance when determining appropriate capital requirement in standardised and IRB treatments. For instance, many banks sell mortgages to investors and buy back the collateralised mortgage securities. With the ENSEC and Freddie Mac Islamic mortgage alternative securitisations, Islamic banks will also be able to trade their booked deals – *sukuk* – which securities will represent differentiated risk. This means that the original credit risk migrates to whether or not the *sukuk* are marketable, available for sale; what is their maturity, are they held to maturity; are the securities meant to be traded, do they have to be marked to market; are they yield or rate sensitive; and what is their granularity, obligor concentration? Moreover, there is the question of a distinction that is covered throughout this book which is that *sukuk* are attached to the asset, even if tangentially, and thereby asset-based. The traditional western asset-backed security is a note secured by a mortgage or other charge on the asset. Thus *sukuk* are less contingent and closer to a full claim on the underlying asset compared with traditional asset-backed securities.

Approaches governing Muslim minorities

The reality is that the supervisory approach to Muslim minorities, whether in the case of the authorised and operational Islamic Bank or Britain or the windows at US and Singapore banks, is ad hoc. Within this broader ad hoc approach, there are two significant and distinct approaches. In the United Kingdom and Singapore, a structured adaptation of existing banking law has been undertaken to formulate a proper way for an Islamic banking activity to be accommodated until such time as either it requires, or the Basel regime provides, a specific approach to regulating Islamic banks or measuring Islamic assets and deposits.

In the United States, the approach is trifurcated between the national and state banking regulators with a further element of significant input from the Federal Deposit Insurance Corp. (FDIC). Until now, the primary method has been to analogise requested authorisations for Islamic instruments to authorised banking powers under federal or state banking statutes.

Deposit insurance schemes

When it comes to deposits, many countries have deposit insurance schemes which have strict definitions of deposits as loans to the bank for which the capital is guaranteed. In specific cases, there may be a graded approach to non-traditional deposits allowing the yield on the deposit to vary; and subject to certain conditions, the capital may also be subjected to loss. In addition to the restrictive definitions, deposit insurance schemes such as the FDIC and its UK and Canadian peers are mandatory for consumer deposits and guarantee the capital up to a specific minimum in the event of a bank failure. As a result, Islamic bankers are obliged to engage either in specific structuring steps to arrive at a *mudaraba* or *musharaka* relationship that is approved by the insurer and, by business process, renders the insurance irrelevant. On the face of it, this is a difficult task, but the competitive pressures facing Islamic banks in markets such as the GCC have resulted in strategies that may be exported that insulate depositors from loss but adhere to the obligatory steps of either *mudaraba* or *musharaka*. To this end, such strategies have already been approved by US and UK regulators.

This approach to supervision in the Muslim minority communities is unlikely to change until there is either substantive uptake of Islamic products, forcing specific regulation, or there are clear directives in the Basel regime. Until such convergence takes place, there are periodic positive and negative effects of the gap in regulatory treatment. For instance, Islamic scholars appreciate and agree many consumer protections afforded in western markets. In the United States, the Truth in Lending Act requires disclosures that allow consumers to compare costs and even accommodates leasehold estates with applicability to *ijarah* mortgage alternatives. But, in some markets, *murabaha* transactions for consumer goods are subject to an additional layer of VAT or may even lose some capacity to transfer manufacturer's warranties to the consumer.[17]

Conclusion

Pakistan may show the way forward for Islamic bank regulation. Years of top-down efforts to implement Islamic banking have produced only modest achievements. But, a novel approach adopted in the early 2000s separates the 'religious' element from Islamic banking and treats it solely from a legal perspective. The result has been unemotional rule-making that has led to clear guidelines, practical risk management analysis, and stunning growth in the Islamic sector. This progress, in turn, has made it easier for State Bank of Pakistan officials to feed their solutions into the global regulatory framework.

In theory, Islamic banks are likely to be more stable than conventional banks. Ostensibly, they have profit-sharing on both the liability and asset side. In practice, Islamic banks have fixed-income assets but have profit-sharing on the liability side. To achieve proper comparability with western practices, there needs to be more convergence between AAOIFI, IFSB, IDB and BIS capital adequacy and risk measurement methods. This is affected by the size or availability of a secondary market. Although the credit process and investment analysis methods may diverge from common credit and investment analysis decision-making, the Islamic approaches also cover the areas in which analytical methods and risk considerations are exactly the same. As a result, the determinants of the underlying approach require true measurement of the risks according to the distinctive product.

---

1 '"First Impression" case affirms right for wire transfer', *Trade & Forfaiting Review*, February 2005, p. 53.

2 Faille, Christopher, 'Senate Hears of Laundering Issues in Islamic Finance' in *Hedge Funds World*, 21 July 2005 available at www.hedgeworld.com.

3 'BMA Progress on Data Disclosure', *Islamic Banker*, issue no. 85, February 2003, p. 32. The article focuses on data relating to the Islamic banking industry, but in a way that is generally reflective of regulatory depth.

4 Hussain, Irshat, 'Customer Choice Drives Pak IB Policy', *Islamic Banker*, January/February 2005, issue nos 108, 109, p. 7. Pakistan, in contrast to Malaysia, does not have a unique Islamic banking law and requires all banks to meet the same capital adequacy and reporting standards without regard to either uniqueness of deposit line or business line: ie, profit-sharing deposits or micro-credit lending.

5 *Ibid*, p. 7.

[6] Spangler, Timothy, Easy as SEC, HedgeFundManager, Issue 17, May 2005, pp. 42–43. Also see Burgess, Kate, 'Regulators test hedge funds' formula', *Financial Times*, 11 March 2005, p. 3. The key tool of hedge fund regulation appears to be controlling the prime brokers through which the funds trade.

[7] Hussain, Dr. Ishrat, 'Pak Anti-Money Laundering Measures Boost', *Islamic Banker*, April 2003, no. 87, pp. 8, 9.

[8] Tricks, Henry, 'British companies prepare to do it by the new book', *Financial Times*, 5 January 2005, p. 22.

[9] McMillen, Michael, 'Islamic Real Estate Finance', presented at Virginia Commonwealth University, 4 December 2004.

[10] Plews, Tim, 'Establishing Islamic Banks in the West: The Case of the Islamic Bank of Britain', in Jaffer, Sohail, ed., *Islamic Retail Banking: Global Challenges and Opportunities* (London: Euromoney Books, 2005), p. 31.

[11] Quoted in *Financial Times*, 11 April 2005, p. 17.

[12] Quoted at www.globalriskregulator.com.

[13] Khan, Tariqullah, Unique Risks of Islamic Banks presented at Workshop on Risk Management and Capital Adequacy in Islamic Banking, Bank Nagara Malaysia, and Islamic Financial Services Board, Kuala Lumpur on 23 September 2004.

[14] *Ibid.*

[15] Khan, Tariqullah and Ahmad, Ausaf, eds., *Islamic Financial Instruments for Public Sector Resource Mobilization* (Jeddah: Islamic Development Bank, 1997) Chapra, M. Umer and Khan, Tariqullah, *Regulation and Supervision of Islamic Banks* (Jeddah: Islamic Development Bank, 2000).

[16] Chapra, and Tariqullah, *Regulation and Supervision of Islamic Banks, op. cit.*, p. 12.

[17] Said, Pervez, 'The view from the regulators in Pakistan' in Jaffer, Sohail, ed., *Islamic Retail Banking: Global Challenges and Opportunities* (London: Euromoney, 2005), p. 202.

14 Changes and challenges

Abdulkader Thomas

Introduction

Islamic financial services companies are still within the early stage of development. With only a 30-year history of institutional development, Islamic financial institutions have methodically expanded their product base and client reach. This methodology is based upon the systemic application of *Shari'a* principles. Given the novelty of the field, Muslim scholars are obliged to engage in the extrapolation of how principles are to be applied under modern financial and commercial circumstances. These are resulting in a number of insights into prospective new developments.

The changing shape of the Islamic market takes it to both Muslim minorities and western institutional investors. This expanse, perhaps unimaginable back in 1963 in Mit Ghamr, is still broadening, but the coverage is not yet deep. This is because the development of new products is restricted to *Shari'a* principles. These rules have a specific immutability, and how to adapt the core Islamic commercial transaction forms to modern financial intermediation requires significant work by Islamic jurists and the process of *ijtihad*.

Key developments

The traditional nominative contracts have been applied by Islamic banks in a way that dominates the primary banking markets. However, twin needs of managing risk and addressing complex needs of business have required new innovation. The evolution of *sukuk* will possibly make this concept a primary tool to grow the market; assist banks and wealth managers with their asset and liquidity management goals; the formulating of advanced derivatives; and managing new regulatory obligations in the global supervisory framework.

The traditional challenge of Islamic banks in the GCC has been the management of excess liquidity[1] in contrast to Islamic banks elsewhere which are typically capital constrained. *Murabaha* purchases and sales of metals on the international metals exchanges have provided a useful but problematic money market alternative. *Sukuk* issuances and their prospective evolution into actively traded instruments such as other bond forms provides an opportunity to develop a true money market turning on the buying and selling of permissible instruments, bank to bank, in an open market instead of the one-off structured and negotiated *murabaha* market.

Sukuk also provide a platform for the logical development of risk management strategies that mimic derivative approaches, including *sukuk*. In addition to the opportunities that are evolving with *sukuk*, Muslim scholars are exploring such contractual concepts and forms as *urboun* and *salam* to determine if these match directly the western market approaches to derivatives including options and futures. However, the full array of financial instrument derivation in the global capital markets cannot be copied by the Islamic market because the Islamic theory of contract and the definition of *riba* means that Islamic bankers are prevented from unbundling rights, obligations and assets in the same manner.

New opportunities

Bankers and their advisers, Muslim and non-Muslim, are obliged to understand that the *Shari'a* has firm boundaries. The basis of Islamic banking contracts in the classical rules of commercial contract has significant implications for the modification of such contracts for modern financial intermediation, the development of derivatives, and execution of hedging strategies. This means that many concepts applied in global financial markets may be mimicked in the Islamic financial space, but that there are limitations to copying. Ultimately, one will find that the Islamic market is more merchant banking in its orientation than detached in its intermediation. As a result, this book often refers to Islamic 'processes' in lieu of either contracts or products.

The implications of bank supervision comprise a major challenge. First, Islamic instruments and processes are not addressed in either the Basel I or Basel II regulations. The distinctions must be addressed in order for Islamic institutions to be included successfully in the global markets. Beyond that, there are issues within some domestic markets. For instance, will Islamic banks find themselves forced to be holders of securities in order to integrate into the global banking regulatory regime, or will they migrate towards more true merchant banking?

The regulation issues and the need for global integration is complicated by the depth of misperceptions that exist in some political and press environments. For instance, some western regulators equate, without due investigation, the Islamic sector with illegal money laundering and the finance of terrorism. Sadly such perceptions are unconnected to reality and are often founded in deeper prejudices in which Islam as a whole and all Muslims are viewed as harbouring violent intentions towards non-Muslims. Although Islamic bankers and their advisers cannot single-handedly overcome such pernicious biases, they can develop strong and transparent compliance regimes that demonstrate the benign nature of Islam, Muslims, and the application of Islamic rules to finance; connecting observers to modernising, integrating global markets such as the GCC and Malaysia and not the disconnected acts of a few criminals with political motives.

Standardisation

Regional and legal variability in the Muslim world and among the supervisors of Islamic banks will be no different than any other place. Even 'unified' markets such as the United States and the European market have substantial variations relating to transfer, income, property and value-added taxes within their borders. Nonetheless, a variety of transactional elements are standardised allowing for the smooth acceptance of either form or jurisdiction in the western capital markets. On the Islamic side, AAOIFI and the IFSB are working to ensure that best practices become widely accepted in the Islamic market, allowing for the same level of comfort to emerge with respect to a wide universe of transacting. To this end, regulators such as the Bahrain Monetary Agency, Bank Negara Malaysia, and the State Bank of Pakistan have begun working within the emerging Islamic best practices, to take aggressive steps to ensure that these standards are widely understood and applied. For instance, the State Bank of Pakistan has published 'Essentials and Model Agreements for Islamic Modes of Finance' on its website. Such progress is only possible in light of a growing *Shari'a* consensus about various processes and methods. With the benefit of key government support, the Islamic regulatory and accounting regime is strengthening and establishing a clear best practices regime.

New markets

'Islamic banking, although a faith-based banking system, is open to and deals with people of all faiths.'[2] The Islamic financial sector truthfully has three unexplored markets before it. Foremost, there is the universe of needs and demands among Muslim majority countries. These have barely been touched. Then there is the requirement of a large number of Muslims living as minorities in Europe, the Americas and Asia. Significant steps are being taken by regulators, even if not formalised or legislated, in the United Kingdom, United States, Singapore and elsewhere to facilitate market demand for local Muslim minorities.

Finally, there is no reason to think that the different Islamic approaches to finance and investment will not appeal to non-Muslims. Indeed, there is some success with *sukuk*, Islamic equity funds, and mortgage alternatives – each enjoying varying degrees of uptake among different segments of the conventional market. For instance, traditional bond and emerging market investors have become consistent *sukuk* buyers. Global investors in the socially responsible and ethical investing sectors have been drawn to Islamic funds. And, the Islamic home finance sector has seen participation from non-Muslims who share the Islamic objection to interest.

Such cross-over requires the dispelling of misperceptions about Islam and Islamic finance in the broader public. It obligates the Islamic sector to succeed in its endeavour to become transparent. Transference to highly regulated markets also means that the Islamic sector has to transmit the correct assessment of the underlying risks to regulators to allow them to incorporate these into their societies.

Conclusion

The primary Islamic emerging markets enjoy deep support from industrialising nations such as Malaysia, Pakistan and Iran as well as the oil rich Gulf Cooperation Council states. The formal support of these nations means that the market is likely to enjoy continued growth as a matter of public policy supported by wealth from new industry and oil surpluses. Innovation, guided by best practices, is the hallmark of modern Islamic banking and finance. This innovation is allowing for the core nominative Islamic contracts to enjoy wider application. But, the improving regulatory infrastructure guiding Islamic banking and finance has not yet been integrated into the global financial supervisory framework represented by the Basel accords. This challenge, coupled with properly guided product development, represents the plane in which Islamic bankers, scholars and their advisers must coordinate the most closely to grow the industry globally.

---

[1] Abedi, Sameer, 'Survival of the fittest: The future of *Shari'a*-compliant retail banking in the GCC' in Jaffer, Sohail, ed., *Islamic Retail Banking and Finance: Global Challenges and Opportunities* (London: Euromoney, 2005), p. 49.

[2] Adam, Nathif, J., 'Converting a conventional retail bank to Islamic banking', in Jaffer, Sohail, ed., *Islamic Retail Banking and Finance: Global Challenges and Opportunities* (London: Euromoney. 2005), p. 41.

Glossary[1]

adl: a trusted and honourable person, selected by both parties in a transaction. Analogous to the Western concept of a trustee

al-kharaj bildaman: the Islamic legal principle that means entitlement to revenue follows assumption of responsibility. Profits, therefore, are based on the ownership of, and responsibility for, capital

al-marhoun: the definite property that is made security for a debt in an *al-rahn* arrangement (see *al-rahn*)

al-rahn: the making of a designated property into security for a debt that may be totally or partially recovered from such property

amanah: gratuitous trust or safekeeping for which there is no liability or obligatory compensation in case of loss or damage. The word is used for both the relationship and the item(s) in safekeeping

bai: contract of sale, sale and purchase

bai' al-dayn: sale of debt or receivables

bai' al-'inah: a loan in the form of a sale, called *'inah* (façade) because it is a sale in appearance only. This is accomplished by buying back what one has sold for a lower price than that at which one originally sold it. The difference, ostensibly profit, is actually a loan

bai' al-wafa': a sale with the right of redemption; literally, a sale of honour. Typically, such a sale takes place when a commodity is sold on the condition that the seller be allowed to redeem the commodity upon paying its price; and the buyer agrees to honour the condition

bai' al-wakala: a sale by an agent on behalf of another

bai' bithaman ajil: deferred payment sale; credit sale

bai' sarf: a sale of currency, or an exchange. Such a sale is subject to strict *Shari'a* guidelines

***daman/kafala*:** guarantee or surety

***fard*:** something required of a Muslim; something that is obligatory

***fard kifaya*:** duty/obligation of the Muslim community, although not all have to perform the duty – ie, there are those that carry out the obligation on behalf of the community as a whole. In the case of Islamic finance, *Shari'a* scholars perform the duty, on behalf of the community, of deciding whether or not a financial product is *Shari'a*-compliant

***fatwa* (plural *fatawa*):** an authoritative legal opinion based on the *Shari'a* (Islamic law): a certification of compliance with *Shari'a* precepts that is issued by a *Shari'a* supervisory board

***fiqh*:** practical jurisprudence, or human articulations of divine rules encompassing both law and ethics. As such, *fiqh* may be viewed as the jurists' understanding of the *Shari'a*, or jurists' law

***fiqh al-mu'amalat*:** Islamic commercial jurisprudence, or the rules of transacting in a *Shari'a*-compliant manner

***fuqaha* (plural of *faqih*):** qualified specialists in *fiqh*, or jurists

***gharar*:** uncertainty or a lack of specificity in a contract regarding the existence of the subject matter of the contract, or its deliverability, quantity, or quality. *Gharar* also involves contractual ambiguity as regards the consideration and/or the terms of a contract. Such ambiguity will render most contracts void

***hadith*:** the narrative record of the sayings, doings and implicit approval or disapproval of the Prophet, peace be upon him. The word is sometimes used in English as a collective noun; and sometimes an 's' is added to make the plural

***halal*:** lawful; one of the five major *Shari'a* categorisations of human acts

***hamish gedyyah*:** security deposit. An amount of money paid by the purchase orderer upon request of the seller to make sure that the orderer is serious. However, if the promise is binding and the purchase orderer declines to purchase the asset, the actual loss incurred to the seller shall be made good from this amount

***haram*:** unlawful; one of the five major *Shari'a* categorisations of human acts

***hawala*:** a bill of exchange or other debt obligation. Currently, used in developing countries as a tool to execute foreign exchange transactions

***ibra*:** to free from responsibility. An act by a person to withdraw his rights, ie, his rights to collect payment from a person who has the obligation to repay the amount borrowed from him

***ijab*:** offer (contract)

***ijarah*:** lease, hire or the transfer of ownership of a service for a specified period for an agreed-upon lawful consideration

***ijarah mawsufah*:** a concept whereby an Islamic lease may be set for a future date (subject to the rent commencing after delivery of the asset)

***ijarah muntahia bittamleek* (or *ijarah-wa-iqtina'a*):** this is a form of a leasing contract used by Islamic financial institutions, which includes a promise by the lessor to transfer the ownership of the leased property to the lessee, either at the end of the term of the lease period or by stages during the term of the contract. In this form of leasing contract, the title to the lease is executed by means of a promise to give it as a gift for no consideration, or as a gift contingent upon the payment of the remaining instalments, or a promise to sell for a token or other consideration, or by accelerating the payment of the remaining instalments, or by paying the market value of the leased property

***ijarah thuma al-bai'*:** literally, lease followed by sale. A contract which begins with an *ijarah* (see above) contract for the purpose of renting out or leasing the lessor's asset to the lessee. Consequently, at the end of the lease period, lessee will purchase the asset at an agreed price from lessor by executing a purchase (*bai'*) contract

***ijm'a*:** the consensus of jurists; considered a binding legal indicator (*dalil*) in the classical jurisprudence

***ijtihad*:** effort or toil (literally); as a legal term it means the effort of a qualified Islamic jurist to interpret or reinterpret sources of Islamic law in cases in which no clear directives exist. Thus, while every toiler or *mujtahid* is a jurist (*faqih*), not every jurist is a *mujtahid*. This is because many jurists serve merely to bear or convey *fiqh*, while others (through *ijtihad*) actually produce it. This explains why *fiqh* may be defined as jurists' law (see *fiqh* above; see also *mujtahid*)

***ikhtikar*:** monopoly or hoarding

***ikhtilaf*:** divergence of opinions among jurists

***istihsan*:** judicial preference for one legal analogy over another, often in view of the public interest. The strict application of *istihsan* would require that preference be given to the soundest of two analogies. *Istihsan* is one of many tools used by jurists in the process of *ijtihad* (see *ijtihad* above)

***istislah*:** public welfare

***istisna'a*:** a contract of sale of specified goods to be manufactured, with an obligation on the manufacturer to deliver them upon completion. It is a condition in *istisna'a* that the seller provides either the raw material or the cost of manufacturing the goods

***jahala*:** lack of knowledge or ambiguity in the terms of a contract, such that one or both of the contracting parties do not have full knowledge of the transaction. *Jahala* is one of the elements of *gharar* (see above) and will render a transaction void

***ju'ala*:** *pre-specified reward based on a contractor meeting defined targets using its own efforts*

***kafala*:** see *daman* above

***khiyar al-shart*:** an option in a sale contract concluded at the time of signing the agreement, giving one of the two parties to the contract a right to cancel the sale within a stipulated time

***khulta*:** mixture; typically refers to the permitted mixing of different asset classes in a security, or to the mixing of permissible and other financial contracts in a company's capital structure. In the investment markets, this is typically applied to either the gross amount of debt to market capitalisation of a company or the proportion of receivables from sales contracts to other assets such as *ijarah* in the structuring of *sukuk*. In both cases the preferred limit is 30 per cent

***mal*:** asset, real goods or services

***manfaa*:** usufruct or benefit derived from an asset. *Ijarah* is defined as a sale of a *manfaa* (see *ijarah* above)

***maqasid*:** the general objectives or higher purposes of Islamic law. These are generally understood to include things such as justice, the preservation of life, the betterment of society, etc

***maslahah*:** public good or benefit

***maysir*:** the forbidden act of gambling or playing games of chance with the intention of making an easy, or unearned profit

***milkiyat al-khadamat*:** the right to a service that may be securitised through a pre-sale, with the *sukuk* holders benefiting from periodic distribution of underlying payments or service delivery

***mu'amalat*:** transactions; generally understood to be financial and contractual in nature

***mudaraba*:** a partnership in profit between capital and work in which one partner, the *rabb al-mal* (investor) contributes money and the other, the *mudarib* (manager), invests time and effort. This arrangement was adapted to European circumstances and called a *commenda*. A modern *mudaraba* is typically conducted between investment account holders, as providers of funds, and the Islamic bank or fund as a *mudarib* (see below). The Islamic bank announces its willingness to accept the funds of investment account holders, the sharing of profits being as agreed between the two parties, and the losses being borne by the provider of funds, except in cases of managerial misconduct, negligence or violation of the conditions agreed upon by the Islamic bank. In the latter cases, such losses would be borne by the Islamic bank. A *mudaraba* contract may also be concluded between the Islamic bank, as a provider of funds, on behalf of itself or on behalf of investment account holders, and business owners and other craftsmen, including farmers, traders, etc

***mudarib*:** the managing partner in a *mudaraba* (see above); generally, a contributor of labour rather than capital

***mujtahid*:** legal expert, or a jurist, who expends great effort in arriving at a legal opinion by interpreting the sources of the law. This is derived from the same root as the word *ijtihad* above

***muqarada*:** in conventional finance, the word is used to indicate bonds; as a *Shari'a* term, it is an alternate term for *mudaraba*

***muqarasa*:** a methodology for plantation owners and agri-business producers to engage in a production profit-sharing arrangement based upon future production

***murabaha*:** sale of goods with an agreed-upon profit mark-up on the cost. There are two types of the modern *murabaha* sale. In the first, the Islamic bank purchases the goods and makes them available for sale without any prior promise from a customer to purchase them and this is termed a normal or spot *murabaha*. The second type typically involves the customer's promise to purchase the item from the institution, which is called *murabaha* to the purchase promiser. It is distinguished from the normal type of *murabaha* which does not involve such a promise by the customer. The *murabaha* to the purchase pledger or orderer is the sale of an item by the institution to a customer (the purchase pledger) for a pre-agreed selling price, which includes a pre-agreed profit mark-up over its cost price, this having been specified in the customer's promise to purchase. Normally, a *murabaha* to the purchase pledger transaction involves the institution granting the customer a *murabaha* credit facility. A *murabaha* to the purchase orderer transaction typically involves deferred payment terms, but such deferred payment is not one of the essential conditions of such transactions. A *murabaha* can be arranged with no deferral of payment. In this case the mark-up will only include the profit the institution will receive for a spot sale and not the extra charge it will receive for deferral of payment

***musaqa*:** a form of agricultural contract in which the owner of productive land shares its produce with another in exchange for irrigation

***musawama*:** a negotiated sale, ie, one in which each of its terms is negotiated by the parties to the sale. Thus, nearly all sales fall under this general category. An example of a non-negotiated sale, also known as *bai' al-amanah*, is a *murabaha* because the seller discloses to the purchaser the exact amount of the original purchase price before agreeing with the new purchaser on a mark-up

***musharaka*:** a form of partnership between the Islamic bank and its clients whereby each party contributes to the partnership capital in equal or varying degrees to establish a new project or to share in an existing one. Each of the parties becomes an owner of the capital on a permanent or declining basis and shall have his due share of profits. Losses, however, are shared in proportion to the contributed capital. It is not permissible to stipulate otherwise

***musharaka mutanaqisah*:** diminishing-balance partnership; one form of partnership, *shirkah* or *musharaka*, that forms the basis for much of modern Islamic home finance. Under such an arrangement, the client partner buys out, over a period of time, the ownership interest of the financier partner

***mutawalli*:** trustee, esp. of a *waqf*

***muzara'a*:** a crop-sharing contract in which one party agrees to till the land of another in return for a part of the harvest

***qabd*:** Possession

***qabul*:** acceptance (contract)

***qard hassan*:** a loan *per amore* in which there is no interest. In Islamic law, all loans are gratuitous contracts. From this perspective, the charging of interest for a loan is a perversion of a gratuitous contract to an onerous one and therefore prohibited

***qiyas*:** analogical reasoning

***Qur'an*:** the Book of Divine Revelation that was delivered to humankind by the Prophet Mohammed (PBOH), peace be upon him. The *Qur'an* is the first source of Islamic jurisprudence

***rabb al-maal*:** an investor or owner of capital in a *mudaraba* contract (see *mudaraba* above)

***rahn*:** mortgage or pledge

***riba*:** interest; sometimes equated with usury, though its meaning is more comprehensive. The literal meaning of *riba* is 'increase'; and *riba* is generally defined as unlawful advantage leading to increase by way of excess or deferment

***riba al-fadl*:** one of two types of *riba* and usually described as the excess over what is justified by the counter-value in an exchange/business transaction where cash is paid by one party and commodities and services are delivered at the same time by the other; or when the same goods are exchanged but in differing quality or quantity

***ribawi*:** a transaction in which *riba* is an element

***rubb-ul-mal*:** see *rabb al-maal* above

***sadaqah*:** voluntary charitable contribution; see also *Zakah*

***salam*:** a contract for the purchase of a commodity for deferred delivery in exchange for immediate payment according to specified conditions

***shahadat al-dayn*:** promissory notes (Malaysia)

***Shari'a*:** the term *Shari'a* has two meanings – Islamic law, and the totality of divine categorisations of human acts (Islam). Because of the second meaning, *Shari'a* rules do not always function as rules of law in the western sense, as they include obligations, duties and moral considerations not generally thought of as 'law'. *Shari'a* rules, therefore, admitting of both a legal and a moral dimension, have as their purpose the fostering of obedience to the Almighty. In the legal terminology, *Shari'a* means the law as extracted by the *mujtahids* from the sources of law

***shart*:** stipulation (in a contract)

***shihama*:** a form of negotiable profit participation certificate introduced by the Central Bank of Sudan in 1998. They were a form of equity-based instrument issued against the government's ownership stakes in the nation's banks, all of which operate on an Islamic basis

***shirkah*:** a contract between two or more persons who launch a business or financial enterprise to make profits. In the conventional books of *fiqh*, the partnership business has been discussed under the option of *shirkah* that, broadly, may include both *musharaka* and *mudaraba*

***shirkatul akd* or *'aqd*:** a sub-category of *shirkah* in which partnership is brought about by means of a contract. Such a partnership may further be categorised as limited or unlimited

***shirkatul milk*:** a sub-category of *shirkah* in which partnership is brought about by means of mutual ownership, as a result of purchase, inheritance, gift, bequest, or commingling of indistinguishable (one from another) assets

shura: consultation

suftaja: a form of bill similar to a bill of exchange between three parties: a payor, a transmitter and a payee

sukuk: participation securities; coupons; investment certificates. The singular, *sakk*, is probably the source from which the word 'cheque' was derived

Sunnah: the way of the Prophet Mohammed, peace be upon him, including his sayings, deeds, approvals or disapprovals as preserved in the *hadith* literature: the second of the two sources of revelation (recited and unrecited revelation) of which the first is the *Qur'an*

taam: complete or whole, as opposed to something that has yet to mature or come to fruition and is thus impossible to value in its present condition

tabarru: donation, gift, contribution. A sum of money 'donated' to an insurer. The presence of *tabarru* makes an insurance transaction permissible and compliant with *Shari'a*

tahawwut: the lexical meaning of this word is to take care of, to pay frequent attention to, to guard. As this is what a hedge fund does for the capital of its investors, the word is used in Arabic alongside '*sanduq*' or fund, to denote a hedge fund. The derivation of hedging in English comes from the notion of placing a hedge around assets in order to protect them

takaful: a *Shari'a*-compliant system of insurance in which the participants donate part or all of their contributions, which are used to pay claims for damages suffered by some of the participants. The company's role is restricted to managing the insurance operations and investing the insurance contributions

tasarruf: disposal, or the power of disposal in financial matters. In *Shari'a* terms, *tasarruf* means any action for which there may be legal consequences

tawarruq: the purchase of goods for deferred payment and their subsequent sale for cash to a buyer other than original seller at a lower price for the purpose of raising cash. This is not to be confused with an *'inah* sale because neither the form nor the intention of *riba* is apparent in a *tawarruq* sale

taysir: the concept of making things easy

***Ulema, 'ulama* (plural of *alim*)**: *Shari'a* scholars or jurists

Ummah: community, nation. Used to refer to the worldwide community of Muslims

***urboun* (*'arbun, arboon*):** earnest money. It also refers to the downpayment advanced by the client (purchaser) to a seller upon entering into a contract of sale in which the purchaser retains the option to either accept or reject the deal at the end of a specified period of time. If the sale is concluded on or before the specified date, the *urboun* downpayment will be counted as part of the purchase price; otherwise, if the buyer fails to execute the contract by the prescribed date, the *urboun* will be kept by the seller

***'urf*:** custom, generally accepted practice

***usul al-fiqh*:** Islamic legal theory; theoretical jurisprudence

***wadia*:** safekeeping (where the 'd' transliterates a '*daal*'). Or a resale of goods with a discount on the original stated cost (where the 'd' transliterates a '*daad*')

***wakala*:** agency; an agency contract, which may include in its terms a fee for the agent

***wakif*:** trust settlor

***wakil*:** an agent under a *wakala* arrangement

***waqf*:** putting aside assets or original property in the name of Allah, or the endowment or assignment of revenues and donating its benefits, generally for religious or charitable purposes, and where the revenues may not be changed to another purpose

***waqf ahli*:** revenues from *waqf* endowments directed toward the endower's family first and then, ultimately, the community's poor

***Zakah*:** literally blessing, purification, increase or cultivation of good deeds. In *Shari'a*, it is an obligation in respect of funds paid for a specified type of purpose and for specified categories. It is a specified amount prescribed by Allah the Almighty for those who are entitled to *Zakah* as specified in the *Qur'an*. The word *Zakah* is also used to indicate the amount paid from the funds that are subject to *Zakah*

---

[1] The editors would like to thank Yusuf Talal DeLorenzo, Abdulkader Thomas and Professor Rodney Wilson for their extensive contribution to the glossary.